The
Experimental Psychology
of Alfred Binet

Translated by

Frances K. Zetland
Claire Ellis

The Experimental
Psychology
of Alfred Binet

Selected Papers

Edited by

ROBERT H. POLLACK
MARGARET W. BRENNER

SPRINGER PUBLISHING COMPANY, INC.
NEW YORK CITY

Copyright © 1969

SPRINGER PUBLISHING COMPANY, INC.

200 Park Avenue South, New York City, 10003

Library of Congress Catalog Card Number: 74-85227

Printed in U.S.A.

Acknowledgment

The editors wish to acknowledge the assistance of Noël Jenkin, Ph.D., Director of Research at the Institute for Juvenile Research, for making the Institute's resource facilities available; Claudine Pernet, for her help in reworking and verifying the translation; Signe Olson, for preparing the bibliography; and Dorothy J. Carter, for providing editorial and technical assistance. This project was supported in part by NICHD Grant No. 5 R01 HD01433 and NIH Grant No. 1 S01 FR05666.

Preface

Alfred Binet has been recognized as the father of experimental psychology by so eminent a French psychologist as Paul Fraisse (1963), but in America Binet is little known for anything other than the famous intelligence test. Even such historians as Boring (1942; 1957), Watson and Campbell (1963), and Herrnstein and Boring (1966) fail to mention Binet's work in experimental psychology.

It is still more surprising that the two most comprehensive theorists of cognitive development, Piaget and Werner, barely acknowledge Binet's pioneering efforts in developing experimental procedures for the study of the perceptual and cognitive behavior of children. American educational psychologists are only now talking about such things as conservation of number based upon Piaget's work of the last 20 to 30 years. This is a phenomenon Binet discovered more than 75 years ago! One could cite numerous findings that have not been acknowledged to this day, but it is better to let the reader enjoy the excitement of such discoveries.

Since Binet's work after 1900 on the intelligence scale and on other clinical phenomena is so familiar, the emphasis of this volume is upon the early stages of his career: 1) his enthusiasm for, and later rejection of, the laws of associationism, and 2) his first studies on intelligence, individual differences, and development.

It is the intention of this book to let Alfred Binet speak for himself as an experimental psychologist. The reader cannot help but share Binet's enthusiasm over the behavior of his daughters on perceptual and cognitive tasks. While his theorizing about his data is often naive and reflects the pervasive associationism of his time, it also testifies to Binet's increasing dissatisfaction with the position. Binet was frequently surprised by his findings, but his eventual devotion to fact over theory and his freedom from dogmatic bias enabled him to interpret his findings objectively. The ingenuity of the stimulus variations chosen and his use of descriptive statistics are as sophisticated, surely, as those of the Geneva group 30 to 50 years later.

The papers in this book have been grouped under three headings: psychophysical studies on two-point threshold, perceptual de-

vii

velopment, and miscellaneous experimental studies. Under each heading, the papers are arranged in chronological order. Only those papers which are experimental or amenable to experimentation have been selected.

The editors accept full responsibility for the brief introductions to each section and for the interpretations of Binet's work. The judgment of the quality of Binet's work, however, rests with the reader.

R.H.P.
M.W.B.

About the Editors:

ROBERT H. POLLACK, Ph.D., was formerly the Program Director in Experimental Psychology at the Institute for Juvenile Research in Chicago. He is now Professor of Psychology at the University of Georgia, Athens, Georgia.

MARGARET W. BRENNER, B.S., is Editor for the Institute for Juvenile Research in Chicago.

Editors' Introduction

I

Alfred Binet was born in Nice, France, on July 8, 1857. He was the only child of a physician father and an artist mother. When he was 15, Binet and his mother went to Paris so that he could attend the famed Lycée Louis-le-Grand and prepare to study law. He received his *licencié* in law in 1878 and immediately enrolled in the Sorbonne to pursue studies in the natural sciences. By 1897, Binet had completed his thesis, "Contribution à l'étude de système nerveux sous-intestinal des insectes," and been awarded a doctorate.

Binet's interest in psychology, however, developed almost independently of his formal education. By 1880, he had read enough psychology at the *Bibliothèque Nationale* to write and publish his first article, "On the Fusion of Similar Sensations." Binet began to work with Charcot and Féré at the Salpêtrière in 1883 and soon became interested in abnormal psychology and hypnotism. During the next seven years, Binet defended Charcot's hypotheses on hypnotic transfer and polarization almost unquestioningly against severe criticism from Delboeuf and the Nancy School. Examination of the facts eventually forced Binet to renounce his support of Charcot.

In 1891, a chance meeting between Binet and Henri Beaunis, director of the Laboratory of Physiological Psychology at the Sorbonne, resulted in Binet's being offered a position in Beaunis' laboratory. A year later, Binet was nominated co-director, and in 1895, Beaunis retired and the directorship went to Binet. This position, which Binet held until his death, enabled him to pursue studies of the higher mental processes, particularly those of thought and intelligence.

In addition to their work together at the laboratory, Binet and Beaunis founded *L'Année psychologique* in 1895. (Beaunis, however, soon resigned as co-editor of the journal.) *L'Année* contained Binet's writings for the most part and by 1908 was largely devoted to the study of practical and social questions.

In 1895, Binet was offered a chair in psychophysiology at the

University of Bucharest while serving there as a guest lecturer. He declined the offer, partly because of the ill health of one of his daughters, and partly because he hoped to secure a position at the College of France. He was disappointed, however, when the College of France chose Janet, and the Sorbonne, Dumas. Binet never held a professorship, but it is perhaps this freedom from heavy academic demands, coupled with the fact that he had an independent income, which provided the lack of restraint essential to the originality and psychological insight which Binet displayed throughout his career.

In 1900, Binet, along with Ferdinand Buisson, was instrumental in organizing the *Société libre pour l'Étude psychologique de l'Enfant,* a *société* of psychologists, school teachers, and school principals concerned with practical problems in the schools. Binet devoted considerable time to the *société* and to its *Bulletin.* After his death, the *société* became the *Société Alfred Binet* in his honor, and the *Bulletin* carried on Binet's tradition of dedication to pedagogical studies.

Another opportunity to work in the schools presented itself in 1904. Binet was appointed by the Minister of Public Instruction to a commission established to improve the teaching of backward children. The members of the commission—educators, medical men, and scientists—were assigned the task of administering special education classes in the public schools. Thus, Binet and Theodore Simon, whom Binet had been working with since 1899, were motivated to develop a series of tests which would enable them to diagnose feeble-mindedness. The result, the 1905 Binet-Simon scale described in *"Methodes nouvelles pour le Diagnostic du Niveau intellectuel des Anormaux,"* was the progenitor of their 1908 and 1911 revisions. Binet was working on the revision of the scale when he died in Paris in 1911.

Binet can best be epitomized as a man with a diversity of interests and a tremendous capacity for hard work. He was continually observing the behavior of his two daughters—a preoccupation which undoubtedly affected his family life. He wrote a small book and several articles on microorganisms and insects. He co-authored, with Andre de Lorde, several plays whose themes centered around abnormal behavior. He was interested in the effects of emotional and other non-rational influences on thought processes, and published a number of studies on suggestibility, esthesiometry, hypnotism, mental fatigue, graphology, and cephalometry. He was a zealous editor and writer, and his tireless research on memory, imagination, judgment, and attention culminated in his historic work on intelligence and individual differences.

And now, some comments on the history of Binet's experimental work.

II

In 1880, the 23-year-old Binet entered the study of psychology as a staunch advocate of associationism. He referred frequently in his works to such British associationists as J. S. Mill, Bain, and Sully, and largely chose to ignore his German contemporaries. Binet continued to adhere to the associationist principles until about 1890, but his increasing disaffection with the position was apparent long before then.

Binet's independence from the associationist tradition could be seen even in his first paper, "On the Fusion of Similar Sensations" (1880). A more rigid associationist might have tried to explain why certain experiences are associated or recalled together. Binet, instead, sought an explanation of why a double sensation is sometimes perceived as single. Relying more on theory than on experimentation, he argued that two sensations fuse and are not perceived as distinct if they are qualitatively similar.

Binet's studies on tactual sensitivity were pursued well into the 1900's. Introspective reports coupled with objective data enabled Binet to categorize his subjects into psychological types on the basis of the position of their limen. He concluded that psychical activity expresses itself in bodily attitudes.

The most elaborately reasoned argument in defense of associationism was *The Psychology of Reasoning* (1886). With dogmatic certainty, Binet asserted that reasoning is nothing but association, and that similar sensations and images, both of which originate in the brain, fuse by virtue of contiguity.

During the same year, Binet wrote "The Perception of Extent by the Eye." Although the laws of association continued to play a part in his theorizing, Binet's belief in them was noticeably wavering. He made no attempt to explain the perception of spatial relationships by association.

The first obvious signs of revolt can be seen in *Animal Magne-*

tism (1887). Binet admitted that he had to stretch some facts and ignore others to succeed in explaining all psychology by associationism. By the time he wrote *Alterations of Personality* (1892), the break was complete. Binet was forced to admit that there must be some psychological laws more fundamental than those of association.

Much of the work during this period was done at the Salpêtrière with abnormal subjects, largely hypnotized hysterics. Although Binet's attention soon shifted to the behavior of his daughters, he did not abandon his interest in the abnormal. In later years, he would continue to study both mental patients and people with supernormal abilities such as great calculators and chess players.

III

By 1890, Binet no longer had a theory to manipulate, nor was he particularly occupied with the vague theoretical questions of the past. It is understandable, then, that his studies over the next five years reflect a vacillation, a groping for a connecting theme, which was typical of no other period of his career. This does not detract from their significance, however, for they reflect the course of his future work on intelligence and his ideas on a reliable experimental approach to the study of psychology.

Binet's earlier research had given him invaluable experience in experimentation. He had come to realize that individual differences had to be systematically explored before one could determine laws which would apply to all people. The method he found most appropriate was that of comparative introspection, or pure introspection coupled with objective observation. In a sense, then, his quantitative data became the vehicle for establishing norms against which qualitative differences among people could be assessed. Although Binet has been called the father of psychometrics (Varon, 1935, p. 39), measurement was not as important to him as the discovery of qualitative phenomena.

This period in Binet's career marks the beginning of his observations of his two daughters, Alice and Madeleine.[1] "Studies on Movements in Some Young Children" (1890) was the first such study of his children. He reported individual differences not only in the

---

[1] It appears that Binet attempted to disguise his daughters' names, calling them Armande and Marguerite in some of his later works. This is the case in Chapter 14 of this book and in his famout *Etude experimental de l'Intelligence*.

way they learned to walk, but also in their personalities. This article also suggested Binet's curiosity about developmental changes in particular functions and about the mental organization characteristic of a particular age.

Binet's ideas on intelligence did not appear until the next paper, "The Perception of Lengths and Numbers in Some Small Children" (1890). Initially, Binet defined intelligence in terms of perception and seemed to envision it as something very general and vague, permeating all conscious psychical phenomena, but not in itself a faculty or function. He implied, further, that intelligence must be studied in the light of such complex mental processes as reasoning, memory, and judgment, and he expressed an interest in the qualitative differences between the intelligence of adults and children.

In "Children's Perceptions" (1890), Binet's studies of perception are continued, but this time they are seen more clearly as investigations into the nature of intelligence. Once again, Binet focused on age differences in intelligence and proceeded to study them through complex rather than simple functions. One can see in "Children's Perceptions" the vocabulary test which would later be incorporated into his intelligence scale.[2]

It is tempting to speculate what the position of present-day experimental child psychology would be if Binet had not shifted his attention to psychometric problems and individual differences. It is quite possible that experimental procedures could have been standardized decades earlier, and that we might have had, long before now, a body of hard normative data on most kinds of childhood behavior.

---

[2] For an insightful discussion of these three 1890 publications, see Wolf, 1966. She writes: "These three papers report crude but unmistakably experimental studies of his two little daughters, and present a singularly important, although neglected, page in the history of child psychology" (Wolf, 1966, p. 233).

REFERENCES

Varon, E. J. The development of Alfred Binet's psychology. *Psychological monographs,* 1935, *46,* (3, Whole No. 207).

Boring, E. G. *Sensation and Perception in the History of Experimental Psychology.* New York: Appleton-Century-Crofts, 1942.

Boring, E. G. *A History of Experimental Psychology.* (2nd ed.) New York: Appleton-Century-Crofts, 1957.

Wolf, T. H. An individual who made a difference. *American psychologist,* 1961, *16,* 245-248.

Fraisse, P. L'évolution de la psychologie expérimentale. In P. Fraisse & J. Piaget (Eds.), *Traité de psychologie expérimentale*. Vol. 1. *Histoire et méthode*. Paris: Presses Universitaires de France, 1963. Translated by J. Chambers, *Experimental Psychology: Its Scope and Method*. Vol. 1. *History and Method*. New York: Basic Books, 1968.

Watson, R. I., & Campbell, D. T. (Eds.) *History, Psychology, and Science: Selected Papers by Edwin G. Boring*. New York: Wiley, 1963.

Silverman, H. L., & Krenzel, K. Alfred Binet: Prolific pioneer in psychology. *Psychiatric quarterly supplement*, 1964, *38*, 323-335.

Wolf, T. H. Alfred Binet: A time of crisis. *American psychologist*, 1965, *20*, 762-771.

Bejat, M. Une correspondance inédite d'Alfred Binet. *Revue roumaine des sciences sociales*, 1966, *10* (2), 199-212.

Herrnstein, R. J., & Boring, E. G. (Eds.) *A Source Book in the History of Psychology*. Cambridge: Harvard University Press, 1966.

Wolf, T. H. Intuition and experiment: Alfred Binet's first efforts in child psychology. *Journal of the history of the behavioral sciences*, 1966, *2* (3), 233-239.

Contents

Section I   PSYCHOPHYSICAL STUDIES ON
            TWO-POINT THRESHOLD   1

  1 On the Fusion of Similar Sensations (*1880*)   3
  2 The Influence of Exercise and Suggestion on
     the Position of the Threshold (*1902*)   13
  3 The Threshold of a Double Sensation Cannot
     Be Scientifically Determined (*1902*)   23
  4 From Sensation to Intelligence (*1903*)   28

Section II   PERCEPTUAL DEVELOPMENT   75

  5 Note on Illusions of Movement (*1888*)   77
  6 The Perception of Lengths and Numbers in Some
     Small Children (*1890*)   79
  7 Children's Perceptions (*1890*)   93
  8 Investigations on the Development of Visual
     Memory in Children (*1894*)   127
  9 The Measurement of Visual Illusions in
     Children (*1895*)   130

Section III   MISCELLANEOUS EXPERIMENTAL
              STUDIES   145

 10 The Perception of Extent by the Eye (*1886*)   147
 11 Studies of Movements in Some Young Children
     (*1890*)   156
 12 The Perception of Duration in Simple Reactions
     (*1892*)   168
 13 Fear in Children (*1895*)   179
 14 Imageless Thought (*1903*)   207

The
Experimental Psychology
of Alfred Binet

Section I

PSYCHOPHYSICAL STUDIES ON
TWO-POINT THRESHOLD

This group of papers has been included neither for its special contribution to our knowledge of tactual stimulation nor as an example of typical psychophysical studies of the time. Its appeal lies in Binet's concern for the kinds of judgmental processes engaged in by his subjects. What a subject did, and to what elements of the stimulus situation he responded, were considerably more important to Binet than either the response itself or the presence of a stimulus-response correlation. This was the case despite Binet's extreme care in collecting data and analyzing them quantitatively in surprisingly sophisticated fashion. The course of Binet's work in any area, regardless of the long time lapses between publications, was always determined by his discoveries about the processes interacting with his quantitative data. The result was often a general conclusion of considerably greater importance than the content of the experiments themselves.

A case in point is Binet's treatment of *Vexierfehler,* or paradoxical judgments, which are the result of the subject's judging the single point as two. Boring (1942, pp. 479-483) covered the German and English literature on the subject, but typically ignored Binet's work in French. The writers cited by Boring attributed these paradoxical "twos" to anatomical reasons or to such factors as practice, fatigue, or the subject's expectations. Binet concluded, as did the German and English authors, that *Vexierfehler* were produced by "autosuggestion," by a self-imposed attitude or response set based on the subject's interpretation of the stimulus. Binet, however, went a step further. He divided his subjects into two groups, the simplists and the interpreters, and he analyzed precisely what went into the judgments of each. Interpreters, for example, showed smaller thresholds with practice and made *Vexierfehler;* simplists did not. He concluded that simplists directed their attention to the cause of the

1

sensation rather than to its particular qualities, whereas interpreters analyzed their sensations and noted distinctions in their quality. Binet was also able to specify the conditions for transforming a simplist into an interpreter. In the end, Binet came to the conclusion that a two-point threshold did not really exist, that the measurements obtained were functions of the type of subject and the instructions.

It is obvious that Binet was an early observer of the effects of instructions and subjective, spontaneous response bias upon psychophysical data. One may question Binet's ultimate conclusion that there is no way of determining a two-point threshold, but later work in a dozen areas of psychology confirms the supreme importance of the variables he studied.

REFERENCE

Boring, E. G. *Sensation and Perception in the History of Experimental Psychology*. New York: Appleton-Century-Crofts, 1942.

1

On the Fusion of Similar Sensations

I

We know that the association of ideas by similarity is one of the two principles which assures the succession of our thoughts. When a sensation, idea, or feeling occupies the mind, these states of consciousness have a tendency to recall previous states that resemble them. If nothing blocks this tendency, the recall is made, and we have a simultaneous consciousness of two states occurring separately in time. Similarity has another property which is less well known and less studied than the previous one, even though there is no doubt of its existence. It consists in the fact that two sensations, two ideas, or two feelings presented together fuse when they are similar. If the resemblance of the two states is perfect, the fusion is total, in that we sense only one state of consciousness instead of two. If the two states resemble each other in an imperfect manner, it is because they are formed partly by common elements, partly by different elements. Only the common elements fuse; the different elements remain distinct. The consequence of this partial fusion is less easily grasped by simple observation than the consequence of total fusion, but the psychological phenomena involved allow us to derive its formula by induction. We experience the two different parts of these two different states in a distinct fashion. As to the two portions which resemble each other, they make only one impression on the consciousness.[1]

Before starting a synthetic study of this "law of fusion," it is perhaps useful to describe it, or at least to describe some experiments which demonstrate the manner in which these phenomena present themselves to us. In order to go from the simple to the more com-

---

[1] Spencer has written in a few words a very precise exposition on this rule. See *Principles of Psychology*, II, Ch. 2.

De la fusion des sensations semblables. *Revue philosophique*, 1880, 10, 284-294.

plex, I will speak first of the total fusion of two states. An excellent example is furnished by the phenomena of tactile sensitivity, in which we find, under specified conditions, identical sensations fusing together. They fuse so completely that the person who is not forewarned that he will be receiving two distinct excitations thinks, while perceiving only one sensation, that only one pressure is being exerted on his skin. This phenomenon concerns a controversial physiological problem about which a few words of explanation must first be given.

Touch is a sense that occupies the largest surface of the body. While special senses such as sight, hearing, smell, and taste, are limited to very narrow parts of the organism, one encounters touch everywhere on the skin and even on some mucous membranes; the nasal cavities, the conjunctiva, the buccal cavity, the throat, the two extremes of the digestive tube, the vagina, and the uretheral canal give us sensations of contact. But certain sections of the general envelope are more sensitive than others. We know, for example, that tactile sensitivity is little developed in the middle of the back. It is more refined on the hand, still more refined on the balls of the fingers, and attains its highest degree on the tip of the tongue. Some of the experiments Weber conducted in this area have remained in science as models of precision. The two points of a blunt compass were passed over all surfaces of the body where he wished to measure the sensitivity. He verified that in the middle of the back, two points had to be separated by 39 lines [the measuring scale of the compass]* to be perceived as two; closer together, the points aroused only one impression. On the chest, the separation necessary was about 20 lines; on the thigh, 16; on the lower part of the forehead, 10; on the palm of the hand and on the tip of the nose, 3; on the edge of the lower lip, 2; on the tip of the index finger, palmar face, 1; on the tip of the tongue, ½. These measures have been repeated, controlled, and corrected somewhat, but not substantially altered.

Weber's experiments have the great merit of establishing, from the point of view of tactile sensitivity, quantitative relations among the regions of the skin. They have another merit, greater still in my opinion: that of raising a new problem. The question has since been posed of knowing how two points of a compass can create, according to the spread one gives them and the region of the skin they touch,

---

* Brackets indicate editors' insertions. Parentheses are always Binet's.

sometimes two tactile sensations, sometimes only one. I will now direct the reader's attention to this problem.

II

Two explanations have been proposed; let us say a word about both before turning from them. The first, as simple as all a priori views, consists in saying that when two points are perceived, each has separately excited a nervous fiber; when we perceive only one sensation, the points of the compass have excited only one fiber. In all cases, one perceives as many sensations as the number of nerves excited. A trace of this explanation has remained in the language under the term of "circle of sensation." If one presses one of the points of a compass on the skin and then seeks to determine how far the second point can be from the first without arousing a new sensation, one describes a space which has the form of a circle or an elipse. According to the theory, this space, capable of arousing only a single sensation, corresponds to the territory of a nervous fiber and is called the circle of sensation.

This explanation is partially true: Undoubtedly, those portions of the tegument which have a very developed sensitivity are richer in tactual corpuscles than those whose sensitivity is still dull. But it is quite a different matter to say that all circles of sensation are an anatomical dimension the territory of a single fiber. It has been verified that there are regions in which the points of the compass can be separated by more than 12 nervous papillae without evoking more than a single impression. Let us add that the limits of a circle of sensation vary significantly with the conditions in which the observer finds himself; under the influences of habit and attention, the circle becomes smaller, and the two points of the compass can sometimes provoke a single impression, sometimes two, with the same separation and on the same region of the skin. If a circle of sensation corresponded to the domain of a single fiber, it would be of invariable size, and neither attention nor habit could modify it. Finally, there is a more conclusive fact than all the others: If one defines on a person's forearm two circles of sensation and places the points of a compass one in one circle and one in the other, bringing them as close together as possible, the person will experience only a single sensation. To be perceived as two, the points of the instrument must be separated by the diameter of an entire circle. If each circle were served by a special fiber, it would be sufficient for the two points to be placed in different circles to be felt as two. (I recall these facts only from memory; you will find them described everywhere.)

We owe to Henri Weber a second hypothesis, known as the "theory of nervous field." It is as follows: For two sensations of touch to be perceived in a distinct fashion, a certain space, a certain number of nervous ramifications, a nervous field, must exist between the two excitations of the skin. The distinct perception of two sensations does not require that the excitations be in two different circles of sensation; there must, however, be a determined distance between the two points. Why is it thus? It is said that it is because two things cannot be distinguished unless they are separated by something. The excitation of two nervous fibers cannot produce two distinct impressions unless the fibers are separated by non-stimulated nervous elements. These elements, which serve to separate the two sensations, are represented by the distance between the points of the compass.

It is difficult to refute so vague a theory, but let us try nonetheless. We are told that it is the non-excited nervous field which arouses in our mind the idea of spaced, and consequently, double sensation. How is this possible? From the moment that a group of nervous fibers ceases to be stimulated, they cease to exist in the consciousness. This fact is certain. Further, we can have an idea of the space which separates points A and B as we move our hand from one of these points to the other, feeling a series of muscular sensations. If, however, we do not do this, we cannot say anything about the relative position of the points; tactile sensitivity cannot give us any information in this respect. This fact has been documented by the work of the English school on the manner in which we perceive space. I think that these reasons suffice to refute the theory of nervous field.

III

The explanation that I propose to substitute for the preceding ones can be summed up in a few words. I suppose that each of the points of our epidermis feels in a special way: tactile sensations produced in such-and-such a region differ qualitatively from those produced elsewhere. For example, when one presses one's finger on the forehead, then on the cheek, the chin, the neck, the nape of the neck, one evokes a different sensation each time. Nevertheless, if the quality of the sensation varies with the area of the skin, it must be supposed that this variation takes place in a continuous manner from one point to another. If two points very near each other are chosen, the difference between the two sensations may be insufficiently marked to be perceived. One could then say that these two sensations were identical for the consciousness and submitted to the same mental laws as if there were no real difference between them.

The distance at which the two sensations begin to be differentiated is not uniform for all of the body, as the local nuances of each sensation vary with a different speed according to the different regions of the skin.

Given this, what happens? When I excite two points of the skin with my compass, I can provoke, according to the separation of the points, either two different sensations or two similar sensations. The two sensations will differ if I choose points on the skin sufficiently far apart for the difference in their sensitivity to be graspable. On the contrary, the two sensations will seem identical when the points chosen are too close, from the point of view of tactile sensitivity, to present a marked difference.

Now, it results from the law of fusion of similar states of consciousness that two different impressions remain distinct, while two similar impressions fuse and have the effect of a single impression. When the two points of the compass arouse two different sensations, the two sensations will remain distinct, and we will separately perceive the two points of the compass. On the contrary, when the two points provoke two identical sensations, these two sensations fuse, and we think we feel only one. This explanation, as we see, is very simple and easy to understand, and it is not one of the least of its merits to expose this important property of the law of similarity: the fusion of similar sensations.

Let us again carefully take up all the parts of this summary. In the first place, what reason do we have to believe that all points of our skin have a different manner of feeling the contact of objects from the outside?[2]

I will develop only one of the reasons that can be given in support of the preceding belief—that which is taken from the phenomenon of localization. It is the most striking. When one touches a person

---

[2] This opinion was defended in Germany by Lotze, Wundt, and Helmholtz under the name of "theory of local signals." While explaining the genesis of the notion of space, these thinkers have been led to differentiate a local signal for each visual and tactile sensation that could be localized.

on any part of his body, the person can say where he has been touched. He will not relate to the arm a sensation which has the head as its seat. An awareness of the origin of a sensation is not innate but acquired, and the way in which it develops is fairly easy to describe. We have learned from experience that when we feel such-and-such a tactile sensation, pressure is applied to the arm; when we feel another sensation, pressure is applied to the toe, and so on. With time, we attach a determined tactile sensation to the sight of our arm, another to the sight of our toe; finally, to each different sensation we attach the sight of a different region of our body. When someone presses, pricks, or pinches our body, the sensation belonging to the affected area arouses an ocular image simply by the force of association; it is a mental law that, when two sensations are perceived in contiguity, they adhere in such a manner that, if one is reproduced, it tends to suggest the other. Here the suggestion is made so rapidly that we picture the image of the touched region almost at the same moment we receive the tactile sensation. Localization is not other than this. As to the position of the point which is the seat of the sensation, it is given to us by our muscular activity.

This generally accepted explanation of the manner in which the so-called sense of origin is formed continuously supposes one thing: Two sensations of contact related to two different parts of the body each possess a local signal which distinguishes it and prohibits it from being confused. Suppose that all our sensations of contact were absolutely uniform. A person pricked on the finger could not say whether he had been pricked on the finger rather than on the toe, because he would have felt the same sensation if he had been pricked on his toe. For one sensation of contact or pressure to be associated with the sight of the finger, another with the sight of the toe, it is absolutely necessary that the two sensations be different; without this, they would be confused, and the sensation which had its seat on the finger would suggest equally the visual image of any other part of the body.

We are now in a position to determine whether the points of the compass which are perceived as isolated really arouse two different sensations; if each of these sensations can be localized in a distinct fashion, this is proof that they differ. Can we localize them? Experience answers affirmatively. I press the two points of the compass transversely on the person's forearm with a separation of 39 lines, which is the separation necessary for a person to sense the two points separately. I then raise one of the two points alternatively, asking the person to indicate whether it is the right or the left which is no longer felt. Each time the person replies correctly, he localizes the sensation without mistaking it for another. This is proof that sensations differ a little from one another. If they differ, they must remain distinct; it is a consequence of the mental law we study.

We have advanced a second hypothesis to explain the fact that two tactile sensations, under predetermined conditions, seem similar and consequently can fuse. It is that the local nuance of a sensation changes in a continuous fashion as one goes from one point to another, so that if one takes two points of the skin that present an imperceptible variation to the consciousness, these two sensations will seem identical. This is precisely what should happen when the points of the compass succeed in arousing only a single impression; the two sensations are similar, and consequently they fuse. All we have to do is prove this last point: two sensations are identical when we receive only a single impression. We have seen that the different sensations of our skin serve as indicators of the place where they are produced. If the skin gave only uniform sensations, we would not know to which part of our body to relate them. This uncertainty must be present to a certain extent if one admits the identity of sensations produced by a compass that arouse only a single impression. Is it true, for example, that on the palm of the hand, the two sensations which are separated by five lines and which fuse are identical? If so, it would be impossible for us to relate each of them to a different point on the skin. Experience confirms this, as each one can prove for himself. Two methods may be employed. The first consists simply in pressing the two points of a compass against the skin at a distance such that they fuse; feeling only a single impression, the person will find it impossible to localize separately the two points— that goes without saying. The second method gives more curious results. One tries experimentally to find the maximum separation that one can give to the two points without their ceasing to be fused, and one marks with ink the points on the skin where the compass is applied. The subject must watch these preparations so that he can try to associate the image of each of the marked points with the tactile sensation which is afferent to it. The subject is then asked to turn his head, and the experimenter excites points on the subject's skin, one after the other, asking him if he can identify the two places where the instrument is pressing. The person will reply no, or, at best, will try to localize and will alternately be successful and un-successful, proving that he is guessing. The impossibility of deter-mining a special spot for each of the two sensations can only be due to one thing: the similitude of the two sensations.[3]

I have attempted to prove that when two sensations of touch re-main distinct, they are of a different nature, and that on the contrary, when they fuse, they are of a similar nature. The proof is made.

IV

It remains only to enumerate some facts of observation which were gathered during the past several years and which can now be ex-plained fairly easily.

If one experiments on the two lips of a scar which have been drawn together and stitched, one will see that the two points of the compass are always distinguishable if one is on one side of the scar and the other on the other. Why is it thus? It is that both of the lips, while being drawn together, have retained the special sensitivity which they possessed when they were separated by the distance re-quired to give a double impression; that which is necessary for the points of the compass to give a distinct impression is not the separa-tion of its branches, but the difference that exists in the feeling of the skin that is touched. The inverse phenomenon is produced on distended skin. Czermak has observed that on the stomach of a woman during pregnancy, one must increase the separation of the compass to produce a double impression. One sees, thus, that the distribution of sensitivity on the cutaneous surface remains the same regardless of whether normal or pathological causes have modified the size of the surface.

When one places the two points of the compass on two different surfaces, for example, the mucous membrane of the lips and the epidermis adjoining it, both points will be felt no matter how small the separation. How is this explained? It is clear that the mucous membrane of the buccal cavity, while a subordination of the skin,

---

[3] In this experiment, one must be careful not to separate the branches of the compass to the maximum distance at which the two impressions are fused, as this distance cannot help but vary during the course of the studies due to the effects of experience and attention. If this precaution is not taken, it can happen that the points of the compass will produce a double impression instead of a single impression; this would obviously change the "determinism" of the experience.

differs from the skin essentially by its texture; the two teguments are of a different nature. Therefore, it is probable that two points—even very close together—on each of the teguments present a greater difference, as regards their manner of feeling, than two points farther apart but both on the epidermis.

Attention has a certain effect on the precision of the touch. It has been observed that, with a great deal of attention, one can, so to speak, split an otherwise single impression and distinctly perceive the two pressures of the compass. This phenomenon can also be explained: A difference between two sensations is translated for the consciousness into the form of a small shock which is felt the moment one passes from one sensation to the other; this little shock is itself a sensation, and we perceive it according to the same rules as other sensations. Now, everyone has noticed that such-and-such a sensation, which passes unperceived when the mind is distracted, will be noted if one pays a little attention. This fact is incontestable, though difficult to explain. If the mind is alert at the moment when the two points of the compass come in contact with our skin, we will perceive the elementary sensation of the shock which separates them; this is all that is needed for the two sensations to remain distinct.

Habit, in general, has the effect of diminishing the diameter of the circles of sensation; following several hours of repeated exercise, one is able to distinguish two points which had previously been fused. Why? Exercise aids powerfully in the differentiation of the sense organs and allows the grasping of nuances of sensation where other people see only identity. This fact is noted in blind people— especially people who have been blind for a long time. Goltz has observed that they have circles of sensation much smaller than those of other people. The reason for this is that, deprived of sight, they are obliged to exercise their tactile sensitivity more often than those who have eyes to guide them. The inequality of precision over various regions of our skin should perhaps be linked to the effect of experience. What is certain is that the regions which distinguish themselves in this area are, by their position, their mobility, and their usage, most often exercising their sensitivity.

V

The collection of facts that I have put before the reader will allow him to form a very clear idea of the manner in which two similar sensations come to be fused. One can perform similar experiments and reason in the same way for visual sensations, which fuse in the same manner as sensations of touch. The process to be used reminds one of that of Weber's compass: Two very narrow strings are placed at a determined distance from the eye; if the two strings are separated or are brought together, their images are formed distinctly or they are fused. The separation required for the two strings to be seen distinctly is inversely proportional to the acuteness of the retinal region on which the images are produced. Let us cite a number. It has been verified that, when images are formed on the midline of the eye, the strings, to be perceived as distinct, must be 150 times farther apart than when they are projected on the macula of the retina. The explanation of this phenomenon is the same as that given for tactile perception. We perceive the image as single or as double according to whether the rays of light diffused by the two strings have excited retinal elements gifted with a uniform sensitivity or a differing sensitivity. In the first case, retinal sensations fuse, and in the second, they remain distinct.

Fusion can occur between a sensation and an idea. Here is an example I have borrowed from A. Bain: "When we look at the full moon, we instantaneously receive the impression of the state which results from the addition of the impressions that the disk of the moon has already made on us. . . . The operation is carried out so rapidly that we pay no attention to it."[4]

[4] This is, if I am not mistaken, the only place where Bain has occasion to speak about the law of fusion (*Sens et Intelligence*, p. 419) .

REFERENCE

Adams, F. (Trans.) *The Extant Works of Aretaeus the Cappadocian*. London: Sydenham Society, 1860.

2

The Influence of Exercise and Suggestion on the Position of the Threshold

I

Volkmann and his students have studied at length the effect of exercise on tactile sensitivity and maintain as a fact that the threshold of sensitivity diminishes considerably with education. Many authors have published graphs in which they follow from session to session the displacement of the threshold as a result of exercise. It frequently happens, however, that observations on the basis of which we formulate laws are constantly verified by second-rate minds until an original thinker questions these laws, studies them, and perceives that the "fact" was indeed erroneous. This is precisely what has happened regarding the influence of exercise on threshold.

Tawney, of whom I have already spoken at great length, verified that, in certain persons, fineness of touch can be improved with exercise, but that improvement is contingent upon one condition: these persons must know the objectives of the experiment and expect a decrease in the threshold. These conditions are ideally realized when the subjects are students in the laboratory; they have prior knowledge from their psychology lessons on the effect of exercise on tactile sensitivity and do not fail to conform to it. The decrease in threshold which Tawney shows in self-suggestioned people is very surprising. Here is one example. Note that the education of touch was performed solely on the subject's forearm (anterior region) and that it produced the following decrease in threshold: The minimum separation for this particular region became 10 times smaller, passing from 50 mm. to 5 mm. Since the regions indicated in the table

Influence de l'exercice et de la suggestion sur la position du seuil. *Année psychologique*, 1902, *9*, 235-248.

[Table 1] were not directly exercised, they profited solely from exercise of the forearm.

Table 1. Education of Touch Through Suggestion

	Period of Determination of Threshold*					
	Before	After	Relation	Before	After	Relation
	Left Side			Right Side		
Dorsal forearm	50	5	10	50	5	10
Back of hand	25	4	6 1/4	25	11	2 3/11
Chest	27	6	*6 /16*	50	5	10
Knee	30	8	3 3/4	18	10	1 4/5
Hip	70	20	3 1/2	88	19	4 12/19
Collarbone	48	14	3 3/7	25	10	2 1/2
Arm	70	24	*12 11/12*	70	33	2 4/33
Inside forearm	48	20	2 4/5	58	24	2 5/12
Thumb	13	5	2 3/5	12	6	2
Abdomen	41	18	2 5/18	27	13	2 1/13
Thigh	60	23	2 14/23	70	12	5 5/6
Cheek	13	12	1 1/12	13	10	*13*
Heel	17	11	1 6/11	15	8	1 7/8
Top of foot	33	20	1 13/20	30	15	2
Back, between shoulder blades	55	30	1 5/6	—	—	—
Lower midback	57	28	2 1/28	—	—	—
Forehead	22	13	1 9/13	—	—	—

* *The numbers are in millimeters and express the minimum separation.* [*The statistical errors in this table are Binet's, and are indicated by italics.*]

An American author cites several other analogous examples. He attributes these amazing effects to autosuggestion and has documented his hypothesis by quite a demonstrative countertest. He directed himself to subjects who, due to an infraction of the rule ordinarily followed in Wundt's laboratory, had not been taught the true purpose of the experiment; he let them think that he was interested only in determining as precisely as possible the threshold of their sensitivity. These subjects underwent as long an education of touch as the preceding persons without gaining the slightest fineness. After 20 days of exercise, their threshold remained unchanged, and in some of them it even increased slightly. Then, by merely warning the subjects that he was trying to understand the effect of exercise, the threshold diminished immediately, thus conforming to tradition. These facts are illustrative of the suggestibility of students of the laboratory and of the degree of confidence one should have in them.

Here is another example. It concerns a person on whom the value of the threshold on the dorsal and palmar faces of the forearm was determined 40 times during five successive days [Table 2]. The threshold did not diminish. On the sixth day, the subject was told that the threshold was being increased in order to determine the

Table 2. Determination of Threshold

Areas	1st Day	2nd Day	3rd Day	4th Day	5th Day	6th Day (Suggestion) Minimum
Forearm Palmar face	26	26	27	—	—	14
Forearm Dorsal face	39	37	36	40	38	10

influence exercised by the suggestion that the threshold was being lowered. Suddenly the threshold, which previously had not diminished, passed from 26 to 14 in one case and from 39 to 10 in the other. The explanation Tawney provides is that of autosuggestion, but this alone is insufficient. I think that the author wanted to say that the person who imagines his threshold will diminish makes a greater effort to analyze and to perceive the two points; that is, he tends to accentuate in himself the attitude of the interpreter. What confirms my interpretation is that Tawney constantly referred to the increase of *Vexierfehler* [paradoxical judgments] during the experiment. Now, these *Vexierfehler,* when they are not the result of an avowed distraction, are explained by an attitude of interpretation.

I was still unfamiliar with Tawney's investigations when the idea came to me of exercising the sense of touch in some of my subjects in order to discover whether a change would occur in their manner of perceiving the contacts. I was well aware of the fact that the study of touch is dominated by psychological questions, and I therefore wanted to determine how the mental habits of a person are modified by exercise.

It is quite rare when two authors, working independently of each other, see a particular question from exactly the same point of view. Tawney was especially preoccupied with the influence exercised by autosuggestion; my preoccupation was somewhat different. I took people who, foreign to psychology, were ignorant of the effect of exercise on the threshold, and I was careful not to suggest it. These people could certainly understand, at length, that their touch became more refined, even though this was not a defined expectation. Thus, the phenomenon of suggestion, as such, played less of a role in my studies than in Tawney's, which does not mean that psychical influences were excluded—on the contrary.

I had the leisure to make complete studies of two people and to sketch those of several others. For the two people, Catherine and Mme Cra . . . , I conducted the experiments during about ten sessions which were separated by long intervals. These people, as we already know, were initially simplists. In the first sessions, they did not commit any errors on the single point and the threshold was obtuse. With education, they both changed type; they arrived at a final phase in which they were constantly mistaken on the single point and had very acute thresholds. During one phase, Catherine was even led to respond with a uniform "two" for all the contacts, exactly as Dr. Sim . . . had done.

These facts are in agreement with those Tawney reported. They proved to us that the categories which we establish between persons relative to tactile sensitivity have nothing definite about them. Through exercise, the simplist achieves the status of an interpreter; he achieves it more or less easily, depending on his intelligence and his aptitude for analysis. From this point of view, then, the experiments revealed a curious difference between my two subjects in the speed of adaptation. In Catherine, the education of touch was made exclusively through exercise; never did I show her the apparatus or give her an explanation. With Mme Cra . . . , I wished to keep the same neutrality, but I was obliged to intervene, as she threatened to become externally fixed in a stationary state. Mme Cra . . . is intelligent and attentive, but her attention is more superficial than profound, and she does not exert much effort. I had to explain various parts of the experiment, initiating her by degrees, sometimes asking a precise question which necessarily made a suggestion, sometimes revealing a bit of information on an important point, sometimes showing the instrument I used for the contacts. Each time I noted the changes in her responses and the way in which she profited from the lèssons I gave her. Chance thus furnished us with two extreme types: one is comparable to a good student who makes rapid progress alone; I allow myself to compare the other to a slow or indolent child who has constant need of his teacher's stimulation.

Let us first talk of Catherine; the history of her education does not lack interest. There is more to be noted here than the decrease of her threshold with exercise. When we spoke of her in our second chapter on simplists, we showed her responding with a correctness which was almost schematic: precise and large threshold, no error on the single point, almost no "two" responses for small separations inferior to the threshold. This simplistic attitude was maintained during the first three sessions without notable change. The sessions were long, the contacts numerous; it is unlikely that our means were the result of numbers given by chance.

During the fourth session, a small change occurred: there were responses of "two" for the single point and for very small separations. These new responses were small in number—a proportion of one to five. By the fifth session, the modification was accentuated; the number of "two" responses was half, that is, one to two. By the sixth session, a new change which was greater still; the number of "two" responses became general, absolute. It was during this session that Catherine rejoined Dr. Sim. . . . Did she remain there? No. Did she retrogress, go back through the phases she had just gone through? Not that either! At the seventh session, a new change was produced; it was indeed a very curious one—one which I did not anticipate. The number of "two" responses remained the same for separations smaller than the threshold, but diminished for the single point; it was as if our subject had begun to distinguish between a single point and the smaller separations. The same fact was noticed in the eighth session, but vanished in the ninth and last, Catherine being troubled by a headache.

Let us summarize the steps of this education: 1) Catherine began with the simplistic attitude. 2) She increased the number of "two" responses. 3) All of her responses were "two" responses. 4) They diminished for the single point. Each of these transitory stages represents a state of interpretation which we have encountered in other persons: the second stage is that of Dr . . . , of Mme L . . . , and of myself; the third stage is that of Dr. Sim . . . ; and the fourth is that to which Marguerite, our virtuoso, arrived after a complete initiation troubled by a headache.

I now reproduce a table [Table 3] in which one can follow in detail the facts I have just summed up.

Table 3. Progress of the Education of Touch in Catherine

Session	4th 2/1901		5th 4/1901		6th [Date not given]		7th 8/1901		8th 11/1901		9th 13/1901	
Separation of Points	Reply 2 pt.	1 pt.	Reply 2 pt.	1 pt.	Reply 2 pt.	1 pt.	Reply 2 pt.	1 pt.	Reply 2 pt.	1 pt.	Reply 2 pt.	1 pt.
0.0	3	13	8	8	12	0	8	7	7	9	14	3
0.5	5	11	9	7	12	0	12	3	12	4	14	2
1.0	8	8	11	5	12	0	14	2	15	1	13	3
1.5	12	4	15	1	12	0	15	1	15	1	16	0
2.0	16	0	16	0	12	0	16	0	16	0	16	0
3.0	16	0	16	0	12	0	16	0	16	0	16	0

Obviously, so many numerical results were not recorded without many words being exchanged. I was careful to write down all the dialogues of the experiments; they were, however, less significant than I had hoped. Catherine expressed herself badly, she made a great number of confusions, and the language of psychology was very foreign to her. As the sessions were repeated, the idea came to her very naturally that her touch should improve. She was thus influenced, as are students of the laboratory, by autosuggestion. The other remarks she made were of less interest, but I will comment on one of them because she repeated it often with insistence. She imagined that I no longer pricked her with the same points I had used at the beginning of the experiment. At the start, I had used only broad points; then, when I noted that she progressed in her perception, I substituted finer points for the broad ones. This illusion, as I see it, is explained through the fault of analysis. In the first session, Catherine perceived large points because of her lack of reflection: she thought that the sensation produced by small separations was the result of the application of one broad point. With experience, she understood the nature of the sensation more clearly and eventually related it to an excitation produced by two small points very close together. Thus she responded "two" for sensations which at the beginning had made her answer "one."

This is not a hypothesis on our part but a simple verification of facts. The peculiarity of the illusion is that when Catherine finally attributes the broad sensation to fine points very close together, she actually believes that she can perceive the fine points; that there are no longer any broad contacts.

Despite this progress in the nature of her response, I think that Catherine is not yet able to distinguish the differences which exist in small separations. The estimations of distance which she so often makes do not give averages which are different for separations below the threshold. It is only after 15 mm. that these averages present notable differences. I present herewith some of these averages of estimation [Table 4]. It is interesting to compare them with those furnished by Marie, our hyperesthetic subject.

Table 4. Average of the Estimation of Separation

Actual Separation	Estimated Separation
Single point	6 mm.
0.5 cm.	8 mm.
1.0 cm.	8 mm.
1.5 cm.	1 cm. 18
2.0 cm.	1 cm. 50
2.5 cm.	1 cm. 70
3.0 cm.	2 cm. 30

Although this method of estimation only gives entirely indirect information on judgments, it permits us to see in our subject an inability to distinguish clearly between the single point and the separations of ½ cm. and of 1 cm.

II

It may be recalled that Mme Cra . . . , during the first two sessions, fixed herself in the attitude of a simplist. In responding to 300 different contacts, she did not once change attitudes; she committed no errors on the single point, nor did she lower her threshold. I then initiated her gradually to a number of particularities of the instrument to see if she would utilize these cues in making a better analysis. On the third session, a rapid examination of her sensitivity demonstrated that she still maintained the simplistic attitude. After the examination ended, I made her feel and touch the points of the instrument, affirming that they had the same fineness. This was a revelation which surprised her very much, because she said, "I felt at certain moments a pressing and not a pricking." One can guess what she meant to say: she made allusion to the abnormal sensations produced by two points very close together. I present here, in a single table [Table 5], the results of the experiments so that one may follow and verify my deductions.

Table 5. Progress of the Education of Touch in Mme Cra . . .

Series	1st		2nd		3rd		4th		5th		6th	
Separation of Points	*1 pt.*	*2 pt.*	*1 pt.*	*2 pt.*	*1 pt.*	*2 pt.*	*1 pt.*	*2 pt.*	*1 pt.*	*2 pt.*	*1 pt.*	*2 pt.*
0.0	8	0	16	0	8	0	4	0	3	1	8	0
0.5	8	0	16	0	8	0	4	0	4	0	6	2
1.0	8	0	16	0	8	0	4	0	4	0	0	7
1.5	7	1	15	1	7	1	2	2	4	0	4	4
2.0	3	5	8	7	2	5	0	4	1	3	1	7
2.5	0	8	2	14	0	8	0	4	0	4	0	8
3.0	0	8	8	16	0	8	0	4	0	4	0	8

After the first lesson, I made a second series of contacts. No change was produced in the threshold. I revealed the instrument and my subject examined it with curiosity. A third series: No change. I resumed the lesson by having my subject feel all the series of separations, each time indicating to her the number of points. New series of contacts (fourth): No change. Repetition of the same lesson. New series (fifth): No change. Last lesson, longer and more precise. I had the subject feel the series of separations and give her answer for each separation; then I would correct it. New series (sixth): This time a change was finally produced. There were responses of "two" for small separations and some trouble with the large separations, but the modification had little importance; one could almost attribute it to a lack of attention.

By emotional means, I finally succeeded in activating this evolution, which was so slowly produced by purely intellectual means. The following session Mme Cra . . . reverted to her former habits of simplistic interpretation. I then warned her that she was making a large number of errors and that hereafter I would signal these errors the moment they occurred. This warning, though made in very polite terms, produced much surprise and a little emotion in Mme Cra . . . ; subjects who are being paid do not like to be reproached, and for cause. From this moment on, there was a change: Suddenly the threshold was lowered, the "two" responses multiplied for small separations, and the *Vexierfehler* became frequent for the single point. Under the stress of emotion, Mme Cra . . . was transformed into an interpreter. Here are the results [see Table 6]:

Table 6. *Transformation of a Subject's Attitude Through Correction*

Separation of Points	Before the Correction		After the Correction	
	1 pt.	*2 pt.*	*1 pt.*	*2 pt.*
0.0	4	0	8	4
0.5	4	0	4	8
1.0	4	0	1	11
1.5	1	3	0	12
2.0	0	4	0	12
2.5	0	4	0	12
3.0	0	4	0	12

I suppose that Mme Cra . . . did not decide sooner to change her mode of interpretation because she feared venturing into the somewhat delicate analysis of large contacts; after all, she wished not to run the risk of committing errors. One frequently encounters this state of mind. If it were necessary to prove that the purely psychological motives which she obeyed in changing her mode of interpretation brought no modification to her tactile sensitivity, I would cite the following fact: In the estimations of distance that she gave me at each response, she almost always, and with striking regularity, attributed the value of 5 mm. to the separation of 1.5 cm.; she made this evaluation when she was in her simplistic period. From the moment in which she became an interpreter, that is to say, in the last session, she was obliged to indicate the distance of separations less than 1.8 cm., since she responded "two" for these separations. Now, the distance she attributed to them was always, and without exception, the same—that of 5 mm. This is certainly proof that she did not perceive any appreciable difference between the separations of .5 cm., 1 cm., and 1.5 cm.

In other people, I saw the transformation from simplist to interpreter take place with much more rapidity; among these subjects were two 16-year-old boys who had been blind from birth, who proved themselves to be simplists for approximately the first 15 minutes, that is, up to the point when I permitted them to touch the points and the instrument. They then asked if all the points were the same. At my affirmative response, they immediately modified their mode of response and became interpreters.

These experiments, which are, as one may see, in such perfect accord with those of Tawney, have a double importance: First, they show us how much a purely psychological cause influences a person's response and modifies the apparent acuity of his touch. While this is not, of course, other than in appearance, it is almost always taken for a reality. In the second place, we understand that physiologists and psychologists who have not taken account of all the circumstances which can exercise a suggestion on the subject have committed a grave fault without knowing it. To see the apparatus, touch it, know that the two points are equal, know that two points very close together give a broad contact, be afraid of being mistaken, receive a warning—these are some of the circumstances affecting the judgments of our subjects which we have been able to recognize. To take no account of them is to work in the dark, to put precise numbers to equivocal responses.

3

The Threshold of a Double Sensation Cannot Be Scientifically Determined

Fechner has made a profound reflection on psychophysical experiments: He noted that, when the subject thought before making a comparison of two stimuli, his judgment was less accurate than if he had stated, without forethought, which stimulus appeared bigger. This observation can perhaps serve as an epigraph to my article. We have, in fact, verified that the threshold of a double sensation can be determined under specified conditions; if, however, one extends the test, requesting the subject's utmost attention, the appearance of the threshold fades and that which was at first clear becomes very vague.

Going into further detail, we recall that in our studies on the determination of threshold, we divided our subjects into two groups, the simplists and the interpreters. The latter did not have a determinable threshold. One could find it only with the simplists, who presented an extremely precise threshold—not a zone but a line. I think that the measures of tactile sensitivity published by so many physiologists are representative of this type of subject. Admittedly, it is strange that so important a physiological measure as threshold is applicable only to certain types of individuals, and there is something very shocking about the exceptions to this rule. Another more serious concern, however, is that every simplist is a future interpreter. In some, the transformation is produced by educating the touch; in others, by revealing the apparatus or explaining the experiment in depth. From then on, the simplist loses every trace of a threshold.

These are not theories or interpretations—they are brutal facts.

Le seuil de la sensation double ne peut pas être fixé scientifiquement. *Année psychologique*, 1902, 9, 248-252.

One need not be a psychologist to verify them. They are not grasped by introspection, but rather by the simple process of recording all numerical responses of subjects and calculating a percentage. I think that the tables we have published are eloquent. Most authors have not yet recognized the nonexistence of the threshold since they continue to publish a measure of it. From whence comes this error? From their negligence, I think. They satisfied themselves with a small number of responses and, above all, they discounted the "two" replies for a single point by attributing this characteristic error to a moment's distraction. I personally know very sincere and conscientious authors who have found the threshold of tactile sensitivity for different regions of the body. They did not record any of their subjects' responses, but, at the time of the experiment, established once and for all, *ne varietur,* the threshold of the explored region; this determination, of course, was accomplished only by a systematic selection: certain replies were kept as correct, others were eliminated. It is an arbitrary method used at one's convenience; I am convinced that whenever one conforms to the conditions of this method, no threshold will be found. Instead, one must 1) note all answers, and 2) prolong and intensify the test.

Furthermore, the threshold, which consists in a relationship between two types of response, is only the exterior and visible sign of a certain state of sensitivity. Just as a sign should not be considered in itself, but always in connection with what it signifies, so, when one speaks of a threshold, one must have in mind the subjective phenomenon of which it is the expression. The psychophysicists have made the mistake in their mathematical conceptions of treating the threshold as if it were a value unto itself, as if it were a quantity. If one is careful to direct attention to the mental side of the question, one quickly arrives at the conclusion that empirical determination of a threshold is of no great value for psychology. I would say further that, even if it were demonstrated that everyone has, for every region of his body, an absolutely precise and constant threshold, one still cannot affirm that sensitivity is a measurable thing. For the threshold to have this significance, it would be necessary that the subjective states to which it corresponds be equivalent. Now, it is nothing of the sort. The words "one" and "two" obviously do not have the same meaning even when they are applied to the same thing, because the focus of attention varies from one individual to another. Focus of attention is of two types: that fixed solely on the exterior stimulus, and that fixed mainly on the exterior stimulus, but also partly on the experience subjective sensation.

We have seen many examples of the first attitude, which is the most natural of all and which fulfills our need to understand the exterior world in an attempt to adapt ourselves to it. Let us recall the initial responses of an unwarned person whose hand we touch with the points of an esthesiometer, asking him to reply as he wishes. Immediately, the person's attention is directed toward the object used for the contact; all his answers evidence a naive preoccupation which can be translated into common language by the phrase, "With what am I being touched?" It is thus that we at first collect answers like these: "It is iron," or "It is pincers," or "It is a pin." The objective orientation is carried to such extremes that certain persons envision complicated forms of the instrument; their descriptions are so precise that they can sometimes be reproduced by a drawing. Needless to say, none bears a resemblance to an esthesiometer. If the unwarned person, thus caught in a natural state, turns his attention back to himself, to his body, to the sensation he experiences, it is, according to my observation, due to the influence of fear. He is afraid of being hurt; fear making the suggestion, he convinces himself that he is actually suffering and cries out. We thus encounter a return of attention to the sensation. Due to the preoccupations which determine it, it is again an adaptive act toward exterior objects and consequently corresponds to a necessity for life relationships.

With a continuation of the experiment, the attitude of attention is modified. Entirely naturally, it seems, the simplistic subject whom I have in mind becomes interested in the number of distinct sensations that he simultaneously experiences. This, then, is the beginning of analysis and interpretation. In some this new orientation is not adopted, but in others the change seems to occur spontaneously. On this point, however, I must express some reservation. Without being aware of it, the subject must feel what I shall call an "ambient instigation"; I myself am unable to perceive what it consists of. The moment never fails to arrive in which, either spontaneously or with a little suggestion, the subject begins a series of responses in which he indicates only the number of points.

Does this indicate a change in the focus of attention? I do not think so. I am making an interpretation here, because, as I have often said, the simplists do not lend much insight into what occurs in their minds. It is my opinion that they continue to direct their attention toward the exterior object; they retain an objective orientation. While it is necessary that they take account of the sensation—without it, no perception would be possible—they nevertheless do not stop there. They skim this stage and pass rapidly from the sign to the object. It is by this insufficiency of the subjective phase that I explain the coarseness of their perceptions. They fail to take account of entirely abnormal sensations produced by very small separations; they neglect to make an analysis of these sensations; they are not surprised by them. The most summary interpretation satisfies them. It is as if they said to themselves: "If there is no double sensation, of what importance is the rest? I will report one point." Naturally, they do not even ask themselves this question; by posing it, they would be conscious, they would understand what they were doing. This is just the opposite of what happens. It seems to me that herein lies the general explanation of the simplistic attitude; I think I am omitting many details, but the overall impression is correct.

I spoke of another attitude of attention: that which I called subjective, to contrast it with the preceding one. This expression is somewhat inaccurate because, in reality, no strictly subjective attitude occurs. With the interpreters, as with the simplists, there is always an intellectual effort to guess the nature of the exterior object which is felt. As with the simplists, the operation supposes two parts: the experienced sensation and the interpretation of it. That which distinguishes the interpreter from the simplist is that the former devotes more attention to the first part of the operation, to the subjective phase. He does not pass hastily over the first stage; he stops a moment and consequently has the time to recognize that he is being made to experience bizarre sensations which correspond neither to the perception of a single point, nor to the perception of two points. He thus makes a more profound analysis than does the simplist. Since this analysis presupposes a return of thought to the sensation, we say that, everything considered, the attention of the interpreter is subjective. One can now see that the expression should not be taken too literally. Despite the faults that the interpreter exposes himself to committing and that he almost always commits, it is not to be disputed that he is superior to the simplist in intelligence; he is more refined, he is more thoughtful, he is slower, he is more conscientious. Further, interpreters are ordinarily of a different age and social condition than simplists.

This theory allows us to understand that there is nothing constant in the classification of subjects, and that one who was at first a simplist can at length become an interpreter. The transformation is not even accidental, but rather the rule.

How, after all, could it be otherwise? What is lacking in the simplist is an attentive analysis of his sensation. Everything which facilitates his analysis, everything which aids in his becoming conscious of himself, hastens his metamorphosis. Now, exercise increases the sharpness of attention; it allows one to notice on the twentieth trial that which was not noticed on the first. In the same way, the sight of the esthesiometer indicates that all the points are of equal size—a discovery which again facilitates interpretation and causes one to note that the perceived sensations resemble contacts now broad, now narrow. Witnessing experiments on others, noticing that some people reply "one" for a small separation, can, above all, transform a simplist into an interpreter. This, then, is an artificial interpreter in whom the weakness of analytical ability has been guided and sustained by a strange coincidence. These interpreters resemble scholars with more erudition than intelligence.

Note that all the classifications we have just made are of mental phenomena. That which distinguishes the simplist from the interpreter is the focus of his attention, his manner of judging. The state of his tactile sensitivity was not taken into consideration. Our analysis did not go that far. But, even if all persons who served as subjects had the same degree of sensitivity, these psychical distinctions, with all their consequences, would nonetheless exist; the interpreters would appear to have a narrow threshold and the simplists a broad one. We have peremptory proof of this truth: A simple verbal explanation suffices to change completely the subject's responses and to displace his threshold by several centimeters, even though it is evident that the exchanged words did not modify his tactile sensitivity. The determination of a definitive threshold is practically impossible; it varies from one moment to another, and the more one seeks it, the less it can be found. Further, the threshold is so dependent upon the mode of interpretation of the sensation that even when it appears to have a clear position, one cannot be sure it expresses the organ's sensitivity.

4

From Sensation to Intelligence

I

Four or five years ago, I conducted investigations of tactile sensitivity among children in some of the elementary schools of Paris and thought that I had verified that the most intelligent and attentive students were the ones with the greatest fineness of touch. Using Weber's compass as the method [see Chapter 1], I had each subject say whether he felt one or two points. The two points of the compass were applied simultaneously to the skin while hidden from the subject's view; the separation necessary for the points to be felt as double, and not mistaken for a unique impression, was supposed to be the measure of the sensitivity of the region. The greater the separation required for a double sensation, the duller the touch. On the basis of this method, I arrived—or rather thought that I had arrived—at a measure of tactile sensitivity according to the size of the separation in millimeters.

More recently, I undertook the same study with adults and found the question to be more complex, and most of all less sensory, than I had anticipated. The nature of the subjects' responses did not directly translate the state of their sensitivity; it reflected, instead, their interpretations—what one might call the degree of their tactile intelligence. One subject, who appeared to have a finer touch than another, simply had a less dull mind, was a more subtle interpreter. I made several attempts to demonstrate the obviousness of this truth.

For example, I observed that many seemingly unimportant psychological circumstances can change the position of the threshold by enormous proportions. We refer to threshold as the minimum separation with which the duality of points is perceived. Now, the thresh-

---

De la sensation a l'intelligence. *Revue philosophique*, 1903, 55, 449-467, 592-618.

old for the dorsal face of the hand is 2.5 cm.; this signifies very simply that it is necessary to give a separation of this value to the points of the compass for a normal person to perceive that there are two points instead of one, and for the number of correct perceptions to be superior to that which would be given by chance.

I say, then, that the position of the threshold, which at first seems to be very precise, varies in a most surprising manner under the influence of small psychological causes. One lowers the threshold, that is, diminishes the necessary separation, simply by revealing the compass and permitting the subject to manipulate it, by explaining to him that very close points give a unique sensation, or finally, by having him witness a tactile experiment on another person. I have seen cases where the threshold was displaced in very surprising proportions after one of the preceding facts; indeed, it is not uncommon for the threshold to decrease by several centimeters. I will cite only one person, who, after the necessary lessons and explanations, presented to me a threshold which was *10 times smaller* than before.

The conclusion of these investigations does not lack importance for the measure of sensitivity. After many hesitations, I clearly concluded that it is impossible to measure scientifically the threshold of tactile sensitivity with the compass experiment and Weber's method. One must be content with an empirical measure which is gross and approximate.[1]

I will nevertheless continue this first investigation and force myself to go into it in depth, making a more deliberate study of the mental operations which give rise to the perception of the number of points. In my former works, I questioned my subjects on what they had felt following a series of contacts; now I question them immediately after each contact. This is a more direct, and consequently more reliable, introspection.

For these new studies, I use a method of exciting the skin which is somewhat different from that of Weber's. I begin by showing my subjects the esthesiometer with its two points separated by 5 mm.[2] I say to them: "I am going to make you feel two contacts successively. Each of these contacts will be produced by the points which you see,

---

[1] A detailed account of these experiments appears in *Année psychologique*, 1903, 9, 79.

[2] I have described this instrument in preceding publications; see especially *Année psychologique*, Vol. 7. I recall here simply that the points are .8 mm. in diameter and that the pressure which they support is 50 grams.

but the separation of the points will not be equal; it will be greater in one case than in the other. You will perceive these two separations with as much care as possible, and you will compare one with the other. You will be required to tell me each time which separation seems larger to you, whether it is the first or the second." These instructions do not permit much liberty, and they oblige the subject to find a difference between the two separations. This is the maximum information that the subject receives; I never apply the points directly before the subject's eyes or teach him to distinguish the large separations from the small ones by tactile sensation; I avoid everything which might perfect his education. Nor do I reveal to him what separations I am going to use, whether the points are separated by 1 mm. or by 1 cm. During the sessions, I do not make any suggestions to him. To guard against boredom and distraction, I sometimes give vague encouragement, but I am careful not to evaluate the responses which are given, not to find them wrong or right. I write them exactly as I receive them, without adding any type of reflection. This is very important.

All the examinations of tactile sensitivity are done on the dorsal face of the left hand. The left hand is placed without stiffness on a table and hidden from view by a screen. I use my esthesiometer for the contacts, saying each time, "Here is the first; here is the second." The interval which passes between the two contacts is about six seconds, sometimes a little longer, but never shorter.

I press the points firmly on the skin and leave them there for approximately one second; I then raise them with a sudden movement. The two contacts are placed at approximately the same point on the hand, but naturally this superpositioning is not rigorous since the separations of the points are of unequal value. As soon as the subject has given his response, I record it without commentary; this takes about 10 seconds. If the subject's response is brief, I can make an average of four double contacts per minute. More often, however, the subject explains his response at length, and in a minute, only one double contact is made. Among the separations which I use, one is constant at 5 mm. and is the referent to which all others must be compared. I begin by making comparisons of very great separations of 12 or 15 mm.; the difference is so clear that few people fail to recognize it. Then I progressively diminish the variable separations by millimeters. In this fashion, I successively compare with the standard all the series of separations from 12 or 15 mm. down to, and including, 6 mm. I follow this descending order. For each variable separation, the comparison is made five times; the small separation is first three times and second twice. When the person refuses to make a judgment on the difference between the two separations or finds them equal, I make one or two additional experiments so that I always have five precise judgments relative to each variable separation. As one can see, this method is a combination of the method of right and wrong cases and the method of minimal change.

The authors who employ a psychophysical method similar to the preceding one generally terminate the trials when they obtain either a correct answer or a false answer. Let us suppose that they follow the order which I have just indicated. They begin by making a comparison between the standard and very large separations of 15 mm.; the difference is clearly perceived. They will then proceed from these large separations to middle separations, which will be less well perceived and give rise to numerous errors. With smaller separations, the errors become greater and greater—so great, in fact, that it becomes apparent that a difference is no longer perceived. At this point, the investigators stop, judging it useless to go further. In the preceding example, if the separation of 9 mm. were perceived to be equal to 5 mm., or if this comparison gave no result, one would think it a waste of time to continue the experiment, making the comparisons between 5 mm. and the smaller separations of 8, 7, 6 mm., etc.

On this point, I separate myself absolutely from those who precede me. This seems a paradox, but I am not certain that the comparison of separations of 5 and 7 mm. is impossible solely because the comparison of separations of 5 and 9 mm. gives inaccurate results. This endeavor is absurd numerically, but perhaps not from the point of view of tactile sensitivity. One should not be too quick to generalize results or reasonings which prove to be accurate in a very different domain. The principle that two quantities equal to a third are equal to each other can serve as an example. Translated to tactile sensitivity, this principle can become completely false: Sensation A barely differs from sensation B and is thus considered equal to it; sensation B, in its turn, is compared with sensation C, from which it differs very little, and the two sensations are again equated. Now, if one compares A with C, it is quite possible that a difference between them will be discovered.

Assuming for myself the task of continuing the comparison of separations whose differences seem, at first glance, well below the threshold, I obtained a result which I would not have questioned, had I stopped when the threshold was reached. I verified signs of a truly extraordinary hyperesthesia in some subjects whose tactile sensitivity appeared initially to be very dull. This method provided me with an extensive quantity of instructive material from which I will draw conclusions in a moment.

II

I arrive now at the facts of observation. I can present them in two different forms: either in a synthetic study where I try to delineate the common attitudes taken by all my subjects, or in an analytic study where I take more interest in differences than in similarities and establish certain intellectual types, ending up with various classifications. There is much risk involved in selecting one of these processes of exposition; I choose the second simply because I am fascinated, above all, by individual differences.

These differences are so noticeable that I am going to present them by means of a classification. I must admit that these classifications are a little subjective, my role as interpreter being quite important. It is very probable that another experimenter would envision a different classification. In any case, that which I expose is valid only for the particular type of experiment I conducted, namely, the perception of difference between two separations of points. It would be a mistake to suppose that for another sensory experience, even a tactile one, the same subjects would be categorized in an identical manner. My classifications do not have this generality; on this point I have proof. When I classified my subjects according to their perception of points using Weber's method, my grouping was quite different; these individuals were described as simplists or interpreters. Here I did not find the same classification, but one should not be surprised at this. The intelligence of individuals is a very complex thing and must introduce a variety of differences according to the point of view under which it is contemplated.

With the benefit of these reservations to which I will essentially hold, I give herewith a general classification of my subjects as conscious or unconscious.

The unconscious subjects

This is a grouping which always has a provisional character. A person is placed among the unconscious because he is entirely incapable of explaining how he compares the separations; this absence of analysis can be due to particular circumstances, to a lack of cultural intellect, to a lack of favorable orientation. Such an unconscious person can become conscious with lessons or with the necessary explanations, but I classify my subjects according to the attitude they assume at the start of the first session.

A subdivision must be made among the unconscious. Some people are not only unconscious of the processes which they use, but believe that they do not use any process whatsoever; they are convinced that they respond by chance. Indeed, this is what happens to them from time to time, since they find no interest in that which they do not understand and therefore suffer from periodic distractions. In reality, however, they do not respond by chance when they are attentive to what is occurring. They consistently give a majority of correct answers, demonstrating that in one way or another, their responses are based on a certain mode of perception.

The other unconscious subjects are convinced that they do a serious job; although they cannot explain the process involved, they are persuaded of the accuracy of their responses.

Catherine. Subject absolutely unconscious of her processes and unable in any way to describe them.

Catherine is a young girl of 18 years of age, working as a cook, and without formal education. I made numerous contacts on her hand, but she was unable to explain how she compared the separations. Furthermore, she had no confidence in her answers; she protested that she did not understand anything about it, that she only knew how to answer, that she often responded by chance. These investigations appeared to her very tedious and monotonous. The following table [Table 1] summarizes the responses made during two sessions; there was no progress from one session to another. Overall, the correct responses outnumbered the false responses, especially for the larger separations; the truth appeared to her through a veil, as one can see from the table of numerical results.

Table 1. Experiments on the Touch of Catherine

	Responses	
Separation of Points	Correct	Incorrect
5—12	8	2
5—11	10	4
5—10	17	7
5—9	14	7
5—8	14	11
5—7	16	10
5—6	18	14

The separations of the preceding table are in millimeters; thus, 5—12 signifies that one of the separations to be compared was 5 mm., the other 12 mm. Naturally, the smallest separation was not always presented first; the two were alternated without regularity. It can be seen from the results that Catherine always gave a majority of correct responses, even for the difference of 1 mm. (separations 5—6, the most difficult of all to perceive on the table), but that the proportion of errors was particularly great for small differences.

Marguerite. Subject absolutely unconscious of her processes; she could not explain them, had no confidence in her answers.

Marguerite, a young girl of 16 years, is intelligent, well-informed, attentive, but showed herself incapable of clearly distinguishing the difference between two separations, even when the difference was as notable as 5—10. Like Catherine, she answered accurately a little more frequently than she answered falsely; when, however, she grasped the difference between the two separations, it remained very vague. Here are the results [Table 2]. With her, as with Catherine, the un-

Table 2. Experiments on the Touch of Marguerite

	Responses	
Separation	Correct	Incorrect
5—10	9	9
5—9	12	7
5—8	12	5
5—7	11	8
5—6	5	7

consciousness of the processes she used was accompanied by a strong mistrust of herself. Marguerite felt that she answered by chance, that she did not understand how to compare the two separations. She eventually became nervous from this incertitude, judged the experiment useless, and begged to end it. Nonetheless she was mistaken; she did not respond entirely by chance because the correct answers were in the majority.

Afterward, I could discern one of the principal causes of error which troubled her. In analyzing her errors, I saw that they fell into two groups: those consisting of finding the second separation too large, and those consisting of finding the second separation too small. The first type of error was committed only seven times, the second, 30 times. This latter error occurred as if the first separation, which had to be retained in the memory longer than the second, became larger; the error of time made it appear too big. I did not encounter this error with such clarity in other persons.[3]

To the two preceding subjects I add Armande, a 15-year-old girl, who sometimes made a rudimentary analysis of her responses, but other times failed to explain how she made the comparisons. Sometimes she said: "I feel a difference," or "I don't feel anything; if I decide, it will be by chance." I requested that she give me answers regardless of whether she felt they were given by chance; she consented only with great hesitation because the experiment did not seem serious to her. "What's the use?" she repeated. "If it's by chance, it lacks meaning." In reality, though, the answers were not given by chance as she believed; they were more often correct than incorrect.

We now arrive at our second category of unconscious subjects. They are unconscious from either a lack of general education, ignorance of psychological terms, or an inaptitude for self-analysis. But they are convinced that they do not respond by chance. If they are asked what process they use to judge the size of the separations, they invariably give the same answer: they feel the difference of separation. It is a sensation to them.

Lucienne. Absolutely unconscious subject.

This is a woman of 38 years, not stupid, of a changeable and emotional temperament, and almost totally deprived of formal edu-

---

[3] A blind person assured me that when the points are removed, the two remaining sensations seem to separate.

cation. She has a certain fineness of touch; of the 29 times I had her compare separations of 5 and 5.5 mm., she responded correctly 20 times and incorrectly only 9 times. She was always sure of her answers, but was unable to explain them. She repeated sentences such as: "I feel the pricking, I feel the space, I feel the separation." To say that it is a sensation is a good means of dispensing with all justification. But one must excuse a person who hardly knows how to read and write.

Chance brings together different people. Mme A., who has a very distinguished mind and who is, further, very intelligent, could not give me responses other than those of the preceding subject. Her thoughts were more highly developed, but her answers remained the same. "I feel the separation," she said. "Since I feel two points, I feel that they are more or less separated." "I feel two points and I feel that there is a separation between these points, and I tell you if it is small or large." "I feel it, I cannot say anything else. I feel the distance." Question: "But how do you know whether the separation is large or small?" Answer: "I am sure of my sensation." "My attention is fixed on the separation. It is almost as if I could see it." "I feel the separation. I have no other indication than this, since I do not see it." Despite several days of questioning, I was unable to obtain another explanation from Mme A. "I feel," she said, and that was enough for her. By being insistent, one needlessly offends her self-respect, because she quickly imagines that one doubts her veracity, her good faith, or her attention—all things which are above the slightest suspicion.

It would be of little use to prolong our study of unconscious subjects; they have nothing to teach us since they themselves know nothing.

III

The conscious subjects

Those who are conscious of the processes they use, and who can explain them in a manner sufficiently clear to convey to us what they mean to say, use four principal methods of comparing separations. These are 1) interpretation based on the form and the single or double nature of the contact; 2) comparison by abstract localization; 3) comparison by concrete localization; and 4) interpretation based on the pricking character of the sensation. I will briefly define these various types of interpretation and comparison, and present some detailed experimental results.

Interpretation based on the form and the single or double nature of the contact. Use of this indicator supposes that one knows that two close points give a single sensation. Consequently, when a person feels a single point in one case, and two in another, he concludes that the first separation is smaller than the second. All those who use this procedure agree that it consists in making two independent judgments which are then compared; furthermore, these are verbal judgments.

Comparison by abstract localization. This procedure alternates most often with the preceding one. I call it the procedure of abstract localization to oppose it to another much more rare procedure which I call concrete localization. Abstract localization excludes the region on which one makes the contacts; the subject does not situate the points on a fixed part of his hand, for example, on a particular metacarpal or an interosseous space. He forgets his hand and situates the points in relation to one another on an undefined surface. He knows that the back of his hand is touched, and he can picture it to himself if necessary, but he does not use this representation of his hand to compare the two separations. He considers the distance between the points, which appear to him in schematic form like small dots; he can picture them as visible points or as touched points, and they are situated on either the same line or two parallel lines. The comparison of their length occurs through a direct comparison of their positions, approximately as if a person showed us points marked in ink on a piece of paper and asked us if the distance between points one and two were equal to that between points three and four.

Comparison by concrete localization. Instead of viewing the hand as a sensitive surface of indefinite form, a subject using this method represents all the particular properties of form that characterize the hand, and from this draws conclusions for the evaluation of the separation of points; for example, if he feels that the points are placed on two neighboring metacarpals, he concludes that the separation of these two bones gives that of the points. This means of comparison seems to be complicated, even in its description; it could not be completely analyzed.

Interpretation based on the pricking nature of the points. All other things being equal, two points close together give a more painful impression—one that pricks more than that of two separated points. This is an indicator which few subjects used.

Without wishing to exaggerate the subdivisions, I think that I can place here an entire group of subjects, the normal ones. These are the ones who use, in various proportions, the processes which I have just described, or at least the first three of these. We will oppose these normal types to some aberrant types who behave entirely differently, due to a particular structure of their minds.

Normal types

I could cite a very great number of these. Three examples will suffice, however, for each presents certain particular traits.

M. Lary used processes 1 and 2, the form of the contact and abstract localization.

M. L., an assistant in my laboratory, is 30 years old, well-versed in the study of psychology, and knows how to observe himself. Even in his first session (February 27, 1902), he showed a certain ability to distinguish separations which were little different, as is shown by the following numbers. He was familiar with the esthesiometer, knew that the points were always the same, and knew that two

Table 3. Experiments on the Touch of M. L.

| Separation | Responses | | Uncertain |
	Correct	Incorrect	
5—10	3	5	2
5—15	7	1	1
5—8		2	2
5—7	4	0	2
5—6	2	3	1

points sufficiently close together gave a single impression. I questioned him after each evaluation; at my request, he summarized in writing the information he had been furnished:

"Two principal processes of comparison (the second will be explained further on). In one case, it seemed to me that there was a direct comparison of the sensations. The sensation of the first double contact lasted a long time, like an infection. At the moment

of the second double contact, it seemed that the points of the instrument were inserted, for instance, between the traces of the persistent sensations. There was a visual localization; the persisting figures
were localized approximately as this sketch represents them:

.   . .   .
1   2 2   1

Moreover, I did not see the hand clearly, nor the points of the instrument. The localization was made on an obscure surface."

These few lines are the synthesis of all the remarks which M. L.
made during the contacts. The synthesis has a good guarantee of accuracy, because the subject explained his evaluations in detail after
each contact. From the first answers given to us, it is interesting to
investigate how M. L. became aware of the process he used. Here
are some of his initial answers:

In comparing 5 mm. and 10 mm., he said: "The second is smaller.
I had a sensation of the first persisting up to the second, and it
seemed to me that the points of the second were interjected between
the traces of the first, which faded at that moment." "The second is
smaller. I made a direct comparison; it was very clear. I did not interpret. The two contacts seemed very clear to me. I saw them on my
hand, separated in one case, and less separated in the other." "The
visual image plays a role; the two pricks were localized in space." "I
have the impression that it was visual. The persisting impression was
at once visual and tactile."

It will be noted that, for M. L., this process results in a direct
comparison of two sensations and not of two judgments. M. L. was
convinced that he did not interpret; he compared. Nonetheless, he
often made errors and thought that points of one separation were included in those of the other, when it was exactly the contrary.

Fifteen days later we had a new session, during which M. L. gave
me some further details on his visual image of localization. "It was
slightly visual. I did not see my hand." Question: "Did you see the
points of the instrument?" Answer: "No. I only saw dots. It was quite
schematic. I saw a black surface." Question: "Did you call forth this
schematic image, or did it come by itself?" Answer: "It came by itself,
it imposed itself on me, it appeared immediately. I did not construct
a visual image in order to understand how the tactile sensation took
place. It seemed to appear immediately, as if it were a sensation. It

looked like those black geometrical figures in which the lines are on white . . .; after I saw the black figures, it was a simple comparison."

M. L. often used the form of the contacts in judging the separations. He used the second process as frequently as the preceding one and described it in the following terms:

"I sometimes had the sensation of two points very clearly separated but without there being any localization, and the sensation of a single point, or of a surface, or of two points in contact. In this case, I interpreted and declared the sensation of two points clearly separated as larger. In general, I do not think that there was localization in this process of comparison; I nonetheless recall having once perceived the two points in contact between the persisting double sensation of separated points, 1 2 1."

What is most interesting in this observation is its clarity. M. L., who was undergoing this type of experiment for the first time, immediately became conscious of the means he employed; we have just seen the precision with which he explained them to us. I did not suggest anything to him, and even in his early responses, before any questions on my part, he described his procedure. For the first contact, he used abstract localization and said so; for the following contact, he took into consideration the form of the contact and said so again. I transcribe these two responses, interesting for their frankness and spontaneity of mental analysis.

5–10. "The second is smaller. I had a sensation of persistence of the first up to the second, and it seemed to me that the points of the second were inserted between the traces of the first, which faded at that moment."

10–5. "I think that the second is larger. I say that because the first gave the impression of a small surface and not of two points."

The process of localization was used 14 times, and the process utilizing the number and form was used 19 times. The other responses were ambiguous and very laconic. Neither of the two processes is more accurate than the other; the two are subject to numerous errors.

M. V. H., a conscious subject, used the form of the contact, abstract localization, and concrete localization.

M. V. H. has been one of my assiduous collaborators for several years. I had only one session with him; I did not propose to determine his threshold of sensitivity, but to investigate by what mental processes he arrived at a comparison of the two separations. I knew that he was trained in introspection, that he had a sure and precise judgment. He was familiar with my esthesiometer, knew that I always used the same points with the same force. The following table shows us that he did not possess great exactitude of perception, since he made errors for the separations of 5—10 and 5—8.

Table 4. Experiments on the Touch of M. V. H.

| Separation | Responses | | |
	Correct	Incorrect	Uncertain
5—12	4		1
5—10	1	2	3
5—8	3	1	3
5—6	2	1	2

After each comparison, he generally made a long and detailed commentary. Analysis of these shows that M. V. H. sought information from three different sources.

1. *The form of the contact and the distinctness of the points.* M. V. H. knew that two points sufficiently close together gave a single sensation, and he often used this notion. For example, after the 10—5 separation: "The second is probably smaller. This is a reasoning out. It must be smaller. For the first contact, I felt two points, but not clearly separated; a sort of tie linked them in the transversal direction of the hand. For the second contact, I felt the two points less; the contact was more pointed." It is clearly the single or double nature of the contact which was taken into consideration here. Another example: "The second is larger. The first was formed by two points which were not very distinct. The second was formed by two very distinct points." M. V. H. was aware of the fact that when he utilized these characteristics, he did so by reasoning; he did not compare two sensations, but two judgments. The same observation has already been given to us by M. L.

"I felt, separately, two dull points," said M. V. H. again, "and on the other contact, two sharper points. I thus had two independent judgments, and it seemed to me that this took place when the two contacts were not produced in the same place on the skin." Again: "The second is a little smaller. This is a reasoning. For the first contact, there was a cold point on a hard place. The second was smaller, on another part of the skin. This was clearly a comparison of judgments. I made two independent judgments; the second judgment was not made with a view toward the first; it was an entity in itself. In these judgments, the tactile character dominates."

2. *Abstract localization.* The subject pictured the two points of one separation in relation to the points of the other, and he verified a relationship between the position of the points. Most often, the four points were on the same line, and those of one separation were between those of the other. Sometimes the four points were face to face on two parallel lines; sometimes a single point of the two separations was between the two points of the other. In all cases, the subject visually represented his hand, but, he said, ". . . in an abstract manner, as a design I would make on paper; I pictured the form of the contact, but in an abstract manner; there was no skin, the hand was not there." Here the subject did not proceed by the comparison of judgments. He compared, according to his evidence, position with position, that is, sensation with sensation. For example, I let him feel a separation of 6 mm., then one of 5 mm. M. V. H. answered: "The second is smaller, surely. For the first, a very pointed point, and another which was fatter and not as strong. For the second contact, a point exactly corresponding to the first, and another which was blunt. Thus the second contact is shorter, because I felt it in the middle of the first. When I perceived that the second contact was in the same place as the first, I immediately forgot that it was the same place on the skin; I no longer thought of it, because it was of no use in the comparison." Question: "Was the second contact judged mainly by comparison with the first?" Answer: "Entirely. I first thought that it was in the same place on the skin; then I felt that one of the points corresponded and that the second was in the middle."

1   1

    .   .   .

2   2

M.V.H.'s Representation

3. *Concrete localization.* This is the most original part of the observation. Abstract localization is relative to two contacts, while concrete localization is at the same time relative to the hand; the

attention is fixed on the location of the sensation. Example: "First contact between the second and third tendon, transversally; I felt it plunge and I barely felt the two points; they were united. The second contact was placed on the tendon of the index finger; one point directly on it and the other beside it. The tactile sensation was different and I concluded that the second contact was longer." (M.V.H. meant to say larger as to separation.) Again: "The second contact seemed longer to me because it touched a tendon which the first contact did not manage to touch." Again: "Perhaps a little larger, the second. Oh! Nothing. I pictured to myself the very point of the skin; it was a very characteristic point, on the tendon of the middle finger. The two points were very close together. The second contact was in exactly the same place on the skin as the first, but it seemed that these two points framed the tendon, while those of the first contact were entirely on top of it. I inferred from this that the second was longer. This is a complex reasoning." It is possible that this tendency to localize the two contacts in relation to the hand stems from numerous experiments on the localization of tactile sensations made on the subject three or four years ago. As a result of these experiments, he had studied the question at length, so the idea of a contact very naturally awakened in him the thought of processes by which one locates the contact on the region of the body which is stimulated.

M. Sim . . . , conscious subject, used the same procedures as the preceding subject, with only slight differences.

This observation is not among those of which I am completely certain; I'm not sure of having done it well. M. S. did not analyze his processes spontaneously and would have been quite satisfied to let me know only the results of his comparisons. I forced him to explain himself further, and several times he complained of my insistence. "You are forcing me," he would repeat, "to become conscious of something which is not conscious." Thus, it is forced introspection. Did I perhaps influence his explanations by some involuntary suggestion? I do not think so, but I do not guarantee anything.

But M. S. gave the best explanations when his judgments were based on the form and number of the contacts. "The first seemed larger," he said. "There was a sensation of two points; for the second, there was only one point. There was no longer a comparison between two different separations, because for each, I was obliged to ask myself whether it was one point or two. It was the result of a judgment based on each of these two sensations. There were two successive operations of analysis relating to each of the separations, with a necessity of formulating them in words. It is not a direct procedure." We are familiar with these sorts of judgments from having analyzed them several times, and we will not insist upon them.

Much more obscure is another process, which consists in comparing the two separations as two different sensations. The explanation which M. S. gave here was extremely vague. I transcribed some of his responses: "For the first, sensation of a large separation. For the second, sensation of a small separation." "I had the memory of the first separation; I awaited the second, saying to myself, 'Here is the separation I will experience if the second is as large as the first,' and then I was immediately surprised when it arrived." "I had the vague impression that there was a sensation of difference; if I made such a judgment, it was so simple as to be almost unconscious. One has something like a rough sensation of a thing one sees with open eyes; one does not need to say that it goes from here to there. One is conscious of the evidence." In summary, all these remarks amount to saying that a sensation of separation is produced. I then posed the question: "What is the nature of these sensations? Are they tactile? Visual? Verbal?" Answer: "They are not very visual. I had the sensation that there was a separation of skin between the two points; it seemed to me that I felt the skin between the two separations." Question: "How did you compare?" Answer: "You made the contacts at the same point. If I felt the first two points sufficiently close together, I couldn't tell, by means of localization, whether or not I had the sensation of the two other points outside of them." With M. L., the process of abstract localization was very clear. M. S. considered it only with doubt, as if with regret. Later, in relation to another contact, he became a bit more precise. "It seemed to me that the second might be placed inside the first." Finally, he gave a more complete answer in which a confusion of abstract and concrete localization stood out: "They were," he said, "sensations of localization of two points, one in relation to the other. One of the two sets of points was localized around the metacarpal of the middle finger, and the other had one point on the metacarpal of the index finger and the other on the ring finger. I have exaggerated the separation of the points to explain it better, but this describes the process accurately." Question: "Do the localizations you speak of have a relationship to your hand?" Answer: "Yes, more or less clearly. Actually, I think that is how I made the tactile comparison of the two contacts; it was the tactile localization on the skin. It mattered little whether it was on the thumb or on another finger. I never thought about where it was. I really had the sensation that my skin was a vague surface which felt." Although this explanation is a little perplexed, it seems to me to be the same as that given by M. L. and M. V. H., our two preceding subjects.

It is strange that, coincident with this constrained analysis, the perceptions are very good; M. Sim . . . showed much sensitivity in the distinction of contacts. Those who analyze the best are not necessarily those who perceive the best; the two functions are independent.

Table 5. Experiments on the Touch of M. Sim . . .

| Separation | Responses | | |
	Correct	Incorrect	Uncertain
5—20	2	0	0
5—15	2	0	0
5—12.5	1	1	0
5—10	1	1	0
5—9	2	0	0
5—8	1	0	1
5—7	2	0	0
5—6	0	0	2
5—5.5	2	0	0
5—5.25	2	0	0

Henri B. used solely the form and number of the contacts.

Henri B. is a sales clerk, 30 years old, with a natural intelligence very superior to his position. He is ignorant of the language of psychology, and some of his responses were unclear. I had explained the esthesiometer to him in previous experiments (I do not mention them because they are not of interest) ; I showed him that two points which are separated only a little give what appears to be a single impression. It is a notion constantly used in his comparisons; with almost every contact, he directed his attention to the number of points. Example: "The first was a single point; the second, two; thus, the second is bigger." Subjects better versed in the language of psychology taught us that when one uses this method to appraise the value of two separations, one makes judgments independent of one another. It is only after the two judgments are formed that one relates them and draws a conclusion. M. Henri B. could not make so precise an analysis for us, but he unsuspectingly confirmed it by the manner in which he made his responses. He did not wait for both contacts to be felt before speaking; when he felt the first, he analyzed it, weighing whether it was a unique sensation or two sensations, and then he answered; he did the same for the second. It is an indirect demonstration of the independence of the two judgments.

A small detail also shows us that the number and the form of the contacts are signs which can be interpreted incorrectly. M. Henri B. sometimes imagined—and I am ignorant of the reasons for this—that certain sensations of a single, but large, point covered a larger surface than two small points close together. It was near the end of the session that he adopted this new interpretation. Thus, he judged that certain separations were bigger than others, even though the first allowed only a single point to be felt; all the judgments given under the influence of this idea were erroneous. These are clearly errors of interpretation; they have nothing to do with sensation, properly speaking.

What makes many of Henri B's perceptions enigmatic is that he frequently evaluated the distances between points, although he was unable to explain on what basis he made his evaluation. Thus, he often said: "For the first, two points; for the second, two points also, but closer together." Often he was even more precise: "For the first, two points separated by 5 mm.; for the second there are also two points; they are farther apart, by at least 1 cm." I was unable to explain the source of this estimation, but it might result from the application of what we have called abstract localization. In any case, the estimation of distance is a judgment based on the sensation and on certain sensory signs; it is not a primitive given fact of the senses. The fineness of perception is average.

IV

Aberrant types

These subjects are distinguished from the average by some special development of a faculty. I had the good fortune to encounter two; one was principally a visual type, the other, verbal.

1. *Visual type*

M. Jean Phil . . . , 38 years old, philosopher and physician, long-time follower of psychology and familiar with experiments.
He seemed to be gifted with a good visual memory. Formerly, he was convinced that he was primarily a visualizer; now he thinks that he has lost some of this ability. Our experiments were few in number, insufficient to determine the approximate degree of perception, but sufficient to show the originality of the mode of interpretation. From time to time, he took account of the number of contacts; he knew that every time he perceived a single contact, the separation was smaller than when he perceived two. Furthermore, he was aware that certain separations were bigger than others, even if he felt the double point in both cases. The characteristic feature was the way he made use of the visual image. He visualized a great deal: "I have a tendency to visualize in order to distinguish the two points." We will emphasize two facts: the richness of the visual images and their function. Their richness was manifested in a large number of responses.

"The sensation which dominated was that of a sliding on the skin," he said. Question: "How?" Answer: "I saw the skin sliding on the aponeurotic plane; I imagined a thin skin, a little rough, slightly pinkish. I saw the aponeurosis very clearly, more clearly than the skin. I remember this from anatomy, from dissection, or sketching. I also saw your instrument (the esthesiometer), and it was clearly yours, because I saw the two steel points in the form I know them to have. I could not have imagined it without them. It would have confused my image to see them gilded." The extent to which this visual representation includes details should be noticed. Is this a voluntary recollection? Almost. "I did not have this representation at first, but I had it as soon as I perceived it was convenient. It was somewhat intentional at first; I looked for something. Then it became a voluntary interpretation. I first perceived the contact (tactile sensation) when I attempted to discover whether I felt the contact on two separate forces of the skin; to prolong the contact and to explain it, I fell upon this interpretation and visualized the two steel points." "I used this expedient to clarify a confused sensation." "The discrimination of points . . . became visual when it was difficult. There were two things: the subcutaneous sensation I felt, which was tactile, and beyond that, the visualization. When the separation was sufficiently large, the tactile sensation was enough. When the separation was small, I visualized by picturing the points of the compass in such a position that I could understand what occurred under my skin." This way of relating the tactile to the visual is not always possible. "In this contact, I felt only one point; I looked for the second (he knew there were two) and did not find it. I visualized the second point, but I was unable to do this in such a way that it rested on the skin; it remained in the air, and the point which touched me seemed a little larger." "When the sensation (tactile) seemed larger, the point (visual) was distorted; it was larger, less clear, and I saw essentially skin."

This subject was able to see four points simultaneously, that is, those of the two contacts to be compared. The points of the first contact (in this visualization) coincided with those of the second. When they did not coincide, they appeared more transparent, more vague, hazier, like the stippling of a sketch, like a shade of sepia, like a blurred photograph. The shadow remained there after the point had vanished. It is incontestable that in drawing the attention of M. Jean Phil . . . to the visual images, in obliging him to explain them to us, we stabilized his visualization. We did not, however, create this disposition; the proof is that similar questions directed to other people have a very different effect.

I could cite, in contrast, Mme H., a 55-year-old lady who had some familiarity with psychological language, and who, despite all my questions, never visualized a contact. She constantly directed her attention to the tactile sensation and gave many details about the tactile sensation itself. She was thus interested in the intensity of the two points and often found that one was stronger than the other; she endeavored to say at what point on the hand they were felt and complained of the changing tactile sensations. She pictured the distance of the points without having any visual representation of her hand. "I did not see my hand, I felt the two points." Question: "You did not picture the instrument?" Answer: "No, I had no vision of the instrument." Question: "How did you feel the distance of the points?" Answer: "It was difficult. Nonetheless, I felt it very clearly. I felt a point on the skin, and then the other point very near it." Question: "Did you sometimes feel your skin slide a little?" Answer: "Yes, that was annoying." Question: "Did you see it slide?" Answer: "No, I did not see it slide, I felt it." This person does not have very fine perceptions.

2. Verbal type

The subject of this observation is a young woman 28 years old, Mme V. H., who was willing to give me two sessions. This is an intelligent woman, instructed in psychology. She knows our technical language and uses it with precision. Several years ago, when M. V. H. was studying the process of localization of tactile sensations, she participated in many of his experiments. As we will see, this particular instruction exercised an influence on her responses. Although her responses slightly resemble those of M. V. H., the psychological character of these two people is very dissimilar; the differences are curiously manifested in spite of analogous cultural backgrounds. Mme V. H. belongs to the verbal type, and we will see what resources she draws from the language.

In the following table, I have summarized the numerical results from two sessions.

Table 6. Experiment on the Touch of Mme V.H.

| Separation | Responses | | |
	Correct	Incorrect	Uncertain
5—12	3		0
5—11	5	1	1
5—10	9	2	1
5—8	3	9	5
5—6	4	7	1

These numbers simply serve to show that Mme V. H. discriminated without tactile sensitivity, since she did not perceive the difference between 5 and 8 mm.

Mme V. H. very clearly explained to us how she compared the separations. She used exactly the same indicators as M. V. H., which were:

1. *The discrimination of points.* Mme V. H. knew perfectly well from her previous education that two points sufficiently close together give a single, indistinct impression. Fairly often, she used this impression to guess the size of the separation. As an example, here is the first response she made when I used two successive separations of 5 and 10 mm. "The first time I very clearly felt one point; the second, I felt two points with a small separation. I then said that the distance was larger the second time."

2. *Concrete localization*. I did not find any clear examples of abstract localization, but concrete localization abounded, especially in the second session. In this I saw a recollection of her former experiments on localization; these left a persistent habit in Mme V. H. that weighed upon her present thought. Localization assumed a particular character; it seemed to be made in very weak visual terms and in most cases was verbalized. Furthermore, the localization seemed to be less a concise and serious reasoning than an image or a metaphor. Here are some examples: "I think that the first separation is larger, because when you touched me, I thought it was spaced as a vein on my hand." She did not say that the two points were placed on one side of the vein, but that their separation was equal to the diameter of the vein. This is a comparison, an image. In another response, she affirmed the poverty of visual representation: "I represented the first metacarpal (she meant to say the second, that of the index finger) and the points astride the metacarpal. I perceived the bone visually, isolated and vague, like a small bone on a table; what I mean to say is that it was without relation to the other metacarpals and without relation to my hand in general. I described to myself in words the position of the points astride the metacarpal; it was troublesome for me." Another time, she said that she pictured the position of points in relation to the metacarpal, but she added that it was not a visual representation. Yet another time, she was ignorant of what the representation consisted of. "I represented their position loosely, something between visual and verbal. Perhaps it was a very faint visual sensation, or perhaps a word which is at the limit of words."

There are both similarities and profound differences between the processes used by M. V. H. and Mme V. H. Both used concrete localization and both represented the region of their hand which was touched. They were even more or less successful in their use of this method of comparison. But Mme V. H. spontaneously brought me up to date on the reasons for using visual localizations. "On this part of my hand," she remarked after having felt a contact, "I tend to have visual images; I think this is because I once did experiments with V. H." Thus, I attribute these similarities to an identity of psychological culture—a fact which proves that experiments leave an impression and make certain interpretations entirely artificial.

There are also great differences in the ideations of M. V. H. and Mme V. H.   M. V. H., in the interval between the two contacts, appeared to conserve the tactile memory of the first contact, even though he often complained that the interval was too long and that the tactile sensation disappeared. Mme V. H., however, had a way of giving up, once and for all, any attempt at retaining the sensory memory of the contact; her memory was incapable of preserving it (even though she often compained of having consecutive sensations of touch which irritated her). She replaced the sensory memory with a verbal evaluation, which, here, is a mnemotechnic process. Above all, Mme V. H. seems to me to be a verbal type who is compensating for a fault in sensory memory.

Here are some quotes of responses in which she explains her mnemotechnic process. "Habitually, I evaluate (the sensation of separation) in centimeters; I always forget the sensations, I only remember the evaluations." The result is that she does not compare sensations, but words: "The second contact is larger," she once said, "because I evaluated the first as 5 mm. and the second as a little more." These are clearly two separate, independent judgments which are compared afterward. M. L. and M. V. H. also indicated that they made similar judgments, but only in certain cases. Furthermore, they made comparisons of sensations or representations. Mme V. H., however, used only one process, verbal judgment; her use of it was so profuse that we can see both its advantages and disadvantages. The disadvantages especially strike me. First of all, this kind of comparison is often deficient because of its indetermination; if the subject has not taken the precaution of making his evaluation in millimeters, he is disconcerted. Example: I applied separations of 5 and 10 mm. consecutively. Mme V. H. said, "The second is smaller than the first. I did not determine the separation in millimeters, but I knew that *it was small;* it was difficult to remember what small meant, so I was not sure." The observation is accurate. The word does not have the fineness of detail the sensation has, and from certain points of view, it is a very inaccurate substitute for the sensation.[4] A second disadvantage is the fact that, as the sensation was forgotten, Mme V. H. could not tell on what basis the judgment was made. I once asked her, "What makes you say that in one case there is a certain evaluation, and in another, a different evaluation?" Answer: "My judgment was not based on anything that I could say, and I did not have the feeling of being exact. On the contrary, I de-

---

[4] I recently demonstrated that language is inadequate in describing sensations. See my book on *l'Etude experimentale de l'Intelligence.*

scribed the position of the two separations to myself with words; sometimes these words were entirely distinct, as if I were speaking to myself, and other times they were more vague." Question: "And if someone were to prevent you from speaking?" Answer: "That could not happen. I cannot prevent myself from judging, for without it I am very uncertain and respond simply by chance."

To the best of my knowledge, internal language, whether it be auditory or motor, plays an important role in the psychological life of everyone. This role, however, is not the same for each person. Language can be the principal element of thought or merely an accessory. To use a simile, it can be either the melody or the accompaniment. In a very recent experiment of a different nature, an American psychologist, Bagley,[5] demonstrated the reality of the distinction which I suggest. He studied how one reconstitutes the totality of a word or phrase of which one has heard only a fragment. He verified that in this reconstruction, one performs an act of ideation which is composed largely of visual images and internal speech. Sometimes the visual element predominates, and speech is muted as our attention becomes fixed on an image. At other times, through an exchange of roles, the visual image becomes vague and serves as an accessory. In this case, a word or phrase is heard or pronounced internally, no longer in a muted fashion, but with clarity and often in an emphatic tone. I think that the preceding analysis is very astute and exact, and true not only for the particular, precise experiments devised by this American author. It seems to me that it represents one of the most important characteristics of our thoughts—verbo-visual—dominated sometimes by the image and sometimes by the word.

It seems to me that in Mme V. H. the development of internal speech is related to two psychological deficiencies. One is the inadequacy of the memory of sensation, and the other is the lack of skill in visualization.

"When I wish to represent an object to myself," she writes in a detailed observation for which I asked her, "I describe it to myself verbally; to remember an object I must also describe it. Even in looking at pictures, I describe them to myself verbally; I always express in words the impression they make on me.

"I was a subject for experiments in visual memory. I was sup-

5 *Psychological review.*

posed to compare lines of different lengths and say which of the two was the longer. The experimenter had asked me not to determine the length by saying to myself that such-and-such a line was 5 cm. long and another 7, and thus, concluding that the second was longer. I had to look at them consecutively and say which was the longer without verbally determining their length. In this case, I was entirely uncertain of my responses. I was infinitely more sure of myself when I could determine them verbally."

So much for memory in general. Here now is what concerns visualization. I myself drew Mme V. H.'s attention to the plasticity of mental images. I told her that certain people can at will transform their images, while others do not succeed in doing so. Thus oriented, she wrote the following lines, which showed that she had a very moderate influence on her mental imagery.

"I have a fairly good visual memory. Sometimes I have visual images which are very clear, but which last only a short time. Sometimes I visualize colorful landscapes, but as soon as I want to see them better, they disappear. These visual images are involuntary; they appear in spite of me, and even an intense effort of will cannot revive them. If, for example, I try to picture M. X., I do not succeed in seeing him as he is in reality. Rather, with effort, I have a sort of very indistinct image of his photograph. The representation is so indistinct that I am not sure I can call it M. X.; on his photograph, I see his head only indistinctly (the same size as in the photograph). If I direct my attention to the door in front of which he is seated, it is impossible for me to see his head simultaneously. It is like a very small, hazy part which emerges from an indifferent whole. This does not prevent me from recalling all the details of the object I think of."

These details show the consequences of this mental type upon the perception and evaluation of sensations under particular conditions. If Mme V. H. cannot compare differences any finer than 5–10 mm., one can justifiably suppose that this prominent sensory obnubilation stems from the fact that she is a verbal type. The words to describe finer differences are lacking in her, especially with regard to what is characteristic of them.

Two hyperesthetic subjects

Hyperesthesia in sense organs is a phenomenon which always draws attention because it includes something of the marvelous. I think that some very authentic facts concerning hyperesthesia exist in science, but a methodical analysis has never been carried out.

I use the term hyperesthesia in a very practical sense; by it, I mean an acuity of perception which is very superior to the average. I do not distinguish between cases in which this hyperesthesia comes from the state of sensitivity of the sense organs, and those in which it must more likely be associated with a particular mode of interpretation. Is it the organ which is keen in the hyperesthetic, or is it really intelligence? In many cases, this would be very difficult to assess.

The common opinion, however, is that hyperesthetic subjects are exceptional subjects and often sick ones. In this research, which actually had a small number of subjects, I was quite surprised to find two hyperesthetic subjects. This led me to believe that hyperesthesia is more frequent than I thought, and that we do not find it because we do not know how to look for it. This is, moreover, a banal truth which might be repeated in regard to many things.

In previous investigations using the method of Weber's compass, I encountered two hyperesthetic subjects. One was Marie, a 35-year-old maid. From the beginning, without past experience, she was able to detect the duality of points placed on the back of her hand when the separation was only 5 mm.; she did not confuse this contact with that which was given by a single point. She was a natural hyperesthetic. The other, on the contrary, was a cultural hyperesthetic. She was a young girl of 17 called Marguerite, intelligent and educated. I gave her so many lessons in the correct interpretation of tactile sensation that she became able to distinguish two points on her neck when the separation was only half a centimeter. The following numbers are taken from an experiment in which I applied one or two points, with separations ranging from .5 to 3.5 cm. The single point was perceived as single 18 times, and as double 3; one can thus say that it was almost always perceived correctly. When the two points were separated by .5 cm., she perceived them as double 16 times; only 3 times did she think she was dealing with a single point. The same proportion of responses held for separations of 1 cm., while for those of 1.5 cm., there was only a single error out of 20 responses. Finally, for separations greater than 1.5 cm., there was a unanimity of correct responses. This is a good case of hyperesthesia because, according to Weber's tables, points placed on the neck must be separated by 5.4 cm. to be perceived as double. Here a separation 12 times smaller was sufficient.

In my recent experiments on differential sensitivity, I again encountered two hyperesthetic subjects. The first is this same Marie, the domestic woman whom I referred to as a natural hyperesthetic. She furnished me with truly very surprising evidence of tactile sensitivity, and I am going to speak of it in a moment. Marguerite did not preserve her hyperesthesia. She, who so brilliantly perceived the duality of points, proved to be a very average subject. I mentioned her when discussing the unconscious subjects because she did not know how to explain the processes she used in comparing the separations, and her perceptions were very obtuse. This fact demonstrates how unstable some hyperesthesias are, probably because they depend on interpretation, or even better, on a certain knack in the interpretation which the subject sometimes catches, sometimes misses.

Our second hyperesthetic shows behavior opposite to that of Marguerite. This is Mme C . . . , a young mother about 35 years old, who was unable to exercise great intelligence in the distinction of points. I was able to educate her sense of touch, but with such difficulty! To me, she seemed to be a victim of tactile stupidity. I was very surprised to establish that, for differential sensitivity, she had perceptions of extraordinary acuteness. I will present these two cases of hyperesthesia in some detail.

First hyperesthetic

This first is Marie; I spoke fairly often of her in previous works because I have used her as a subject in many experiments. She is a domestic, approximately 35 years old, and does not have a brilliant intellect. Nonetheless, she is not absolutely lacking in judgment. Her characteristic traits are carelessness and a complete lack of self-esteem. She is interested in very little, and not at all in experiments on touch. She must be constantly stimulated in order not to become distracted.

The exactitude of her responses was, at times, curious. In the first session, she proved to be able to grasp an extremely small difference in separation; she accomplished this immediately, without previous practice. I speculated that, with education, her hyperesthesia could increase further; when I investigated, however, I did not find this to be true. During the course of three months, from December 19, 1901, to March 19, 1902, I had seven sessions in esthesiometry with her. Sometimes her hyperesthesia manifested itself the first time, sometimes it disappeared completely. This inconstancy of hyperesthesia was not produced from moment to moment, but from session to session. I have often said to myself that if I wished to give another person proof of the results, I rather doubt I would be able to convince him of their authenticity. Perhaps similar causes could be used to explain the misadventures of so many hypnotizers who announce that their subjects possess an extraordinary hyperesthesia and then do not find anything with the control. It is clear that, in this case, an isolated examination does not present conclusive authority. One must have patience and only form an opinion on the basis of all the investigations.

I will present here the results of the investigation of sensitivity during seven sessions.

Observations

Table 7. First Session (December 17, 1901)

| | Responses | | Separation |
Separation	Correct	Incorrect	Judged Equal
5—7	4	0	1
5—6	7	0	3
5—5.5	8	1	6
5—5.25	5	0	0

FIRST SESSION—the decreasing order has been followed. The separation of 5—7 was presented five times; the separation of 5—6 ten times; the separation of 5—5.5 fifteen times; and finally, the separation of 5—5.25 five times. In general, for each pair of separations, an alternate order was followed: the larger was presented alternately first and second, but all regularity was avoided. The difference of 5—5.25 was perceptible.

Table 8. Second Session (December 23, 1901)

| | Responses | | Separation |
Separation	Correct	Incorrect	Judged Equal
5—6	8	3	2
5—5.5	2	2	1

SECOND SESSION—the decreasing order has been followed. This subject had chilblain on the left hand. The difference 5—6 was perceived; that of 5—5.5 was not.

Table 9. Third Session [Date not given]

Separation	Responses		Separation Judged Equal
	Correct	Incorrect	
5—8	25	28	2
5—7	15	12	1
5—6	9	8	1

THIRD SESSION—three series of experiments. In each of them the decreasing order was followed. Deplorable conditions: the subject had chilblain on the left hand, and at the end of the session, admitted to a continual state of distraction. No determinable threshold. The separation 5—8 was not perceived.

Table 10. Fourth Session (January 8, 1902)

Separation	Responses		Separation Judged Equal
	Correct	Incorrect	
5—7	3	0	0
5—6	23	5	6

FOURTH SESSION—good disposition. The difference 5—6 was perceived.

Table 11. Fifth Session (January 17, 1902)

Separation	Responses		Separation Judged Equal
	Correct	Incorrect	
5—10	12	0	0
5—6	8	1	4
5—5.5	9	0	8

FIFTH SESSION—good disposition. The preceding order of stimulants was used. The difference 5—5.5 was perceptible.

Table 12. Sixth Session (January 29, 1902)

Separation	Responses		Separation Judged Equal
	Correct	Incorrect	
5—6	11	0	5

SIXTH SESSION—good disposition. The difference 5—6 was perceived.

Table 13. Seventh Session (March 19, 1902)

Separation	Responses Correct	Incorrect	Uncertain
5—20	2	0	0
5—15	2	0	0
5—12.5	2	0	0
5—10	2	0	1
5—9	1	0	1
5—8	2	0	0
5—7	1	0	1
5—6	0	0	2
5—5.5	6	8	10
5—5.25	0	1	1

SEVENTH SESSION—*mental disposition appeared good. The skin on the hand was irritated, and the subject complained of the contacts feeling very painful. (The previous day she had done her laundry.) No fineness of tactile perception. The separation 5—8 was barely perceived.*

These summary results could raise some doubts. One might wonder how the separations followed each other, and if I did not by chance follow too obvious an order, which my subjects were able to guess. I will, thus, go into some detail. The contacts were made successively on the back of the left hand, in the same place as much as possible. This was much easier with Marie; the point of the instrument produced a depression which remained visible for a fairly long time. Six seconds passed between the two contacts to be compared. This time is a little long, but it was necessary to enable me to modify the separation of points by means of a screw. (I was later able to change this inconvenient method.) I will remind the reader that Marie had her eyes closed, her head turned toward the right, and could not see her hand. Even as gross a deceit as looking at the hand and the instrument would have been to no avail; how could the subject, suddenly spying the esthesiometer, perceive that the separation was sometimes 5 mm., sometimes 6 mm.? To be aware of this, it would have been necessary to view the instrument very attentively. Instead, that which is to be feared is unconscious deceit—the little conjectures of an attentive subject who detects by certain signs that we are going to make him feel a large separation and then a small one; the noise made by the experimenter and the time it takes to change the setting of the instrument can be used as clues, sometimes even by a subject who is honest and not aware that he is cheating. After studying this question carefully, I was unable to understand how Marie might have been able to guess what I did.

The principal characteristic of her hyperesthesia was its inconstancy. Some days it was very clear, while on others it disappeared. Sometimes it was possible to verify certain material conditions (chilblain, etc.) which influenced the tactile sensitivity.

At each session I asked Marie the reasons for her judgments. I asked her this often and ended up annoying her. It was with great difficulty that I obtained explanations; they are scattered throughout six sessions, and I have grouped them here under certain primary headings.

1. Apparent size of the points. Marie knew that I always used the same size points, but she remarked that the points seemed finer when they were far apart than when they were close together. Many of my subjects knew that points close together gave a single sensation, but they never said that two distinct points gave a sensation of being finer than two less separated ones. Marie alone said this. I transcribe some of her remarks: "When the points are closer together, they give the effect of a single point, like a nail. The point seems fatter than if the separation were larger, even when they are double." "I feel the points as finer when they are more separated."

2. When the points are close together, they press more. This is a perceptual indicator which we have not encountered before. Marie mentioned it in the second session and referred to it frequently in a variety of ways. For a large separation, she said that the points were softer; for a small separation, harder. Once she said that when the separation was smaller, she felt the points more, as if they penetrated deeper into the skin. When the separation was larger, it did not pinch the skin as much; it was less hard on the hand, less painful.[6]

These are the only signs of sensation she was conscious of; there was no effort at localization. "I pictured my hand as if I were seeing it." Question: "Did you think about the position of the points on the hand?" Answer: "I did not think of that. I did not realize whether it was on a bone or between two bones; the nerves of my

---

[6] With a special instrument, I measured the degree of penetration into the skin. Points of the same nature and supporting the same weight penetrate deeper when they are closer together, all other things being equal. On Marie's hand, the penetration varied from 1 to 3 mm., depending on the separation of points.

hand do not serve me for that." Two months earlier, she had already given me the same responses. "I pictured my hand as if I saw it; I only pictured the distance and did not think of the points." Thus, the indirect method of localization was not employed.

Did she use language, the other indirect method? I had some difficulty in making myself understood to Marie. It was a question of translating fine psychological distinctions into the common language, which is very vague. Marie is like those ignorant people who, when they want to make you understand a thought they have had, put it in the form of a dialogue: "I said to myself . . . ," etc. This is, above all, a convenient way of expressing oneself, and one would be mistaken to conclude that internal speech intervened. Even if it did, that would not be proof that it was in the foreground, that it played a principal role.

I think it interesting to record the dialogue exchanged between Marie and myself. One can understand what difficulty a psychologist experiences in speaking of psychology with an illiterate domestic. Question: "How did you compare the second sensation with the first?" Answer: "I tried to recall how the first one was." Question: "Did you recall it as a sensation of touch?" Answer: "Yes." Question: "You did not recall it in words, as words which you say to yourself?" Answer: "Oh, no." Question: "Did the sensation of touch remain in the memory?" Answer: "Yes, up until I answered you." Question: "You did not feel it going away as time passed between the first and second sensation?" Answer: "No, no. When you touched the first time, I tried to remember the first point, and when you touched the second time, I compared them with one another."

This explanation was very vague. When I resumed my questioning two months later, I had forgotten Marie's earlier responses. "When you pressed the first time, I said to myself that it was small or that it was large; the second time I compared the two as if I saw them." Question: "Explain yourself. What do you mean by 'as if you saw them?' Did you represent the points as if you could see them?" Answer: "No, I compared the first sensation of touch with the second." Question: "Did you compare in words? Did you say, 'The first time I said to myself that it was fairly large; now I say to myself that it is large; therefore, I conclude that it is larger the second time than the first.' This is what a comparison in words would be." Answer: "No, I did not compare the words; I did not bother with that. Sometimes the sensation remained in my mind when I did not feel it on my hand any more. I thought, 'This time it is smaller, or this time it is larger.' When the second one comes, I lose the touch of the first, especially when it occurs in the same place; it is the impression of the first which remains in my mind." I do not present this dialogue as a marvel of precision and clarity. All I can conclude from it is that Marie probably preserved the memory of the tactile sensation which she experienced, and that she succeeded in comparing tactile memory with tactile sensation.

In conclusion, Marie could grasp a difference of half a millimeter with a separation of 5 mm. To be sure of the separation, I constructed a more precise apparatus. With it, the points were moved by a micrometric screw which allowed me to present variable separations with a twentieth of a millimeter accuracy.

Second hyperesthetic

Let us examine the case of Mme Cra . . . ; I studied her during two sessions, each lasting approximately two and a half hours with long rest intervals.

The hyperesthesia of this person is as difficult as Marie's to verify regularly. In certain series it would be quite apparent, but then a short time later or in another session, I would be unsuccessful in trying to find it. Evidently it is a very transient phenomenon.

Some details concerning the singularity of this hyperesthesia will not be superfluous. It is, indeed, hyperesthesia, since Mme Cra . . . was able to distinguish between separations of 5 and 6 mm.; the proportion of accurate responses for this comparison was well above that which would be given by chance. Here is a summary of all the re-

Table 14. *Comparisons Made by Mme Cra . . . of the Separations of 5 and 6 mm.*

Series	Responses Correct	Incorrect	Uncertain
1	12	1	4
2	5	4	1
3	1	3	1
4	5	2	2
5	9	2	4
6	16	3	3
Total	48	15	15

sponses given by series; by this, I mean an uninterrupted series of contacts made under appreciably similar conditions. If, for example, we interrupt the trials with a rest and then begin again, it is a new series.

The number of accurate responses was slightly greater than three times the number of incorrect responses. It seems incontestable to me that Mme Cra . . . clearly perceived the difference of 1 mm. in 5, but she was not consistently able to do this. The second and third series were fairly bad, as was the fourth. In these series, her hyperesthesia seemed to vanish. Series one, five, and six, however, were excellent. I made the same calculation when the separations to be compared were considerably larger. To arrive at high numbers, I put together all the responses given for the separations of 5—10, 5—11, 5—12, 5—13, 5—14, and 5—15. There were 74 correct, 25 incorrect, and 22 uncertain responses. Thus, although the difficulty was significantly less, it seems to me that Mme Cra . . . was no more exact in the comparison of these last separations. It is almost a paradox. We reported this singular fact in the first pages of this article.

With great difficulty, I obtained from Mme Cra . . . an explanation of how she went about making her comparisons. She used two indicators: the greater or lesser duality of the points and their pricking nature. It is curious that Marie, our other hyperesthetic, also used this latter sign. Here are some responses given by Mme Cra . . . :

Separation

5—6   "The second is larger. For the first, I felt a single prick. For the second, I felt two." Question: "Is it because of this that you thought the second was larger?" Answer: "Yes."

6—5   "The second was closer together. I felt the two points clearly the first time and less clearly the second time."

5—6   "Both the same; a single prick."

6—5   "The second was more separated. I am only guessing that; I did not feel it very clearly."

5—6   "The second is more separated. I clearly felt the two pricks, more than the first time."

6—5   "The second is closer because it pricked me more." Question: "You mean it gave you pain?" Answer: "Oh, yes."

5—5.5 "The second is separated more; it pricked less strongly."

In this small number of separations, one can see that Mme Cra . . . had to compare 5 and 5.5 mm. She made the comparison ten times, giving six accurate responses, one wrong response, and three expressions of uncertainty.

Confronted with these results, I wondered whether it might be possible to cultivate this singular hyperesthesia and augment its degree. This is an experiment I would like to take up again if I can find the occasion.[7]

V

I will try to draw some conclusions from the previous experiments. Once again, what strikes me is the great variety of individual differences. There are, so to speak, no two subjects who perceive and, above all, who compare, the separation of points in the same way. Even with such a simple operation, individual psychology plays an enormous role. We have limited the number of processes employed to four, but there are certainly many more. We have cited only the most typical—those that people best succeed in describing.

Having thus designated the role of individual psychology, I would like to extricate what is essential in this work on perception and interpretation. The analysis should be able to separate, if this is possible, two very distinct parts: the sensation and the interpretation.

In the preceding experiments, I was unable to do this for a reason which I think I understand. If the interpretation of my subjects remained too elementary and obscure, it is because they primarily sought to do well on the comparison of separations which I asked of them. Introspection came afterward, as an addition; they thus did not have the liberty of mind necessary to examine themselves well. I resumed the experiments in another manner, putting introspection in the foreground.

Here is the way in which I proceeded. I said to my subjects that I was going to make them feel points with various separations. Their task was not to evaluate the separations or to determine whether

---

[7] I have since observed that most subjects, when put on the track, recognize that two points close together produce a more painful sensation than two separated points applied with equal force. They do not, however, think of using this as an indicator. Sensations are probably rich in unused signs.

they felt one point or two; I told them this was a useless determination since there would always be two points. They were supposed to devote themselves entirely to describing to me what they felt; they were even supposed to describe, as much as possible, the sensation and the interpretation separately. I was careful, following this verbal explanation, to question them at length after each contact. As is my habit, I transcribed their responses word for word.

To finish the experiment, I asked them to perform the following operation. When they arrived at the perception of a single point, they were supposed to make an effort to imagine that they perceived two; conversely, when the perception of two points was obtained, they were to imagine that they felt only one. In both cases, they were to describe to me, as well as possible, how they carried out the operation. By this artifice, I hoped to make the part of sensation, rather than that of interpretation, very acute. Actually, I think this procedure is good.

These new experiments were conducted in a very long and detailed manner on about ten persons. I will not summarize all of them, but only those which seem interesting to me.

We must first eliminate the responses of some subjects. Two young girls, whom I patiently questioned about what they felt as tactile sensations, systematically limited themselves to answering that they felt one point or two. There was no means of making them abandon these stereotyped responses. In vain, I taught them that the contact of one point or two on the skin could produce more than 20 different sensations. Nothing better demonstrates the persistence of an initial orientation by means of inertia. These persons had at first been exposed to "Weberism"; by that I mean that they were practiced in guessing the number of points of the compass when applied to the hand. This preoccupation with number anesthetized all the other sensations.

Happily, I encountered this obstacle in no other subjects. It is true that the other subjects were all intelligent adults, possessing specific knowledge of psychology. They were M. P. and M. L., chief of operations and assistant in my laboratory; Dr. Sim . . . , one of my students; M. George A., professor of philosophy; and Mme H., who was often a subject in experiments on sensation. I also underwent the experiment.

In general, it seems very difficult to distinguish between sensation and interpretation. Some people spontaneously declare the difficulty they experience in describing the sensation without making reference to the cause behind it or to the appearance of the skin—in short, to the details which are not part of the sensation itself. When we vigorously limit ourselves to describing the sensation, the description becomes very brief. Thus M. A., despite my express recommendation, never ceased to allude to the object which produced the sensation, the apparatus, or the form of the depressed skin. He said to me, "One clearly has the impression that one interprets to be precise. It seems to me very difficult to distinguish what one really feels." M. L. expressed the same difficulty. He said, relative to the contact made by points separated by 5 mm., "I have a sensation of pricking, and next to it, a slight cold contact which does not prick. I cannot arrive at this without exteriorizing. It is impossible to describe the sensation. It is not words which are lacking, but the sensation itself; even if language were richer, the sensation could not be described without relating it to other points which surround it or to the object which produces it."

This assertion was repeated by many others, and I think it is important. As M. L. says, *it is impossible to describe the sensation.*

It is especially when one obliges the subject to transform his perceptions that one gets a clear idea of the process he uses. This process is a multiple one. We will again encounter some of our preceding descriptions, but we are going to be more precise.

First of all, there is the process of verbal judgment, which intervenes fairly often. M. V. H. first used this process in a rather gross form. I made him feel two points separated by 5 mm., and he analyzed himself thus: "It is a line. I asked myself whether I could feel two points, and in asking this, I said to myself, 'If they want me to, I can easily get used to the fact that it is two points, and call it two points.' " It seems that this is a purely verbal convention. M. L. furnished us with a more precise example of judgment, which, even though remaining verbal, seemed to be a little more frank. For the contact of two points separated by 5 mm., he said: "Two points, by interpretation. I had the impression of a pricking contact; and next to it, the impression of a kind of tickling produced by a conical point. There was a pricking sensation and a zone of slight tickling." Question: "How did you go from there to two points?" Answer: "Because I knew it; it is stipulated that it is called two points; it is a question of nomenclature." This process of verbal interpretation seems to me the one in which interpretation is most distinct from sensation; the work of the mind does not compose a part of the sensation. Dr. Sim . . . presented me with a similar mode of interpretation. When he found the points only silghtly painful, he judged them to be separate because, he said, when they were close together, they pressed in the same spot and were more painful. We thus understand fairly well how this first type of interpretation is called judgment by the subjects. It does not involve a modification of sensation by the activity of the mind; rather, the activity of the mind is exerted in judgments which evolve in a distinct manner, at least as much as possible. Here then is a first mode of interpretation: that of sensations by judgment.

The second mode of interpretation is very different, and takes place through images instead of judgments; that is, in large part it is accomplished by reference to previously perceived sensations which one revives for the necessities of interpretation. It can also be accomplished by some slightly different processes, but in this case the sensation which one experiences is always modified as a consequence. It is a sensory process, in contrast to judgment, which is a verbal process.

We were able to understand this sensory process, thanks to the artifice which we employed with our subjects: transforming the perception into a different one—for example, replacing the perception of a single point with that of two. This metamorphosis is not always successfully carried out; there are sensations which are rebellious, that is clear. Some are not sufficiently ambiguous to lend themselves to contradictory interpretations. It is even more curious that, in certain cases, one does not know whether a certain perception is reached voluntarily or whether it would have happened without the cooperation of the will. Some of my subjects provided me with a strange reason for these data; when they paid attention to the perception, they did not know whether their will had been acting upon it or not.

The sensory process seems to me to be of two different natures: tactile or visual. In the first case, the attention is fixed on the tactile sensation, and memories of touch are used. In the second, visual images intervene.

The first, the tactile operation, is fairly difficult to analyze. This is understandable; it is not easy to make the distinction between actual sensations of touch and tactile images. I confess that it is even in part by supposition that I admit to these tactile images.

The case most clearly belonging to this variety is perhaps my own. I am going to reproduce the notes that I wrote when the experiments were conducted on me. At the time, I was starting to study the question, but was far from having a comprehensive view of it. The points were applied to me, and I wrote: "A sensation of points. It pricks a little. I do not really know if there is one point or two. In making an effort to understand, I tactually represent the points going into the skin, and I try to discover if these representations agree with my sensation." Another contact: "I feel two points, but in fact, I am constructing them in some manner; it is not clear. My thoughts go from one to the other; I think of them one after another, and it seems that I reinforce them. The localization remains very vague; I know that it is in the middle of my hand, but I do not picture my hand." Another contact: "Properly speaking, I do not have the sensation of two separated points, as two points marked in ink on a piece of paper. It is a coarse, confused, vague sensation. And against this sensation, which is like a cloud, I try to make an idea prevail. I adjust it to my sensation, and see if it matches. If it matches, I am satisfied. I am further aided by the conviction that there are two points." In the other written responses, there was an outline of visual elements.

Some other subjects have also described diffuse sensations in which they tried to imagine a sensation that was a little sharp. I suppose that this mode of interpretation, whether artificial or natural, is produced by an evocation of images which come to be confused with the actual sensation; but since the sensation and the images belong to the same sense modality, it is difficult to distinguish them and to follow their interplay.

An interesting variation is associated with the same process: Perceiving two points and wishing to feel only one, one is forced to forget the other by not paying attention to it. One thus neglects it while knowing vaguely that it exists. I do not understand how it is possible to accomplish this suppression with a simple effort of attention. Perhaps this example has not been completely described.

In any case, this tactile interpretation defines the impression, makes it more distinct, more precise, and makes it easier to retain in the memory.

We arrive, in concluding, at visual interpretation. This is the one most clearly explained to me, undoubtedly because the visual image stands out more clearly than the tactile image.

It often happens that the association of the tactile sensation with the visual image is so firm, so stable, that the subject thinks he is not making an interpretation or adding anything to the sensation. M. L. furnished us with a very typical example of this. He explained to us that he felt two points and that it was slightly visual; it was entirely schematic since he did not see his hand, but only the points as if they were on a black surface. I asked: "This schematic image—did you summon it, or did it come by itself?" Answer: "It came alone, it imposed itself on me, it came immediately. I did not produce a visual image after a tactile sensation in order to know how the tactile sensation occurred. It seemed to be given immediately, as if the image itself were a sensation." M. L. would be the first to realize that this appearance could not be reality. Since there was a visual element in his procedure—we described it above under the name of abstract localization—it is evident that it was not a sensation. Vision was not directly in question, it was visualization. But the association was so rapid, so external to the subject, that it gave the impression of being a characteristic of the senses. Fifteen years ago, we encountered similar facts in experiments with hysterics, and it is these phenomena which can account for what is called the *transportation of the senses.* An insensitive hysteric, when pricked with a point, is able to visualize it mentally. The production of visual memories cannot be considered as a result of a conscious and deliberate interpretation; nonetheless, it is an acquisition of experience and an addition to the dull sensation.

For one to be conscious of the work of interpretation and the role played by the visual image, either the tactile sensation must be ambiguous enough to warrant interpretations or one must voluntarily assume the idea of transforming this sensation in a variety of ways and of playing with it. I had the good fortune to find four subjects who, each in his manner, described this somewhat delicate phenomenon to me. I find that their descriptions have a common basis which may be summed up thus: In explaining the tactile sensation, a certain visual image is adopted as a hypothesis. For example, one imagines two steel points—those of the esthesiometer being applied to the skin at the point at which the contact is felt. One adopts this visual construction when one wishes to feel two points. In this case, I suppose that the tactile sensation is something vague and blurred, spread out in a zone, and by itself without precise meaning. One tries to see if the visual image of two points can be adjusted to the tactile sensation; one follows the image of the two points. Mentally, one lowers the image to the skin, seeing if the points can be applied to the tegument or if they refuse to be placed there; or, a little differently, one seeks tractability on the part of touch. One asks whether the tactile sensation can be transformed into the visual sense, whether it lends itself to the combination. Tactually, one examines whether one feels something comparable to the two visual points. If this combination, this tactile-visual construction, is accomplished, if, above all, it lasts for a certain time, it will be judged probable or certain.

M. Sim . . . , to explain how, at will, he could feel one point or two, tells us, always in relation to a particular experiment (and I note in passing that the responses of the subjects are given after a contact; it is direct introspection) : "When I wish to feel only one, I imagine a balancing game with the apparatus, and press on the side of the one which I wish to feel. I bend it further, then I lower it again when I wish to feel two." The apparatus is represented visually. For another contact, M. Sim . . . is unsuccessful in feeling two points and gives this reason for his failure: "At first it is clearly two, but then it fuses; and so I prefer to judge immediately rather than wait. Once they are fused, I can no longer separate them." Question: "Can't you do it as a visual image?" Answer: "Yes, but not as a tactile sensation. I have a tendency to place the two points of the visual image against the edges of the tactile sensation, but the latter does not double. It seems to me that there are three points: a tactile one in the middle, which is real, and two visual ones which do not exist except in my imagination." Another time, this same subject gave a general explanation of the procedure: "When I feel two points in an ambiguous fashion, one is always felt more than the other. I direct my attention to the doubtful one and try harder to feel it. Accordingly, I tell you whether there is one or two." Question: "Is it simply your attention which is directed on it?" Answer: "Yes, attention, and comparison with the other." Question: "Do you use special images?" Answer: "Yes, visual images. Visually, I picture better the one which I do not sense very well. I develop it further than it appears to me in the ambiguous tactile sensation. In summary, I try to make something clear from something doubtful." Question: "Is it the visual image of a point?" Answer: "No, it is that of a separation. It is hardly visual, it is vague. It is, rather, an image of movement." Question: "What difference is there between when it succeeds and when it doesn't?" Answer: "When it succeeds, I feel something at the place where I try to localize the point visually. If it does not succeed, it is very simply because I do not feel anything; I only feel the point I have departed from. When it is a doubtful case, it is because one of the points is felt less than the other. I attempt to feel the less felt point by representing it there to myself visually. When I feel only one point and wonder if there are two, I use the same process."

This process thus consists in imagining something and trying to discover whether this something goes along with the experienced sensation. It is clearly the process of hypothesis and tentative verification.

M. L. gives information which agrees with the preceding concerning the transformation of a perception at will. Here are some examples of transformations which have not succeeded. "I thought of the two points of the apparatus visually, and I tried to separate them and see one far from the other. I did not have the impression that the sensation varied because of this effort." Another example of failure following a contact with the two points separated by 5 mm.: "I only felt one point. I tried to represent the two points of the instrument as two needles separated from one another, but that had no results." Question: "Why did that give no results?" Answer: "There was no association between visual and tactile images. With my eyes, I followed the two points toward the skin, and I hoped that the moment I arrived at the skin, I would feel the splitting; but that did not occur. There was a contradiction between the two images." Thus, although the subject had hoped for modification of the tactile sensation, the latter resisted. In another instance, the failure was in the visual image and was described at length and in great detail: "One point, from the beginning; a little painful, pricking strongly. I tried to picture the two points of the apparatus, at which time I tried to follow them to the contact. I saw them poorly and did not succeed in picturing the two points on the skin. There was a blurred area; there was no coinciding of the tactile and visual images. It was a sort of conflict of images." Question: "Did you have the two tactile contacts in your imagination?" Answer: "No. I did not succeed in producing the imaginary contact." Question: "When you felt the two points spontaneously, did you have these images of the needle?" Answer: "No, I had only the very vague impression of two points separated by a distance and very weakly visualized. I tried to represent the points of the instrument in a less schematic fashion, and I was hoping that, at a given moment, the visual image of the points in contact with the skin would provoke the tactile image."

M. George A. described very well the role of the visual image in certain cases. In connection with a contact of two points separated by 5 mm., he said: "I had a double contact of points very close together. From a tactile point of view, I did not know whether I felt two distinct things, but I had no difficulty picturing two white points close together, then separated by a darker line. At the same time, I heard the sound of the instrument." Question: "What did the sound do?" Answer: "It added something to the point; I represented the mass. During the experiment, I had a great deal of difficulty paying attention to the sensation, and I asked myself what what going to happen." Question: "Did your visual image come as fast as the tactile?" Answer: "Unless I made an effort to set it aside, it came simultaneously."

From these explanations, it seems clear that the visual image disentangles a confused tactile sensation and makes it more precise. Moreover, it is not only a visual image; it is something more complex. Since the sound of the instrument is a part of it, it must also involve a notion of the object. M. A. sees as clearly as M. L. that, in simple cases, the visual image comes as quickly as the tactile one.

We owe to M. A. an explanation of the process of adjusting the image to the sensation. For him it was an instinctive act: "When the sensation began, I immediately tried to relate it to an object. As soon as I had a sufficient interpretation, I no longer bothered about the object; then only the impressions and the pains persisted." Here is his complete description of the operation: "I had the impression that it was double." Question: "Was it visual?" Answer: "I did not picture the instrument; I saw two bars. I also pictured the depression of the skin at the point of the contact." Question: "Without this visual image of the bars or the depression, would you have felt one or two of these vague contacts?" Answer: "It becomes intermixed. There are moments when I have the sensation of two contacts; then I see two bars. Then I feel only one contact, and finally I come back to two. To confirm my sensation, I have to interpret it. But after I have chosen, the image is then controlled by the sensation. If I have chosen two, I very clearly see the two points, and I say to myself, 'Do I really feel two of them (tactually)?' And then, sometimes, when it does not seem to me that I feel two, the sensation of a single point, which seems fatter to me, is suddenly substituted for that of two points, and I begin the same control again." Question: "What does this control consist of?" Answer: "I direct my attention to the sensation. I say to myself, 'Do I feel two or one of them?' I do not oscillate; I represent to myself and adopt one or two. If it is not one, I adopt the other." Question: "What makes you decide?" Answer: "I find that it is clearer, and I also want to answer. From the first contact, I develop an idea for myself, and then I change it." Question: "Is this control a joining of images with the sensation?" Answer: "It seems more simple to me. It seems to me that what is real is that these two points which I represent visually touch me; and then I ask myself if this sensation is going to change. If it does not change, I say there are two points. If I feel two points less clearly, I say there is only one; then I picture it and feel only one point."

I thought it interesting to dwell upon many details of the preceding facts because they allow us to explore the inner parts of a perception. We see clearly that the mind uses two processes of interpretation, sometimes alternately and sometimes cumulatively; one is verbal, and the other sensory. Properly speaking, the verbal process is the judgment which is manifested apart from the sensation, as an independent activity. On the whole, the sensory process is fairly complicated, with its operations of invention, adjustment, and realization. Its particular characteristic is that it cuts across the sensation and modifies it profoundly. I have already stressed these two modes of psychical activity elsewhere (*Étude expérimentale de l'Intelligence*). I find them here without looking for them. It seems to me that their existence, duality, and independence are among the most important questions of psychology.

From another point of view, these investigations teach us how prominent a role the mind plays in the perception of the exterior world. It has been a long time since Helmholtz said that the outside world only gives us signs, which are interpreted by our intelligence. The development of this idea seems to be contrary to the virtual principle of all psychophysics, according to which a sensation is produced by a stimulus, handed over to the intelligence, imposed on us both as form and as intensity, and composed of a homogeneous quantity. In opposition to this, we can suggest that sensation is something formless which we cannot even describe in words, and that its precision and significance are produced by the interpretation which we give it. Thus, due to this intellectual alluvium, a sensation produced by the same stimulus varies profoundly from one person to another, receiving the imprint of each personality. If, on the one hand, it depends on the stimulus, it no less depends on us: each advance we make in its analysis can have as much practical importance as an increase in the intensity of the stimulus which produces it. Hyperesthesia produced by a perfection of the ability to interpret is of an importance as undefined as the resources of our intelligence. This is perhaps the most precise and striking fact which can be cited to prove that in external perception, the exterior force does not dominate us; rather, it is we—our intelligence—who dominate it.

Section II

PERCEPTUAL DEVELOPMENT

Binet's studies on perception reflect an increasing reliance upon formal, controlled experimentation; his armchair speculations of the past would not be repeated. The reader will find in Binet a genuine concern for methodology—for the standardization of stimulus conditions—and this is reflected in his studies of the Mueller-Lyer illusion and the development of visual memory. His sensitivity to every nuance of the subjects' behavior and to the "demand" characteristics of the experiment is nowhere more clearly illustrated than in these papers. Moreover, he is constantly alert to the implications of his perceptual data in understanding complex cognitive functions.

Binet is always the psychologist, focusing on the behavioral changes of his subjects and finding new ways to alter relevant stimuli. This experimental ingenuity is particularly clear in his analysis of the Mueller-Lyer illusion. With the exception of work done in 1896 by Heymans, the comparison of small and large figures was so original that no one else has repeated the study with any other geometrical illusion. The separate study of the componential subfigures waited 69 years for replication (Pollack & Chaplin, 1964; Pollack, 1964). Binet's study on the perception of lengths and numbers is a classic example of a conservation experiment. Once again, he drives to the heart of the problem and then delights us with several variations of the basic experiment. The same is true in the paper on children's perceptions.

While Binet plays the role of an experimental empiricist in these studies, he nevertheless provides the foundation for a developmental theory which is still discernible in the later contributions of Piaget and Werner. Students of Piaget will notice the striking resemblance of the content and even the interpretation of these five selections to the work of their mentor. Binet could have been a forerunner of Piaget—a forerunner less philosophically sophisticated, but with the same predilection for synthesis of data into a larger developmental

75

schema. In addition, the two men are remarkably similar in their ability to empathize with their subjects and to find meaning in their data. Compared to similar work in the American literature, theirs soars with inspirations.

Aside from these basic similarities, Binet and Piaget differ in several ways. Binet, for example, is more attentive to experimental detail. He takes greater care in the systematic manipulation of variables and in the precise description of experimental conditions. His style is uncluttered and lucid, and is not, as Piaget's has been described, difficult to understand. After Binet's break with the associationists, he never again allowed a preconceived epistemology to force his observations into predetermined categories or stages, and he was considerably less bound to a fixed view of developmental progression than was Piaget.

Because of their own interests, the editors count these papers among their favorites. They represent findings in large part unduplicated because the majority of developmental psychologists are unfamiliar with them. These colleagues are hereby invited to share in the delights of discovery and to derive perhaps equal inspiration from a first-rate experimental psychologist.

REFERENCES

Heymans, G. Quantitative Untersuchungen ueber das "optische Paradoxon." *Zeitschrift fuer Psychologie*, 1896, *9*, 221-255.

Pollack, R. H. Simultaneous and successive presentation of elements of the Mueller-Lyer figure and chronological age. *Perceptual and motor skills*, 1964, *19*, 303-310.

Pollack, R. H., & Chaplin, M. R. The effects of prolonged stimulation by components of the Mueller-Lyer figure upon the magnitude of illusion. *Perceptual and motor skills*, 1964, *18*, 377-382.

5

Note on Illusions of Movement

The exact nature of sensory illusions, so-called illusions of movement, is not yet well known; the following fact, which Mr. X, an eminent micrographer, shared with me, seems to me an interesting contribution to the study of these phenomena.

One day, Mr. X was studying under the microscope a *Stentor coeruleus* contracted into a ball and animated by a slow rotating movement around its longitudinal axis. The observer was trying to reproduce a picture of the *Stentor* in a sketch; he had already drawn the contour of the animal and the granular bands which stripe it. Only his right eye was used for the observation; his left eye was kept constantly closed. With his right eye focused alternately on the animal and on the sketch, he suddenly saw the bands of the sketch begin to turn. This movement took place in a direction opposite that of the image and with a speed of rotation a little less than that of the animal. Surprised, Mr. X was curious about what he would see if he looked at the sketch with his left eye, which, until that moment, had remained closed. With only his left eye open, the illusion was again reproduced; the movement of the sketch continued in the same direction as it had with the right eye, but it was a little slower. It should be remembered that during his observation under the microscope, the observer had never looked at the animal with his left eye. The illusion, however, took place after a prolonged three-hour observation and to a certain degree was probably determined by fatigue.

We would not have thought it useful to publish this observation, which in many ways resembles the examples of illusions of movement reported by Helmholtz and by so many other authors, if it did not exemplify a new phenomenon. This phenomenon consists in the participation of both eyes in the illusion, even though only one eye—

Sur les illusions de mouvement. *Revue philosophique*, 1888, 25, 335.

the right one—had been open during the observation under the microscope. The same type of illusion definitely occurred for both eyes, since the apparent movement of the sketch was produced in the same direction.

6

The Perception of Lengths and Numbers in Some Small Children

I summarize here the first results of a series of studies that I am currently pursuing on the phenomena of perception in small children. I intend to study two subjects: 1) the perception of lengths, and 2) the perception of numbers.

My studies were done solely on the two little sisters I mentioned earlier, who are, so to speak, constantly before my eyes. The elder is four years old; the younger, two and one-half. One is calm, reserved, reflective; she pays a great deal of attention to the experiments when she is well disposed. The second is more gay, more exuberant, more giddy, and one must have a great deal of patience to do observations on her. We have, therefore, two very different types of children for our study.

Perception of lengths

The experiment is set up in the following way: On a large sheet of white paper, I draw in ink two straight lines placed side by side and separated by a space of 1 to 2 cm. A fixed ratio of 24:40 or 3:5 exists between these two lengths, and the child to whom I show them is asked to indicate which one appears longer or shorter to her. If one uses only two lengths, the correctness of the child's response can be due to chance; therefore, it is necessary to trace on the same sheet of paper two similar lines a little below the first pair. Below these, trace another two lines, being careful not to put all the longer lines on the same side since this could serve as an indicator to the child. If the child correctly chooses the longer line all three times, it is probable

La perception des longueurs et des nombres chez quelques petits enfants. *Revue philosophique*, 1890, 30, 68-81.

that she can estimate the difference in length by sight. Moreover, one can exclude all chance in the responses by readministering the test, reversing the drawing in relation to its margins. It must also be noted that the absolute length of the lines can exert an influence on the perception of their difference, and that doubtless there are certain lengths which are more favorable than others to this estimation. Therefore, it is necessary to add to our original drawing a series of lines which maintain between them the ratio of 24:40, but which have different absolute lengths. As a last consideration, I always arrange it so that the absolute difference between the two lines is no less than 1 mm.

According to this method, I made five sets of drawings containing lengths with ratios equal to 24:40, 32:40, 34:40, 36:40, and 38:40. These constitute a scale with which to measure the estimation of length. I am not publishing these drawings here. It is unnecessary because anybody can construct similar ones if he needs to.

Before using these drawings in my studies on child psychology, I submitted them to the examination of adults, who were generally successful in recognizing the longer lines without error. I must point out, however, that for the drawing with a ratio equal to 38:40, two adults committed several errors. One of them was even mistaken on the drawing where the lines were in the ratio of 36:40.[1]

Let us examine how the children behave in front of the drawings. It is necessary, first of all, to take some precautions with them to hold their ever-fleeting attention. Thus, the first care must be to show them only two lines at a time, hiding the others with a movable screen; if one shows the child the entire sheet, it is quite difficult to keep her glance from wandering over all the lines. Moreover, it is very useful to solicit the child's attention in advance, showing her the two lines to be compared only at the last minute. These are little precautions, but they seem to me indispensable. I am certain that if one neglected them one would very often obtain negative results signifying only one thing: the experimenter did not know how to operate. The experimenter is obliged, to a point, to adjust his method to the subjects he is addressing. There are certain rules to follow when one experiments on a child, just as there are certain rules for adults, for hysterics, and for the insane. These rules are not

---

[1] According to Weber, the smallest difference that one can grasp between two lines is equivalent to about 1/50 of the shorter one, but this number varies with the individual and with exercise.

written down anywhere; one learns them for oneself and is repaid in great measure. By making an error and later accounting for the cause, one learns not to make the mistake a second time. In regard to children, it is necessary to be suspicious of two principal causes of error: suggestion and failure of attention. This is not the time to speak on the first point. As for the second, failure of attention, it is so important that it is always necessary to suspect it when one obtains a negative result. One must then suspend the experiments and take them up at a more favorable moment, restarting them 10 times, 20 times, with great patience. Children, in fact, are often little disposed to pay attention to experiments which are not entertaining, and it is useless to hope that one can make them more attentive by threatening them with punishment. By particular tricks, however, one can sometimes give the experiment a certain appeal.

The first observations were done on the elder of the two little girls. I showed the drawings to her, explaining that she was to put her finger on the longer line; I noted that she could recognize almost without hesitation the longer line on the first four sets of drawings. Several times she was able to go from one drawing to the next without committing an error. I used my control procedure, which consisted of reversing the drawing in relation to its margins, and she was not deceived. It was not the same for the fifth set containing lines in a ratio of 38:40. There, several errors were committed, and I consider this ratio as constituting, for the moment, the limit of her power to discriminate. These results were obtained without any preliminary exercise.

The little two-and-a-half-year-old did not behave differently. It is true that at the first testing, she committed many errors. This was due simply to the fact that her attention was not well fixed, as the following will show: Two days later, repeating these experiments, I saw with genuine astonishment that she could go through the first four sets of drawings, as her sister had done, without committing a single error. One cannot attribute this result to chance. The total number of lines contained in these four sets was 32; if the child had guessed every time, it is probable that she would have been mistaken a certain number of times on such a long series. Moreover, I was able to subject this little girl to the control procedure (reversing the drawings) without her committing an error. Nothing was more surprising than to see this child of two and one-half years place her index finger successively and with assurance on each of the two lines saying, each time without a mistake, "There, that's the smaller one; there, that's the bigger one," as if it were not enough to indicate only one of them. Like her older sister, the little girl began to commit errors only when she compared the lines in the fifth set. The ratio 38:40 constitutes, then, a limit for her also.

The few people who witnessed these experiments were particularly astonished at the speed with which the children recognized the longer line; there was, so to speak, no hesitation. Moreover, it is a well-known fact that the small child does not know how to reflect, to retain his judgment. Thus, if the child cannot perceive the difference in length at first glance, he will not perceive it at all.

I next tried to find out whether the same children could compare two lines which were no longer shown simultaneously, but successively, letting 10 or 15 seconds elapse between the two perceptions. I obtained quite confusing results. They appear to me chiefly related to the fact that the experiment requires an effort of attention that the child is incapable of making. In fact, to compare accurately two lengths seen 15 seconds apart, it is necessary to try to retain the memory of the first length during the 15-second interval. A child is not always disposed to do this; here we are confronted with a failure of attention, the stumbling block I alluded to above.

These experiments, however, have had the advantage of revealing to me a possible cause of error. I showed, in turn, two lines of different lengths traced on two sheets of paper. The older of the two little girls succeeded each time in choosing the longer line; she never made a mistake. Her assurance raised my suspicions. I asked her how she did it, and she told me, very naively, that she had noticed a black dot on the sheet with the longer line; this black dot, always small, served as her guide in discovering the longer line. Other examples of unconscious falsification were observed in the course of the studies. I will cite some of these later, and it will be seen that observations on children present nearly the same causes of error as occur with hysterics.

I had the opportunity to try Beaunis' ingenious instrument for studying memory and the comparison of angles on one of my little subjects. This instrument is composed of two half-circles, each furnished with a movable ray that can make all the desired angles. I studied the conditions under which the two children could recognize that one of the angles was smaller than the other. A preliminary study showed us that an adult can easily perceive a difference equal to 2/40 of the smaller angle. Some people can, many times in a row and without making a mistake, perceive a difference of 1/40; others cannot perceive a difference smaller than 3/40.

In all my investigations I placed the two half-circles next to each other on a large, well-lit, white sheet; the two diameters were on the same line. The child, situated between the two, was obliged to turn his head to the right to study one and to the left to study the other; consequently, it was impossible for the child to perceive them simultaneously. The perception was always successive. This evidently rendered the comparison much more difficult, because it required an effort of attention and memory greater than that of the comparison of two lines presented simultaneously. I was always careful that the daylight fell perpendicular to the diameter of the half-circles. Moreover, in the successive trials I placed the half-circles in random order, presenting the larger angle sometimes to the right of the child, sometimes to the left. To avoid any reference marks, I was particularly careful to change the direction of the radii so that each half-circle sometimes had the larger angle, sometimes the smaller. Beaunis' apparatus lent itself easily to these precautions, and I found it very useful.

I have summarized in a table [Table 1] the experiment done with Madeleine (four years and three months).

Table 1. Comparison of Angles in Madeleine

| Date | Comparison Between | | | Replies | |
				Correct	Incorrect
March 14	70	and	80 degrees	4	0
	60		70	3	0
	50		60	5	0
	40		50	5	0
	40		48	3	0
	40		46	4	1
	40		45	2	2
March 25	60		65	7	3
	50		55	6	4
	40		45	13	3
	40		44	9	1
	40		43	8	2
	40		42	3	3
March 27	40		42	4	6
March 28	40		44	9	3
	40		43	5	7
March 30	40		44	5	1
	40		43	8	4

Examination of this table shows that the child improved a little during the beginning of the experiments. She became capable, after some exercise, of recognizing angular differences which at first passed unperceived. Eventually, the distinction between 40° and 45° was made with such surety that one overlooked it because the child had come to perceive a lesser difference: that between 40° and 43°.

Can we determine exactly the smallest perceptible difference for the child we are examining? One maintains for certain that she can never distinguish 40° from 42°, and yet she distinguishes with a certain ease 40° from 44°. In regard to the comparison of 40° with 43°, one cannot be so affirmative; it all depends on the child's degree of attention. If we take the total number of responses, we find 25 correct as opposed to 13 incorrect. It seems to me that this result is not explained entirely by chance and that the perception of the differences plays an undoubted part. After all, I am rather inclined to admit that the smallest perceptible difference for Madeleine is, for the moment, equal to the difference between 40° and 43°, in other words, to 3/40 of the smaller angle.

If we review the results of our experiments on the perception of lengths, we can see that, in both of these studies, the power of discrimination in the same child is shown to be nearly equivalent. That is, Madeleine, in comparing two lengths, is sensitive to a difference equal to 4/40 of the smaller one. It is with genuine satisfaction that I state this final agreement between studies pursued in completely different ways. I now consider it completely established that there exists in Madeleine—and probably in other four-year-old children like her—a remarkable acuteness of perception. In this regard, Madeleine differs very little from an adult.

I am well aware that comparisons between children and adults are somewhat artificial and schematic, because that which one calls the "adult" individual corresponds no more to a unique and well-determined type than that which one calls the "healthy" individual. As I said above, one adult can distinguish 1/40 of the smaller angle; another, 2/40; and another, only 3/40. To which of these individuals should the child be compared? To be absolutely correct, it would be necessary to wait until the child one was studying became an adult. One could then compare him with himself at different stages of evolution and thereby determine the exact influence of age on perception. While waiting until I can make such a comparison, I take the mean number for the adult, which is equal to 2/40 of the smaller angle, and compare it with the results of the experiments I have just summarized. Now, it is evident that the difference between 2/40 and 3/40 is entirely minimal, and that it can in no way express the relationship which exists between the intelligence of an adult and that of a child. If one could succeed in measuring intelligence, that is, reasoning, judgment, memory, the power of abstraction—and this does not appear to me absolutely impossible—the number expressing the mean intellectual development of an adult would represent a relationship quite different from the number expressing the intellectual development of a child.

If I insist on these facts, it is because they appear to me completely new. I have not found the least mention of them in the works on child psychology that I have consulted and therefore take the liberty of pointing out this subject of study for future observers. It would be important to know whether I have dealt with a regular or an exceptional case. For the moment, however, I am content with pointing out that it would be interesting to know if, as my observations seem to indicate, intellectual development begins with those lower functions which attain a very high degree and almost end their evolution at a moment when the higher functions are in a rudimentary state.

Perception of numbers

I asked myself how the perception of numbers occurs in children who do not know how to count. Before knowing how to count, a child accustoms himself to an idea of numbers. He knows what it is to have many marbles or very few of them. He therefore makes use of an instinctive and probably unconscious numbering system before becoming acquainted with verbal numbering, which we are charged with teaching him. Authors, moreover, have made many interesting observations on this subject. Preyer reports some of them. He speaks of a 10-month-old child from whom it was impossible to take away one of his nine pins without his being aware of it. At 18 months, he knew perfectly well whether he was missing one of his ten animals. This same child used to bring his mother two handkerchiefs and then take them back to their place. One day, when given only one of them, he began to look for the second with a look and intonation that indicated his desire to regain it.

Although observations of this type appear to me of great value, they remain a little superficial because, in general, they are provoked by chance. The question of instinctive numeration deserves careful examination through methodical experiments.

The little four-year-old girl that I am studying fortunately does not know how to read or count, and her parents were wise in postponing the beginning of her instruction as much as possible. For amusement she was taught some names of numbers and some letters, but that was done by fits and starts, as if by chance. When the experiment began, this is what her knowledge in computation amounted to: She knew how to count up to three objects, that is, she could distinguish three beans from two beans, three books from two books, etc., and count them correctly. Beyond the number three, she said the numbers entirely by chance, and the spoken enumeration was no longer of any help to her. I insist on this point. If one showed her a group of four objects she would say, for example, that there were six of them. Her word "six" did not have, as one might think, the value of our word "four," because on another occasion, if one again showed her a group of four objects, she would say an entirely different number, for example, twelve.

At the risk of repeating myself excessively, I will say one more time that the first requirement of these experiments is to hold the child's attention. I prefer to be alone with her in her room so that no stranger distracts her. I try above all to interest her in the experiments, and I watch to see that she does not get bored. Sometimes the little girl says, "I'm beginning to get bored," or rather, she expresses the same feeling more cunningly by saying, "I'm afraid of fatiguing you." From that moment I suspend everything. Sometimes I have the good fortune of hearing her say, "Again! It's fun." I am sure, then, that her attention is aroused, and I seek to profit by her good mood.

These studies can only be done by the method of right and wrong cases. I am always careful to indicate the total good and bad responses so that the reader may judge for himself if the conclusions are due to chance.

To determine whether the child can perceive numbers without knowing how to count, I placed before her two groups of similar objects and asked her to indicate which group had the greater number of objects. By varying the difference between the two numbers, it was possible, by trial and error, to arrive at the smallest perceptible difference. I made use of diverse objects—coins, pens, counters, and particularly beans. These had the advantage of interesting the child more than objects of a more regular form. In taking account of these experiments, I will use the generic term of counter.

First, I placed two groups of counters of the same size next to each other on a table; one group contained 18 counters, the other only 15. The separate counters were distributed irregularly on the same plane. The little girl quickly recognized the more numerous group. I then modified the two groups, sometimes making the group on the right more numerous, sometimes the one on the left. The relationship of 15 to 18 remained unchanged, however. Six trials were completed, and the child's response was invariably correct. To increase the difficulty, the relationship of 15 to 18 was replaced by that of 16 to 18. In nine trials, no errors were committed by the child. With the relationship of 17 to 18, the child responded correctly eight times and made one mistake. With the relationship of 21 to 22, the child responded correctly four times and made four mistakes.

These initial facts indicate that this little girl, although she cannot count to four, is capable of comparing 17 units with 18 and of finding very easily that the group of 18 is larger. The correctness with which this comparison is made is a confirmation of the above experiments on the perception of lengths. But we will return to this subject a little further on.

Now it is necessary to ask whether the child can compare entire collections without counting them. My opinion is that she has a perception of totality; if she judges one group more numerous than another, it is because it occupies more space on the paper. Properly speaking, then, this would not be enumeration, that is, the perception of an entity composed of discrete elements. The idea behind this explanation came to me during the course of the experiments I am now going to describe.

I had in reserve a collection of green counters which were smaller than the white ones. More precisely, the white counters were 4 cm. in diameter, the green ones $2\frac{1}{2}$ cm. My idea was to substitute 18 green counters for 18 white ones. The total group occupied a smaller surface, and when I tried to make the child compare the group of 18 green counters with that of 16 white ones, she was always wrong. As I said before but will repeat again, and as I verified once more for surety, she was capable of comparing groups of

17 and 18 white counters similar in diameter and of recognizing the more numerous group. It seemed obvious to me that if she committed an error in her comparison between two groups of counters of different sizes, it was because the total dimensions were different; that is, the group of 18 green counters occupied a smaller surface than the group of 16 white ones.

I allege, therefore, that the child had mechanically, and of course unconsciously, substituted the perception of the whole for that of its discrete elements, although she continued to indicate that she was trying to perceive numbers. The childish phrase she used was always the same: "There," she said, pointing toward one of the groups, "there are more of them here."

I next explained to the child that she misunderstood what I was asking of her. I made myself clearly understood by showing her two groups, one formed with 3 green counters and the other with 2 white ones. The child, comprehending my explanation, said immediately that there was a greater number of green counters but that the white ones were bigger. To support this explanation, I did some experiments on less numerous groups. Before a group of 4 green counters and another of 3 white counters, she found the green ones more numerous three times in a row, the position of the groups being changed each time.

I then did some experiments with more numerous groups to see whether the child, as a result of the preceding explanation, would continue to perceive the discrete elements as she had done with 3 or 4 counters. Before two groups, one formed with 18 green counters, the other with 14 white counters, the child found the latter group more numerous. Moreover, I could progressively diminish the group of 14 white counters to 10 without the child changing her mind. (The subtractions, of course, were done outside of her view.) Even reduced to 10, the white counters appeared more numerous than the 18 green ones. It was only when I reduced them to 9 that the 18 green counters appeared more numerous.

These repeated failures were not due to a decrease of attention, because the child always responded in the same way. They were not due to the fact that the child had forgotten my explanations; if I showed her 4 green counters and 3 white ones, she said, as I taught her, that the green counters were more numerous. I believe these experiments prove only that the child, when perceiving a large number of discrete objects, has very great difficulty in perceiving them other than as a solid entity.

The idea came to me of studying which of the small numbers the child could actually perceive in discrete form. I thus attempted to verify whether the child could correctly recognize the more numerous group of counters in the following cases: 2 green counters, 1 white one; 3 green counters, 2 white ones; 4 green counters, 3 white ones; 5 green counters, 4 white ones.

A great number of trials were done with these numbers and were nearly always successful; I say "nearly" when in ten responses there were nine correct ones. In the following cases, however, the group of white counters was judged more numerous: 6 green counters and 5 white ones; 7 green counters and 6 white ones, etc.

It seemed well demonstrated to me that, under the preceding conditions, the child was unable to compare numbers higher than five or six. Since comparison is fundamental to perception, it follows, then, that this child could not correctly perceive a number higher than six. However limited her instinctive enumeration, it goes much beyond learned verbal enumeration which, in the child examined, did not exceed the number three.

I am dwelling for a long time on these experiments because they are very intricate; if I had not recorded them in complete detail, the methods I used might have been misunderstood. I am convinced that these experiments contain interesting psychological information. In short, they show us that, in the child I studied, the perception of the whole occurs more easily and more correctly than the perception of numbers. Moreover, they permit us to establish with some certainty the limits of the perception of numbers, that is, of numeration properly speaking.

New experiments on the perception of numbers

The reader may be astonished by the results we have found. In the little children under our observation, the perception and comparison of lengths occurred with remarkable correctness; on the other hand, the perception of numbers was extremely gross and defective. I asked myself whether there was a real difference between these two modes of perception or whether the difference I found was merely attributable to my methods of observation. Consequently, it appeared necessary to study again the perception of numbers using slightly different procedures.

This is the way I set up the new experiments: I brought together

on a table a small number of objects such as 2 pens, 3 grains, 4 counters, etc., and drew the child's attention to them. When she had had
time to perceive their number, I took all the objects and hid them
in my hand. I then put one on the table before her and asked, "Are
there any more of these?" If the child responded affirmatively, I
placed a second object before her and so on. I tried, of course, always
to pose the question in the same words and tone of voice so that no
response was dictated. Moreover, in putting the counters back on
the table, I tried not to place them in the same order as before.

Let us take, as an example, the test done with 3 counters. If the
child, upon seeing the second one, says that there are no more, she
commits an error of underestimation; the number she has retained
is inferior by one unit to the correct number. If the child, upon seeing the third counter, says that there are no more, her response is
correct, and there is nothing more to say about it. If, on the contrary,
the child says there are more, she commits an error of overestimation,
the counterpart of the error of underestimation. Since one is then
obliged to suspend the experiment, showing no more counters to the
child, one does not know whether the error of overestimation rests
on one unit or on several. It is good not to forget this. Finally, in
order not to confuse the child's memory, it is indispensable that one
not change the numbers each time, but do a series of trials on the
same number.

These experiments can be considered an application of the
method of right and wrong cases with this distinction: the chances of
error in each experiment are higher than the chances of a correct
response. If, for example, the child must retain the number three
(and she can indicate the numbers one, two, three, or four), calculation of the probabilities indicates that while errors due to chance are
in a proportion of 3:4, correct responses are in a proportion of 1:4.
That is, correct responses versus erroneous responses form the ratio
1:3.

A last observation: In our preceding experiments, the child
showed her ability to perceive numbers by an act of comparison.
Here the procedure is different. The child proves that she can
perceive a number of objects by recognizing them, that is, by bringing in an act of memory.

The results are illustrated in the following table [Table 2]. The
first column indicates the number of objects presented to the child,
and the second, the number retained [i.e., the child's response].

Table 2. Perception of Numbers in Madeleine and Alice

Madeleine (52 months)					Alice (32 months)				
3 2	5 5	3 3	4 5	4 3	2 2	4 3	3 3	2 2	3 3
3 3	5 4	3 3	4 4	4 4	2 2	4 3	3 3	2 2	3 3
3 3	5 6	3 3	4 5	4 4	2 2	4 3	3 3	2 2	3 3
3 3	5 4	3 3	4 4	4 4	2 2	4 3	4 4	2 2	3 3
3 3	5 5	4 4	4 4	4 4	3 2	4 4	4 5	2 2	3 3
4 3	5 4	4 4	4 4	5 5	3 2	4 5	4 3	2 2	3 3
4 4	5 5	4 4	4 4	5 5	3 3	3 3	4 2	2 2	3 3
4 4	5 5	4 4	4 4	5 5	3 3	3 3	4 3	3 3	3 3
4 4	5 4	5 5	4 4	5 6	3 3	3 3	2 2	3 3	3 3
4 5	5 5	5 4	4 4		3 3	4 3	2 3	3 3	4 3
4 4	5 4	5 4	4 4		3 3	4 5	2 3	3 4	4 3
4 4	5 5	5 5	4 4				2 2	3 2	4 3
4 4	5 5	5 6	5 5					3 3	4 4
	5 6	5 4	5 5						4 4
									4 3
									4 4

Summary:

Madeleine	Number to be remembered	3	4	5
	Correct answers	8	24	14
	Incorrect answers	1	9	12
Alice	Number to be remembered	2	3	4
	Correct answers	15	24	5
	Incorrect answers	2	4	15
Three weeks later Madeleine	Number to be remembered	3	4	5
	Correct answers	16	10	10
	Incorrect answers	0	1	1

Despite the difference in procedure, these new studies entirely confirm the preceding ones by showing us that the perception of numbers in our two little subjects occurs within very restricted limits. We can easily fix the initial limit for Madeleine at the number four; with practice, at the number five. For Alice, the limit is not as high; she recognizes with certainty only the number three.

We will observe that there is no gradual transition between the numbers that these little intelligences can retain. One of these children can retain the number three. She makes no mistakes, so to speak, on this number; the errors that she commits are entirely insignificant. Add one more unit and everything changes. The number of errors becomes suddenly, sharply, much more considerable.

The errors of underestimation are more numerous than the errors of overestimation; in Madeleine, there are ten underestimates and six overestimates, and in Alice, seven of the former and two of the latter. It seems that in these children, the number of objects retained by the memory has a tendency to be reduced.

7

Children's Perceptions

That which is called intelligence, in the strict sense of the word, consists of two principal things: first, perceiving the exterior world, and second, reconsidering these perceptions as memories, altering them and pondering them.

In the two studies that follow, we shall try to determine what, in particular, perception and ideation represent in the two children, aged two and five, who were submitted to our observation and on whom we have already published some short notes.

We examined the perception of lengths and numbers in a preceding note. In regard to numbers, we saw that these children, who did not know how to count, could not perceive numbers of objects greater than five or six. These experiments make us appreciate the value of those carried out on certain higher animals: monkeys and bears, for example, have been made by various contrivances to perceive a certain number of objects. Because the more intelligent animals hardly exceed what small children can do, it is to them that they must be compared. Like children, animals merely perceive the *totality* of a group of objects, whereas adult humans, thanks to the use of language, actually *count* them, which is quite different. When we compare the animal to the adult human, we are therefore committing an error. I recall likewise that in the perception of lengths, small children can demonstrate a shrewdness of perception; but it seems to me that one must not extend the conclusions of these experiments too far. A child is above all utilitarian. If he succeeds in correctly estimating certain lengths, it is because he needs to in order to keep from bumping into objects and from hurting himself. This is all the more necessary because he has walked alone for a long time when he reaches the age of three. I do not

Perceptions d'enfants. *Revue philosophique*, 1890, *30*, 582-611.

believe, however, that the child is capable of correctly perceiving all distances. On the contrary, I am persuaded that he often makes gross mistakes as to the distance of a far object, like a roof or a steeple, which he is not in the habit of touching. Correct perceptions take place only for the environment within his reach, the development of his faculties being regulated by practical need.

We shall now examine new forms of perception, insisting particularly on those which require an effort of interpretation.

The perception of colors

Appellation Method. Let us first consider the method which must be followed for studying the perception of colors in young children. The most complete studies on the subject are those of Preyer, who used several methods. He began by repeating several times the names of a small number of colors, each time placing the corresponding color in front of the child. He then asked, "Where is the red one? the green one?" and so on. The response, correct or not, was written down.

This was the first form given to the experiment. After the child became familiar with the trials and showed himself capable of distinguishing several colors, Preyer changed his procedure. He placed the colors successively in front of the child and asked him to name them. The colors consisted of colored ovals placed in a box. At the end of a certain time, Preyer permitted the child to choose for himself the colors to be named. Sometimes he gave the name of a color and asked the child to find it in the box.

All these tests have in common the requirement of the intervention of language and the memory of color names. I entitle these the appellation method. Preyer admits that experiments of this kind do not reveal the exact state of the perception of colors because, to be successful, the child has to associate the idea of the word "red" or "green" with the corresponding color. Perhaps this act of association becomes possible well after the child is able to distinguish red from green.[1] On the other hand, Preyer seems to think that the difficulty in associating a name with a given color is the same in regard to the act of association; if the child names green, for example, less easily than yellow, this is due solely to the fact that he perceives green less well than yellow.

[1] *L'âme de l'Enfant,* p. 6.

I followed Preyer's method in studying chromatic sensitivity in a little girl between two and a half and three years of age to whom I had not taught any names of colors. At the moment I began my experiments, she was acquainted with the color names she had heard her older sister use, but she was completely ignorant of their meaning. If one drew her attention to a color and asked her to name it, she responded entirely by chance: blue was called yellow, and a moment later, the same blue was called green, then red, etc. One could see that associations between colors and their names had not yet been formed—not even incorrect associations. An exception must be made for red, which was very often called blue. This little girl's older sister, who had not been taught color names either, behaved quite differently. She educated herself entirely alone and at two years and nine months could correctly name red, yellow, green, blue, white, black, gray, and brown. This can give an idea of the importance of individual differences in the same family and in children supposedly receiving the same education.

The first experiment, like the ones to follow, was done with some Holmgren wool. It took place on the 19th of March. (The child was then two years and eight months.) At first, I showed the little girl seven skeins of green yarn (of different shades) and three skeins of red yarn. She did not know the names of either of them. I taught her to repeat after me the word red when I pointed to the "red" ones and the word "green" when I pointed to the green ones. After this preliminary education, she gave me red and green when I asked for them.

	Red	Green
Correct	10	10
Incorrect	0	0

The following morning I took three samples of red, three of yellow, three of green, and I spent a long time teaching her the names of these colors, making her repeat them after me. I then spread out the skeins before her, asking her to point to the color whose name I said or to name the color I put in her hands. After six questions, I regularly repeated to her the names of the colors. Here is a summary of these first results.

	Red	Green	Yellow
Correct	20	12	12
Incorrect	0	8	8

It follows from these first observations that the child continually confused yellow and green; at the name of yellow, she sometimes pointed to the yellow, sometimes to the green. When she was presented with one of these two colors, she indiscriminately called it yellow or green.

The preceding experiments were done in three sessions. On the 23rd of March they were begun again, after I had given a new lesson in colors to the child.

	Red	Green	Yellow
Correct	6	1	2
Incorrect	0	5	4

Green and yellow being unceasingly confused with each other, I omitted the yellow skeins.

	Red	Green
Correct	5	5
Incorrect	0	0

I replaced the yellow skeins.

	Red	Green	Yellow
Correct	6	2	2
Incorrect	0	4	4

On March 25, I repeated the same experiment, using two skeins of red, two of green, and two of yellow.

	Red	Green	Yellow
Correct	9	6	5
Incorrect	0	3	4

On March 27, equivalent results:

	Red	Green	Yellow
Correct	6	3	2
Incorrect	0	3	4

On the first of April I resumed the lessons. To combat the confusion which had established itself in the child's mind between the name of yellow and that of green, I temporarily omitted the green skein, and I did two series of interrogations with the red and the yellow. In the first series, I asked the child to point to the color whose name I said; in the second, I asked her to name the color to which I pointed. Here are the results of the first series:

	Red	Yellow
Correct	4	4
Incorrect	0	0

Evidently, if the child makes no mistakes on the yellow, it is largely because she can easily distinguish it from red, which she has recognized correctly up to now. In the second series of experiments, where the child herself must say the names of the colors, the results are quite different.

	Red	Yellow
Correct	6	0
Incorrect	0	6

The child continued to call the yellow one green. However, I was careful, as always, to correct the error as soon as it was committed. I alternated each time: I presented the yellow skein, then the red one, then the yellow one, and so on. It can be seen that the idea of the word "green" seems to have become almost indissolubly linked with the color yellow.

I added one more color, a skein of white yarn, and I began the two series of experiments again. If the child must designate the colors when their names are called the following results are obtained:

	Red	Yellow	White
Correct	6	6	6
Incorrect	0	0	0

There is no error made. If on the contrary, the child must say the name, the results are no longer equivalent.

	Red	Yellow	White
Correct	6	2	4
Incorrect	0	4	1

Yellow was called green four times, and white was once called gray. As always, this child found it more difficult to name the color I presented to her than to select the color corresponding to the name I gave.

On the fifth of April some experiments were done on red and green. First, by designation of the color:

	Red	Green
Correct	6	6
Incorrect	0	0

Then, by designation of the name:

	Red	Green
Correct	2	2
Incorrect	0	0

Two days later, April 7, I did the experiment simultaneously on five color and obtained the following responses by requesting the child to designate the named color:

	Red	White	Green	Yellow	Dark Brown
Correct	10	5	5	3	11
Incorrect	0	6	7	6	0

Then, requesting the child to name the color that was indicated:

	Red	White	Green	Yellow	Dark Brown
Correct	6	1	6	3	9
Incorrect	0	9	2	4	0

Several facts are evidenced here: first, the new color, the dark brown, was not confused with any other. The child said on seeing it, "This is like chocolate." Perhaps this comparison helped her. Green tended to be well designated; whenever a response was incorrect, it was because of the confusion with yellow. For that matter, it is the same with yellow, which was confused with green. As for white, it was confused sometimes with green, sometimes with yellow—a little more with the latter color.

We added a sample of blue and received the following replies when the child attempted to designate the colors whose names we gave her.

	Red	Green	Yellow	White	Brown	Blue
Correct	2	1	1	4	2	3
Incorrect	0	1	1	1	0	0

The green, the yellow, and the white were confused with one another; the red, the brown, and the blue remained distinct.

The preceding experiments were voluntarily terminated for four months. At the end of this time (25th of August), I asked the child to designate the names of colored samples that I gave her. I got the following series:

	Yellow	Red	Blue	Pink	Green	Brown
Correct	0	3	4	0	3	0
Incorrect	4	1	0	3	0	3

The yellow was called green; the red was once called blue; the pink was called red; and the brown, black. The pink suggested something to the child: "This is like wine, but it is not to drink."

Having the child designate the sample at the sound of its name, I obtained:

	Yellow	Red	Blue	Pink	Green	Brown
Correct	0	3	3	2	2	2
Incorrect	3	0	0	1	1	1

Yellow was three times taken for green; pink once taken for red; green once taken for yellow; brown once taken for green.

In the first days of September, two samples, one orange and the other violet, were added to the preceding ones.

When the child said the names, we had:

	Green	Red	Blue	Yellow	Pink	Orange	Violet
Correct	8	8	8	5	5	6	5
Incorrect	0	0	0	3	2	0	3

When the child indicated the sample named:

	Green	Red	Pink	Blue	Orange	Violet	Yellow
Correct	2	3	3	2	3	3	1
Incorrect	1	0	0	1	1	0	2

In the second half of September, I again obtained, by designation of name:

	Green	Red	Pink	Blue	Yellow	Orange	Violet
Correct	1	4	4	3	0	2	2
Incorrect	2	0	0	0	2	0	0

By designation of color:

	Green	Red	Pink	Blue	Yellow	Orange	Violet
Correct	3	3	3	3	3	3	2
Incorrect	0	0	0	0	1	0	2

Every time a mistake was made with yellow, it was because of the confusion with green. It should be noted that violet was confused with blue.

If we recapitulate the preceding results, we have:

	Red	Green	Yellow	Blue	Brown
Correct	134	78	51	26	24
Incorrect	1	38	60	1	4

	Pink	White	Orange	Violet
Correct	17	20	14	12
Incorrect	6	17	1	5

The number of experiments is much less than that of Preyer's, who did not stop until the child had correctly named the colors. I did not go that far because I thought that it would be more useful to use other methods on the same child. After giving her such frequent lessons on color, I resolved to let nature take its course. I am watching her. Without further lessons, from time to time I ask her the name of a color, hoping to see which colors will be the first she will learn to name correctly on her own. The observation is in progress; I will give the results later.

For the time being, one can draw from the above the conclusion that the color which was correctly designated the largest number of times is red; in Preyer's child it was yellow. Further, in designating the color red or in saying its name, the child never hesitates.

The strange confusion in the child's mind concerning green and yellow must be remarked. Was the confusion due to the colors themselves? Does this little girl not clearly see the difference which exists between them? Is it a question of dichromatism? Or is it a confusion of words?

Preyer's method does not provide a solution to this problem because it does not allow for the study of the perception of colors, except by errors in the ability to designate. I thus took a detour. I wanted to see if the same child could find a color that was first shown and then mixed in among other colors. This is, if you wish, the recognition method substituted for the appellation method.

The appellation method places the child in somewhat artificial conditions. He is required to learn the names of colors and to perform a reasoned perception. It is clear that the child, left to himself, does not recognize colors by their names. but by their visual memory; the recognition method is much less different from his habits than the other method.

Recognition Method. I began these few experiments at the same time I undertook the others. One day I used the first method, the next day, the other.

The first experiment was done with three samples of red, three of yellow, and three of green. I presented one of these samples to the child and made an effort to have her look at it with attention, handle it, etc. Then I took back the sample, which I mixed with the eight others, and I asked the child to find it and give it to me. Here are the results:

	Red	Green	Yellow
Correct	9	9	9
Incorrect	0	0	0

These results were obtained on the same day that we obtained the following series. They are clearly different by the appellation method:

	Red	Green	Yellow
Correct	6	1	2
Incorrect	0	5	4

The comparison of these two series shows that the child is entirely capable of distinguishing yellow from green. If she is often mistaken when Preyer's method is used, it is simply because she has difficulty associating each color with a distinct word. Preyer suspected this to be the case.

Two days later I tried the same kind of task, complicating it a little. I collected seven samples of very distinct colors—red, yellow, green, blue, brown, light pink, white—and obtained the following results:

	Red	Yellow	Green	Brown	White	Pink	Blue
Correct	1	1	1	1	1	1	1
Incorrect	0	0	0	0	0	0	0

To reply correctly, the child is obliged each time to choose from among the seven colors in such a way that the accurate response precludes any possibility of chance.

It is clear that recognition of the color under these conditions is so easy for this child that she never makes a mistake. I thus tried to complicate it a little by allowing some time to pass between the moment when the child was presented with the color and that in which she was to find it. With a 30-second interval, the results were:

	White	Blue	Red	Pink	Yellow	Green	Brown
Correct	1	1	1	0	0	0	0
Incorrect	0	0	0	0	1	1	0
Hesitation	0	0	0	1	0	0	1

The pink was first confused with the white, then recognized. Yellow was confused with blue, and green with yellow. The brown was confused with the yellow and then recognized. The next day, the same experiment with the same conditions:

	Red	Yellow	Green
Correct	1	0	1
Incorrect	0	1	0

Yellow was confused with blue.
The next day:

	Red	Yellow	Green	Blue	White	Pink	Brown
Correct	1	0	1	1	0	1	1
Incorrect	0	1	0	0	1	0	0

Yellow was confused with white, and white with yellow. From this time on, the child was able to sample all the colors without error, and I had to cease the investigation because the results were always the same. During this time, however, the child was unable to *name* correctly yellow and green, which proves that the confusion is one of words and not of colors. How, by what chance, a crossing or a sort of knot between the verbal associations of green and yellow was produced we cannot say; but everyone knows by personal experience that in trying to learn the names of objects, one sometimes commits a mistake which one has great difficulty overcoming.

This cause of error should not be forgotten when Preyer's method is used. It would be incorrect to admit that the difficulty of learning and retaining a name was the same for all the colors. This is only true in theory. In practice, when a verbal association is accidentally made wrongly, it creates an enormous obstacle for different associations with the same object, because one must begin by forgetting the first to make room for the others.

Interpretation of designs

Our study of perceptions will remain incomplete if we do not examine how a child perceives a design, an engraving, a photograph, that is, the imitation of an object. These are very complicated things —certainly more complicated than perception of a weight or a length —and it is by convention and habit that we are not aware of the enormous difference which exists, for example, between an object and a penned drawing of it.

I had occasion to observe for the first time in little Madeleine, when she was a year and nine months old, that she recognized with great certainty familiar objects sketched in outline. The objects were: a hat, a bottle, a glass, a table, a chair, an umbrella, and a bowl. Since above the sketch of the bowl was a cloud of smoke, the child concluded that the bowl contained hot milk.

Needless to say, if a child is to recognize an object from five or six pencil lines which reproduce only its essential characteristics, she must have not only a good memory of visible things, but also a well-developed ability to identify objects.[2] In a sketch, there is neither the color of the object, nor its real size; the third dimension is suppressed, and the position of the object is entirely changed.

But the little girl I observed did not recognize all sketched objects, and one can even say that she did not recognize some of the most familiar. Thus, I noted that if, at the age of a year and nine months, she understood the sketch of a table, a chair, or a bottle, she did not at all understand sketches of isolated parts of the body. A mouth from the front or in profile, a nose in profile, an ear, a finger represented in its normal size, with the nail and the three joints clearly drawn, were not recognized. The child did not know what they were. After about three years, I repeated the experiment; Madeleine was then about four years and four months. She remained hesitant and surprised in front of the preceding sketches and could not understand them. It is impossible not to be struck by this fact. How is it that a little girl, who understood at a year and nine months the sketch of a horse, did not understand at four years the sketch of a nose or an eye?

Why this difference? Undoubtedly, it is easy to answer that the child only recognized in our drawings that which she had already seen, and she had never seen her nose and arms alone. This reason seems inadequate to me. What was missing in the child which prohibited her from seizing the meaning of the preceding sketches was

2 Although I only report observations and experiences, I cannot help but recall that observations made on primitive men led to very different results.

that she did not have, to the same degree as we do, the talent for analysis. We, the adults, can easily represent to ourselves the different parts of the body as complete entities. Our representation need not be the copy of a previous perception; we can fractionate one of our perceptions and picture only a part of it. It seems that the child did not carry out this job of disaggregation as easily; she had seen the object in its entirety and, to recognize it, she needed to receive again the entire impression. Now, this was missing in the preceding drawings and consequently explains why she did not understand them.

I examined to what point Madeleine could understand emotional signs, showing her drawings and photographs published by Darwin in his book on the expression of emotions. The responses of the child were generally very precise. In front of the first plate, which contained six photos of children crying, Madeleine did not hesitate; she said that the babies were crying and were bad. She had often had occasion to see her little sister cry and thus was not mistaken. I then had her look at two photos of a young man. The first showed him in a natural state. In the second, he simulates pain with a strikingly real expression. Madeleine said, on seeing the second photo: "His face is not nice. He looks as if he is going to cry." The child here confused pain with crying. In the same plate, the third photo showed the forehead of a woman expressing pain. On her forehead there were large rectangular wrinkles. Madeleine certainly saw the wrinkles, but she did not understand what they meant.

The third plate gave examples of a sentiment well known to children—laughing. It was very easily interpreted. The first figure was of a young girl smiling. Madeleine said it was a lady who laughs. The second figure showed another young girl who was clearly laughing. Madeleine saw this. She had more trouble with the third photo in which a young girl was smiling very slightly. Figures 4, 5, and 6 showed an old man: first, in his normal state, impassive; then smiling naturally; then showing an artificial smile with the corners of the mouth strongly retracted by the galvanization of the large zygomatic muscles. For Madeleine, in the fourth figure the man was serious, in the fifth he was laughing, and in the sixth he laughed and was not nice.

In the fourth plate, two photos dealt with anger. The first showed a lady who had a sneering expression and whose upper lip was raised on one side to expose the canine. Madeleine was completely mistaken on this photo, as she found that the lady was nice. In the second photo, we see an angry little girl. Madeleine said the girl was nasty.

The fifth plate was not well interpreted. From a portrait of a young girl expressing disdain, Madeleine found that it was simply a lady who was asleep. The error came from the fact that the person had her eyes half closed. Two portraits of young men expressing disgust were no better understood. These were, Madeleine said, men who cry.

Finally, let us finish with the sixth plate, which contained expressions of anger and of resignation. The man who represented anger looked to his right. It was only the direction of his glance which struck Madeleine. "He is looking over there," she said. The expressions of resignation provoked a curious commentary: "It is a man who says, 'Well! I had put something there, and I no longer find it. Perhaps a thief took it.'"

In summary, Madeleine seemed to interpret only smiling and crying with precision and certainty.

Distinction between dream and real life

Children often remember a word whose meaning they do not understand. They repeat it because the sound amuses them or because they give it a new or original meaning, which we often find difficult to understand. There is a word that the two little girls whom I study repeated early; it is "dream." "I dreamed that," they often say, or "I am going to dream, Mommy. Did you dream of me? It is a dream!" etc. I took pains to have them indicate to me, with as much precision as possible, the idea they had of "dream." It is a common observation that children dream and that the memory of what they dreamed can reappear during the day, but does the child know he has dreamed? When does he begin to be aware of it? When does he learn to distinguish this memory from those of real life? And how does he achieve this? To know that one dreamed last night and that one is at this moment wide awake, is to know and distinguish true from false, reality from illusion. How does the child get out of this difficulty?

To study this question, there must first be proof that, when the child tells of an unusual event, he is reciting a dream. Very often, nothing can be affirmed. When the younger little girl was three, she told me of an accident that had happened to her. She had fallen into a barrel in which there were frogs. She had called for help but there was no one, no one! Finally, mamma had come, calling, "I'm coming, I'm coming!" This dramatic tale, told with sincere emotion, did not correspond to anything real, and many people hearing it concluded that the child recounted one of her nightmares. I am not certain of that. Imagination can do what dreams do, and it is very possible that, in the child, imagination works in a silent, unconscious fashion and gives him visions which he takes for realities.

One can only admit the existence of a dream if the child speaks of it in the morning when he awakes, if his first words are, "I have just seen such-and-such a thing," and if there is some emotion in the telling. When, in addition, the child is agitated during the night, when he talks aloud, without awakening, and especially, when his words agree with what he retells when awake, then there is no more doubt. It is indeed a dream.

At what age does he child begin to distinguish between his dreams and his other memories? Little Alice, who was three, had not yet been able to make this distinction. The elder, on the contrary, had done it for about three months, that is, since she was four and one-half. But this distinction, although it seems to me incontestable in fact, still remains undecided on many points. Here is a conversation which will exemplify the difficulty of the question. The little girl told how she saw her father, in a dream, kill a little boy with his cane. Some time later, her father came back to the story.

Father: Do you remember that you said papa killed a little boy with his cane?

Child: Yes.

Father: Where was this?

Child: In a hollow place.

Father: Is it true?

Child: Yes, but in a dream.

Father: Then papa didn't kill the little boy?

Child: Yes, yes, you killed him.

Father: But it was not a real boy that papa killed?

Child: Yes, it was a real boy. And then, I dreamed that mamma burned a devil with a match.

Father: Tell me, what do you mean when you say when I dream.

Child: I mean that it was awful. It frightens me when I dream.

Father: How do you know that it was a dream when you saw me kill a boy?

Child: Because I do not really see you chase boys. If you killed a boy in the courtyard, it would smell bad.

Father: Then it didn't smell bad?

Child: No, it was a dream.

Father: Then it is not true that I killed a boy?

Child: You killed him just the same. It was a dream.

Father: What is it to dream?

Child: That means it is not for real; that is all I can say.

Father: How do you know that it isn't real?

Child: Because I don't see you in the courtyard chasing boys.

Another day, the father asks the following question:

Father: Would you lead me to the place where I killed the little boy?

Child: I can't, since it was a dream.

We do not think it impossible to interpret correctly the child's responses and to show that they are not contradictory. This is incontestably a question of a dream, because it was on awakening that the child had told for the first time that she saw her father "kill a boy."

Despite the vividness of the memory, the child did not hesitate to say that the event was unreal; "It is not for real," she repeated. She said further, "It is true, but in a dream." Later, when she said, "It's true; yes, yes, you killed him," there was no contradiction. I think this means simply that she was not lying and that she really dreamed what she recounted.

The feeling of self

Several authors have examined how the child learns to know himself and to distinguish himself from all that surrounds him. In these episodic studies, I do not take up questions from first principles. I simply try to cite some forgotten facts or to report a curious observation; that is, to manage, in some fashion, to sketch the expression of the child. As far as the development of the sentiment of "self" is concerned, I will simply note the forms of language which the two girls I studied used to indicate themselves.

It has been noted for some time that children often speak of themselves in the third person. Everyone has heard a child say, in speaking of himself, "Peter was bad," and other analogous sentences. This is the rule during the first years: A young child calls himself by his name, just as he calls each person and each object by its name.

Some observers conclude that the child does not have a distinct idea of his "self," of his person. If he indicates himself as he indicates other things in the exterior world, it is because he has not yet learned to distinguish between the self and the not-self, which is so great for our adult conscience. Language would thus be a faithful reflection of the development of the successive stages of the child's personality. The child has no clear consciousness of himself until he uses the words "I" and "me."

This opinion does not seem accurate to other observers, who maintain that there is, in all of this, only an effect of imitation. The child talks as he is taught to talk, or in more exact terms, he talks as he hears others talk around him (as no one teaches a child to talk). If he does not indicate himself by the word "I," it is because his parents call him by his proper name. To be better understood, they refer to themselves as papa, mamma, grandfather, etc. The child imitates them in this, as in all else.

Of these two opinions, which is more accurate? I collected from the two girls several observations in support of the first opinion. The elder of the two, during approximately the first three years, indicated herself in the third person; this is the rule and can be explained by imitation of the parents' language. But the other, who is 18 months younger, was raised under very different conditions: Instead of being uniquely surrounded by parents who, in order to be better understood, indicated her and themselves by name, she spent her days with her older sister. Now, the latter does not have the good intentions of her parents. When she speaks of herself to her sister, she says "I" and "me," and she indicates her sister by the word "you." The younger child is thus accustomed to this language, having heard it from the age of 20 months, which amounts to saying that she has almost always heard it. Add to this that the younger child admires her older sister in what she says and does and imitates her fervently. Nonetheless, it must be noted that the younger child, for all this, does not lose the habit of speaking of herself in the third person; today she is more than three years old and still does not say "I."

It seems to me that chance has provided all the elements of a decisive experiment to show that the influence of imitation is an insufficient explanation; when it works in the opposite direction and should produce just the contrary of what is usually observed, then the result remains unchanged. It is thus that the child experiences a real difficulty in indicating herself by the colorless words "I" and "me" and finds it easier to use a more significant term like her own name.

For a long time, the little girl of whom I speak indicated herself by her name, or rather, by a diminutive of her name—Zizite rather than Alice. She would say, pointing to her chest with her finger: "This is Zizite." She would also say: "It is Zizite who knocks." "This bread is for Zizite." "That is Zizite's doll," etc. As I noted this past April 20 (she was then two years and nine months), she would sometimes repeat, but without understanding it, the word "mine" which her sister had said in front of her. The elder had said at the table, indicating her own plate, "This is mine." Alice, pointing to her own plate, replied, "This is Zizite's mine." This expression is entirely exceptional; she much more frequently says, "This belongs to Zizite."

Little by little the personal pronouns were introduced into her sentences, but they were not used all at once. At two and three-quarters years, she commonly used "you" and "me," but a curious detail is that she made a special application of them. For example, the pronoun "me" occurs in sentences such as, "Me will run." "Me will do it anyway." "Me" functions as subject of the sentence. She does not say, "This belongs to me, it is for me," she prefers to say, "It belongs to Zizite, it is for Zizite."

Three months later, when she is three years old, her language improves further. I write down word for word a large number of her conversations with her sister, and I can study the finest nuances of her language in these documents. While regretting that I did not take up this procedure earlier, I will indicate in a few words what I learned from it.

To indicate people not present, she correctly says "he" or "she" or "one." Thus, when her sister says, "Father is ill," she replies, "Poor father, he is ill. One must lie down when one is ill."

She also correctly uses the pronoun "we," as this little scrap of conversation will demonstrate. The two girls are in bed, without light, and they chatter. The elder says, "Are there not rats on the floor?" The younger, not understanding very well, replies, "Yes, we are on the floor." Then, the elder: "No, no, we are not on the floor because they would eat us." The younger: "We are in our beds." I could cite twenty such examples. A curious thing is that the only imperfections of language which remain to her concern the designation of first and second person singular; it seems she has more difficulty indicating them than the third person.

For the second person, the irregularities do not amount to much. Sometimes she says to her sister, "You [eu] put earth in the vase. You [tu] will be little tomorrow." Sometimes you [tu] is replaced by you [toi] as in the sentence, "You [toi] do not have dolls." In the same way, you [te] can be replaced by you [toi], but not constantly. In general, she manages to use the second person fairly well.

But, as to the first person, the grammar mistakes are considerable. The child uses several designations, most of which are incorrect, and she uses them either alternately or simultaneously. She thus indicates herself most often by her name. The most striking thing is that this happens in conversations with her elder sister, who continuously uses the pronoun "I." Here is an example:

> *Madeleine:* Wasn't I funny when I was small? I was in the cabbage.
> *Alice:* Are you now big?
> *Madeleine:* Yes, but I haven't been for long.
> *Alice:* Zizite is also big.
> *Madeleine:* You are even bigger than I am.

At other times, Alice indicates herself by suppressing all pronouns, and the verbs which follow are in the third person. In expressions like "once," "saw cows," or "is thirsty," she is speaking of herself, implying probably the name Zizite. Always, the surprising fact is that she uses these detours to reply to her sister who speaks entirely correctly. Still another example among many:

> *Alice:* Nenene (Madeleine), did not hear what you said earlier.
> *Madeleine:* I did not say anything at all.
> *Alice:* You said, "The balls are in the big room."

Madeleine: No, I didn't say that.
Alice: But heard it just the same.

It is not the younger sister who imitates the elder, it is sometimes the elder who imitates the younger and surpresses, for example, all pronouns when speaking of herself.

A third way of indicating herself consists of saying the name and following it with the third person pronoun. For example, she says, "Zizite, she doesn't speak," or "Me says that, me doesn't speak." She understands "mine" and "yours," but she does not use these words.

She never uses the word "I." When we have her memorize stories in which she encounters this pronoun, she begins by repeating it badly. It is then modified, and eventually she eliminates it from the story. Here are three lines which she memorized; instead of saying:

> *While I listen to you,*
> *Fearing that I will fall on the way,*
> *Good angel, give me your hand.*

She says:

> *While me there listen to you,*
> *Fearing me there fall on the way,*
> *Good angel, give me your hand.*

[In the French *je* (I) is replaced by *moi y* (me there).]

From all that precedes, it seems to me that the manner in which the child indicates herself is not the result of education and imitation, and it is not, as it was thought, a negligible phenomenon. It is something original and particular to the child. This I consider well established by the observations I have made.

At exactly three years and two months, the little girl used the word "I" for the first time. She repeated several times during the day the following sentence: "I don't know." At the same time, however, she indicated herself by her name in other sentences. Two days later, she found a new use for "I." She said, "I don't want to," to refuse something that she was asked to do. Assuredly, she understands that she speaks of herself, but when I ask her what the word "I" means, it is so new in her mouth that she replies that she does not know. Her older sister, now four years eleven months, cannot say more. "When you say 'I eat,' " she is asked, "what does the word 'I' mean?"

She replies, "It means to play"; if the inaccuracy of her reply is explained to her, she cannot find another.

Ideas on things

The objects of the exterior world are complex wholes giving us a large number of sensations and ideas which vary from one individual to another. It is common to say that the simplest object is not seen by two people in the same way. When an ignorant man, a painter, and a botanist look at the same flower, each one draws from his sensation a different state of consciousness.

I think it would be interesting to know how children perceive and represent to themselves objects which are familiar to them, and what particularities strike them the most in the outside world. I therefore made several observations on the two girls I am studying. I took them separately, each one having her turn, and asked them to tell me exactly what such-and-such a well-known object was; for example, a table, a knife, a doll. I will not emphasize the indispensable precautions, for example, prohibiting the child from telling funny things to be amusing. One can determine fairly easily whether or not the answer is seriously made. My best means of control is to resume the questioning after sufficient time has elapsed for the child to forget everything, both question and answer. During the course of a year, I questioned each of the little girls as many as fifteen times about each object and even left an interval of five months between two of the periods. It was easy, with these precautions, to eliminate the fantasy responses and to retain the serious responses which express a lasting psychical state.

A few words now on the manner in which I arranged the answers to each question. I reproduce, for brevity's sake, only four or five series of replies for each child; but I give the complete series, and it is always preceded by the same number so that it is recognized. Also, all definitions preceded by a certain number were given by the child during the same interview. We will later see the importance of this indication.

Each reply was collected in its entirety, including her hesitations and errors; I have not changed anything. As to the question, it was always made in the same terms: What is a knife? and so on.

Here is the way in which the older of the little girls described familiar objects during the course of her fifth year (between exactly four years three months and five years).

A knife: 1. A knife, that's to cut meat. (February)
           2. A knife, it cuts meat. (March)
           3. A knife? That means something that cuts. (September)
           4. A knife? That's to cut meat. (October)

A horse: 1. That's to pull a carriage, with a man inside. Then the coachman whips the horse; then the horse runs.
           2. It runs, it bites.
           3. It is something that walks.
           4. A horse, that's for running.

A lamp: 1. That's to light, in order to see clearly in a room.
           3. It's something that lights, which allows us to see clearly.
           4. A lamp, that's to see clearly.

A clock: 1. It is put on the chimney piece to see what time it is. One says 3:30.
           4. A clock, that's to tell time.

Bread: 1. That's to eat.
           2. One eats it.
           3. That's to eat.
           4. Bread, that's to eat.
           5. That's to eat.

A table: 1. It's to put lamps, books, a tablecloth, napkins, many of father's books on.
           3. It's to set the table on.
           4. A table, that's to put out dinner, to eat.

A bird: 1. It flies in the air, it sings.
           3. It flies in the sky.
           4. A bird, that's to fly.
           5. A bird, that's to fly.

A house: 1. That's to put children in, so they don't get cold. (This answer was given during the winter.) Then one closes the doors very gently when the children sleep; then the parents go to sleep also and everyone sleeps.
           2. One goes inside, and then the little children can run, get on the horse, do everything.

3. A house? When someone wants to rent a house. he rents it, then he stays inside it all the time. (Answer given during the summer when the child's parents were in a rented house.)
4. A house, that's to rent.
5. That's to live in.

A doll:

1. That belongs to little children to amuse them; they dress it, they undress it, they put it to bed.
4. A doll, that's for playing.
5. A doll, that's to play with.

Mother:

1. That scolds little children when they're not good.
2. That beats little children when they are not good; that sends them out in the hall. (There is a large hall in the house inhabited in winter.)
3. That's a lady that the children love very much.
4. A mother is to watch over the children.

A dog:

1. It runs, it bites, it has a tail; they are very bad, dogs.
3. That's to have in one's home.
4. A dog, it runs.
5. A dog, that's for running.

A wolf:

1. It jumps on little children, it devours them. It's very bad, the wolf; it's worse than a horse. The kicks of wolves hurt.
3. It eats all the big people and all the little girls.
4. A wolf, that's to eat.

Water:

1. That's to bathe oneself. (Answer given at a period when the child took a shower every morning.)
3. That's to drink with wine.
4. Water, that's to drink.

Potatoes:

1. That's to eat with green beans.
3. It's something to eat.
4. That's to eat.

A carriage:

1. Men get inside; one whips the horse, and the horse runs.

3. That's a horsey, that pulls the carriage; then there are ladies in the carriage.

4. It's a horse which pulls the carriage, and then there are ladies inside.

An omnibus: 1. That's to put many ladies inside. It has windows. There are three horses, they run; one does ding (word intended to imitate the sound of the conductor) ; they run.

4. An omnibus, one gets inside and the horses pull it.

5. An omnibus, it's to run.

An armchair: 1. That's to sit in.
3. That's to sit.
4. An armchair, that's to sit.

A bottle: 1. That's to put wine in.
4. A bottle, there's wine in it.
5. One puts wine in it, and then one pours it out when the children are thirsty.

A pencil: 3. That's to write.

A balloon: 4. It flies in the air.
5. A balloon, it flies.

A hat: 4. It's to put on one's head.
5. It's to go out.

A flower: 4. It's to put in the room.
5. A flower, that's to pick.

A worm: 4. It's dirty, it's not clean; that causes pimples on the face.

A village: 4. It's a place where there are many people, many people.

A garden: 4. That's to walk in.

A snail: 4. That's to be squashed, so that they don't eat the salad.
5. It eats the salad, and then one squashes it so that it doesn't eat in the garden.

Boots: 4. That's to put on to go out.
5. That's to put on to go out.

A box: 4. That's to put something in.
                   5. That's to put something in.

A piece   4. That's to eat.
of sugar: 5. That's to eat.

A handker-   4. That's to blow the nose.
chief: 5. That's to blow the nose.

A mouth: 4. That's to eat.
                   5. That's to eat.

A finger: 4. That's to hold a fork.
                   5. That's to hold a fork.

A string: 4. That's to attach something.
                   5. To make a package.

Now I will transcribe the answers of the younger child collected while she was between two- and one-half and three- and three-quarters years old.

A knife: 1. Cuts little children. (February)
                   2. To cut children. (March)
                   3. That means to cut. (September)
                   4. That's to cut children and then cut meat and then cut chops. (September)
                   5. That means cut children. (October)

A horse: 1. Bites.
                   2. Bites children.
                   3. It's the horse's coachman, who says "Git-up" to his horse.
                   4. That means to walk on four legs.
                   5. That means he goes with wolves.

A lamp: 1. Doesn't bite.
                   2. It's to light.
                   3. That means see clearly.
                   5. That means see clearly in the night when one's asleep.

A house: 1. Doesn't bite.
                   3. Don't know.
                   4. That means to go in the house and then see Friquet. (Friquet is the name of a little bird

whose cage is suspended in the vestibule and which is seen immediately upon entering the house.)
5. Don't know.
6. That means go into the house.

Bread:
1. For the little bird.
2. To eat with cold cuts.
3. That means to eat, to push with bread. (We often recommended to the little girl that she push the meat on her plate with bread and not with her fingers.)
4. That means to eat with meat.
5. That means to eat with meat.

A table:
1. Doesn't bite.
2. That's for dinner, to write.
3. That means to eat dinner.
4. That means to eat.
5. That means to write and then eat.
6. That means to dine.

Potatoes:
1. To eat.
2. To eat.
3. That means to eat with bitter sauce.
4. That means to eat with meat.
5. That's to eat with meat.

Water:
1. To drink.
2. To drink.
3. That means to fill one's jug. (In the courtyard of the house, there is a pump where one goes frequently to fill jugs.)
4. To wash hands.
5. That means to run and then to wash hands.

A dog:
1. To hold.
2. That means it sits up and begs. That means a man leads it by a string.
4. It bites.
5. It means go on four legs.

A carriage:
1. Doesn't bite children.
2. To go.

> 3. Put many stones, many stones, much sand, much sand. (The child has a small carriage which she uses for this purpose.)
> 4. Don't know.

Mother:
1. It's pretty.
2. It's pretty.
3. That means spoil the children. Mothers give many candies, many little boxes.
4. That means she spoils all the little children.
5. That means spoil the children.

Father:
1. Is pretty.
2. Is nice.
3. That means to write with pens. (She has often seen her father write.)
4. That means eats everything.
5. That means he spoils all the children.

A wolf:
1. Eats little children.
2. Eats little children.
3. That means eats all the little children.
4. That means eats all the little children and then all the meat.

A spoon:
1. It eats soup.
2. To eat.
3. That means to eat.
4. That means to eat with meat. (The child eats pieces of meat with a spoon.)

A bed:
1. Lay down the children.
2. To lie down.
3. That means to go to sleep at night and then not wake up.
4. That means to go to sleep at night.
5. That means to sleep at night.

A bird:
1. To fly.
2. It lays an egg.
4. That means it flies after swallows.
5. The birds eat all the grains.
6. That means swallows.

A pencil:
1. Writes on a book.

2. To write.
3. That means to write on a book.
4. That means to write.
5. That means to write.
6. That means to write.

A chair: 1. To sit.
2. To sit.
3. That means to sit.
4. That means to sit.
5. That means to sit.

A garden: 5. That means there are flowers in it.
6. That means there are flowers in it.

A snail: 5. That means it shows its horns.
6. That means squash it.

Boots: 5. That means one walks with them.
6. That means one puts them on one's feet.

A box: 5. That means put candies inside.
6. That means put something inside.

A balloon: 5. That means flies in the air.
6. A red balloon, red, red. That means it flies in the air all alone, all alone.

A hat: 5. That means put it on your head.
6. That means put it on your head. That means hello. (She repeats a fragment of a story which one tells to children: "My hat on my head, I salute you, you fool," etc.)

A flower: 5. That means put on one's hat.
6. That means to smell.

A lobster: 5. That means pinches hard.

A worm: 5. That means crush it with your boot.
6. That means one touches it with one's hands, one irritates it.

A village: 5. That means to stay all the time in the village.
6. That means one sees everybody pass by.

A piece of sugar: 5. That's to eat.
6. That means put it in the mouth.

A handker-   5. That's to blow one's nose.
chief: 6. That means to wipe the mouth.

A mouth: (Difficult replies)
               5. That means it eats all the animals.
               6. That means to chew.

An eye: 5. That means to see clearly.

A string: 5. That means to harness horses. (One of her fa-
               vorite games is to play "horse," harnessing her-
               self with strings.)
               6. That means harness horses.

In all cases we have just reported, the object of the question posed
to the child seems to be to invite her to make a definition of things
or a definition of words; but it is clear that a little child is incapable
of defining. When you say "definition," you imply a certain work of
reflection, of comparison, of elimination, etc. The little children that
we studied respond immediately without thinking, and their replies
express very simply the first images which were evoked by the name
of a certain well-known object.

Thus, one should not attach too much importance to the phrasing employed. When the little girl is asked what a horse is, she replies, "It's the horse's coachman, who says 'Git-up' to his horse." One
should not interpret the sentence word for word, note that the response does not correspond to the question, and conclude that the
child does not know what she is supposed to say. The only fact to
be retained is that, when one speaks of horses to the little girl, the
first image evoked is that of a horseman who says "Git-up." One
must apply this interpretation to all the cases. The experiment, in
summary, is analogous to one which might be done on an adult if
one said to him suddenly, "I'm going to talk about a horse," and
several seconds later asked him the representations evoked by this
word. For that matter, Galton proceeded in this way, but such a form
of interrogation would not have been as easily understood by the
children as the form we adopted.

This reservation does not allow us to avoid studying the phrasing
which the children used in their responses. It often happens that
several responses in the same series begin in the same way; that is
one of the reasons why I retained the indication of series. Thus, five
or six responses which follow each other all begin with the word "to"

(to drink, to eat, to hold, etc.). In one entire series, the child answers each time: "That means to say . . . ," or else "That is something which. . . ." The child has, by chance, encountered a formula which satisfies her. She takes it over and uses it many times, repeating it until she encounters another which she adopts in its turn, having abandoned the first one en route. This abuse of one single formula shows the taste for repetition and rhythm which is characteristic of the child, as I will show further on. Sometimes the child is not content to repeat just the words; she also wants to repeat ideas. Thus, by pronouncing the word "horse," one leads her to say what she thinks of it: The first image is that of an animal that bites. The child replies, "It bites." Then, without transition, one talks to her of a lamp, then of a house, then of a table. The child wants to repeat the response which she has found, but it doesn't belong to the new question. Therefore, she modifies it a little, but keeps it nonetheless: "A lamp doesn't bite; neither does a house." This is what leads her to make such an unusual reply. The idea would seem absurd if one did not know how she was led to it, because it is impossible that this is the first image which the word "lamp" suggests to her. Everything is explained, on the contrary, if one thinks of this taste for repetition, of the continuation of the same idea, which, in this case, leads the child to try a sort of classification of objects based upon the unique characteristic of biting or not biting.

Each child does not always make the same reply to the same question. There are variations which are without great importance and which are easily explained: they are due to changes in habit or to the acquisition of new ideas. Thus, during the winter, the house is considered a shelter against the cold; during the summer, the family inhabits a rented house, and it is the idea of "renting" which occupies the child's mind. When she takes showers, water reminds her of this daily experience; later, when the showers have ceased, other associations of ideas are made with the same word. If variations of this type are put aside, I think that one will be struck by the great uniformity of responses. Sometimes, seven months apart, the same sentence is repeated. If the words change, the idea the child has of the object often remains the same. It seems that she continues to see it from the same point of view.

This idea, what is it? It is easy to characterize it for an entire group of objects—for all the objects which the child is accustomed to handling and to using, such as a table, a knife, a bed, a chair, a pencil, a piece of bread, etc. These words evoke in us complex ideas: in particular, the visual image of the form of the object. For me (undoubtedly because I am a visual type), the word "table" gives me an image of a plank supported on legs, and it is thus that I would define it, if I were taken unawares.

Let us look at the replies of the two little girls. The visual aspect of the thing is rarely taken into consideration. Instead, the answer usually deals with the use of the object: "Bread is to eat; a knife, it's to cut with; a chair, that's to sit in; a table, that's to put lamps or books on." This method of representation is not at all an effect of whim or fantasy, since one finds it in the questioning periods separated by more than a seven-month interval, and since it is common to the two children. This clearly shows us with what eye these two children look at the exterior world; they are, as we said above, utilitarian before anything else. Talk to them of bread, and they do not stop at the form or the color. Bread, above all, gives them the memory of something which is carried to the mouth and eaten: "Bread, that's to eat." Strictly speaking, this reply is reasonable and any adult could give it. Here is another, however, which is completely surprising, which a sensible person is probably completely incapable of making, but which, nonetheless, is only an exaggeration of the point of view which we have just indicated. One asks the child what a snail is, and she answers, "A snail, that's to be squashed." One could not be more utilitarian. In other cases, when one questions the child on objects which are not within her reach, which she does not handle, she may amuse herself by giving a description which one could call disinterested or artistic. But I think that this is an exception, and the general rule is that the child is constantly attentive to the useful aspect of things.

One last remark: What sort of ideas does the child create when one does not mention any particular object, but uses a generic term such as dog, horse, carriage, etc.? Does the child have a general or abstract idea without precise determinants, or rather, a particular memory well detailed and colored? In many cases, it is difficult to know. When the child says of a dog, "It runs, it bites, it has a tail," what dog is being represented? Is it the red dog the child saw at the Luxembourg Gardens being chased by a guard? And, in her memory, does she see the end of a pathway, a dog that runs, and a guard throwing stones at it? Or rather, does she have only an abstract and impoverished idea of some dog? We do not know, and we could not ask the child without making suggestions to her. In a large number of other cases, no doubt is possible: the child gives particular details without being invited to do so. Relative to one object, she speaks of other objects, and sometimes she tells us of an event or describes a picture, like the picture of the carriage or the omnibus in which so many details are indicated. Nothing looks less like abstraction than this way of representing things.

Internal perceptions

I am separating, under a different heading, the replies that the two little girls gave to questions which were a bit more delicate, such as hunger, thirst, and anger. Their replies seem to me very characteristic.

Replies of Madeleine (between four and four- and three-quarters years) :

What is it to be afraid?
1. To be afraid of wolves, be afraid of snakes.
2. It is to lose Little Thumb in the woods. The animals bark, then Little Thumb cries. That is what it is to be afraid.
3. It means to be afraid of wolves who will eat you. To be afraid, that's when you play hide and seek, like Lucie. She cries a lot when we play hide and seek. Then we are afraid.
4. It means to be afraid of wolves, not to be eaten.

To be sad?
1. When mamma doesn't want us to go in the room alone. Then Zizite cries. There.
2. When mamma has beaten the little child when it wasn't good, teasing its little sister, pushing her. Then mamma scolds the little child who did this.
3. That means to cry.
4. It's to cry.
5. It's to cry.

To be angry?
1. One is angry when the children are not nice to the parents. They are spanked, and then they say, "No mamma,

I don't want to do this or that." And then they are put in the black closet.
2. It means to not be satisfied.
3. It means to not be nice, to spank the children when they are not nice.
4. It means to be nasty.

To be jealous?
1. That means to try on Cinderella's slipper. Cinderella's sisters tried the slipper, then their foot was too big. It was tried on Cinderella, and it fit her. Then the sisters of Cinderella were jealous.
2. That means to want the doll of another girl. It's not nice to be jealous.
3. That means to be nasty.

To love someone?
1. That means that one likes to be nice to people; always kiss them when they leave, and then say hello to them when they come, and then kiss them.
2. That means to kiss.

To be unhappy?
1. That means not to have children.
2. That means that the children are dead.
   (Two answers that certainly do not have much value; the child repeats what she has heard said.)

To be hungry?
1. One eats cutlets, potatoes, everything, beans, everything, everything, everything.
2. It means to eat everything.
3. It means one must quickly make lunch.
4. It means to eat.

To be thirsty?
1. One drinks all the wine.
2. It means to give a drink.
3. To be thirsty, give something to drink.

To be tired?
1. One rests in an armchair when one is tired.
2. One must rest.

3. To be tired? One must rest.

To be sleepy?
1. One lies down, one takes a nap.
2. That means to sleep.
3. That means you must lie down when you are sleepy; when one is not sleepy, one must get up.
4. That means to sleep.

To be cold?
1. That means it freezes.

To be hot?
1. That means not to be cold.

Here, now, are the answers of the younger child:

To be hungry?
1. That's for eating.
2. That means to eat all day long.
3. That means to eat meat and then potatoes and then push with bread.

To be thirsty?
1. That means to drink everything, everything, everything, everything.
3. That means to drink the entire glass.

To be sleepy?
1. That means to lie down.
2. That means to lie down at night and then to sleep well and not wake up.

To be tired?
1. That means to rest in a chair.
2. That means to sit down, to rest in a chair, and then in another chair.

To be angry?
1. That means to get angry.

To be sad?
1. That means to cry.
2. Then the little girls are dead when the ladies are sad.

3. That means to cry.

To be jealous?
1. That means to say, "Want the pipe, want the balloon." That means to say that. (She imitates a little girl who demands the sugar pipe or balloon seen in her sister's hands.)

To be afraid?
1. That means to be afraid of wolves, of monkeys.
2. That means to be afraid of wolves when they are in the woods.

To love someone?
1. That means to kiss them.

That which especially strikes me in all these replies is the definitions of physiological needs such as hunger, thirst, and analogous states. The replies of the two children are the same—the same ideas and sometimes the same words. The child does not direct attention to the need itself, but to the means of satisfying it, that is, to the exterior events which are afterwards produced. Thirst, for example, evokes the image of a full glass which one empties completely, while fatigue leads to the thought of an armchair in which one can relax. Perhaps the child has difficulty in perceiving the internal psychological phenomena.

To end this short study, if we glance at the path we have followed, we will retain the following facts relative to the two girls under our observation:

1. They show a great ability to compare lengths.
2. Among the colors, red is the first to be designated correctly.
3. A design representing the entirety of a known object is easily interpreted. Difficulties arise, however, in interpreting the fragments of an object or the signs of an emotional state. In all of this, the child does not seem to analyze her perceptions.
4. The child has difficulty in the use of personal pronouns, which probably indicates a certain difficulty in perceiving her own personality.
5. At four and a half, a little girl can account for her dreams.
6. In recalling objects, the child is above all attentive to the use of the object.

8

Investigations on the Development
of Visual Memory in Children

Our investigations were carried out in the primary schools of Paris
on more than 300 boys belonging to the elementary, middle, and
upper classes. The children in the elementary class are, in general,
7 to 9 years old; those in the middle class, 9 to 11 years old; those in
the upper class, 11 to 13 years old. The pupils were called into the
principal's office in groups of four, the experiments on each of them
lasting from 10 to 15 minutes divided by a rest period. The pupils,
especially the older ones, appeared to take an interest in the experiments, after having shown at first a slight timidity which we endeavored to dispel. Their attitude varied greatly according to the neigh-
borhood and according to the school; each group of four pupils often
had a homogeneous attitude, one of the children probably setting an
example that the others followed unconsciously.

Our experiments can be described briefly in the following manner: A line sketched in pencil on a white pasteboard was presented
to the child, who considered it for a moment and tried to retain its
length in his memory.

To measure the accuracy of memory, one must not compare the
recalled length of the line with the real length. It is necessary, instead, to make the comparison between each person's memory and his
accuracy of perception when asked to compare two lines that are
placed before his eyes simultaneously. In directly comparing two
lines, it is possible that a person may commit an error of 1 or 2 cm.;
if the same subject commits an identical error when reproducing one

With Victor Henri; Recherches sur le développement de la mémoire visuelle des enfants. *Revue philosophique*, 1894, 37, 348-350.

of the lines by memory, this is an error of comparison, not of memory.

How can one measure the accuracy of an act of memory and of comparison? When one does experiments with lines, one can use several different procedures; we have chosen two principal ones: visual recognition and reproduction by the hand. Recognition consists in finding again from memory a standard length from among those on a table containing that length mixed in with several others (method of scales); reproduction consists in drawing from memory, at the end of a certain time, the length which was shown as standard. One can execute two analogous operations without bringing in memory: instead of recognizing the standard in a series of lengths, one chooses it by direct comparison; likewise, instead of reproducing this standard from memory, one copies it while viewing it.

It is important here to mention the rule we adopted for calculating the children's errors. Each time a child failed to indicate the line equal to the standard, an error was carried to his account; this error was called positive when the line that he wrongly indicated was longer than the standard and negative when it was shorter. To facilitate comparison, they are reported as percentages.

We summarize the results in the following manner:

1. *Influence of age.* We have established some comparisons between children of different ages by classifying them in three groups according to their class in school; these groups correspond to the primary, middle, and upper classes, between which an average difference of two years exists. In all types of trials relative either to memory or to the direct comparison of lengths, the exact responses are in relation to age. The children of the elementary class are inferior to those of the middle class, and the latter to the children of the upper class. They commit a greater number of errors, and their errors are more serious; that is to say, they are farther from the standard. Thus, for the experiments on memory using the method of scales, the children of the elementary class commit on the average 73% errors, those of the middle class 69%, and those of the upper class 50%.

2. *Comparison and memory.* The errors are less numerous in the comparison and in the direct reproduction than they are when one brings in memory; the direction of error is the same, however.

3. *Direction of errors.* There is a tendency to elongate the short lines and to shorten the long lines.

In the experiment on recognition, which consists in finding visually a standard line among a scale of lines, errors are negative for the lines of 68 mm., 40 mm., 16 mm., 4 mm., and even 1.5 mm. We are ignorant of whether a limit exists—a neutral length, that which the Germans would call *Indifferenzlänge*—for this kind of ocular mensuration; nevertheless, if the limit exists, it must be less than 1.5 mm. for the subjects who served in our experiments.

In the experiment on reproduction by the hand, the children reduce only the longer lines, 16 mm. and above. On the other hand, they increase the lines of 1.5 mm. and 4 mm. This observation indicates that the *Indifferenzlänge*, the neutral point, must exist somewhere between 16 and 4 mm.

4. *Influence of age on the direction of errors.* The smaller children diminished the long lines more than their elders did.

Not being able to give here all the tables of our work, we reproduced only one of them [Table 1]; it expresses the results obtained by the method of recognition or method of scales.

Table 1. *Results of experiments on the memory of lengths studied by means of the method of scales**

	Length Serving as Standard	Number of Errors	Positive Errors	Negative Errors	Number of Correct Responses
Elementary Class	16 mm.	48	5	43	52
(85 children)	40	80	14	66	20
	68	91	20	71	9
Middle	16	44	8	36	50
(70 children)	40	84	20	64	16
	68	79	18	61	21
Upper Class	16	28	3	25	72
(70 children)	40	55	24	31	45
	68	68	24	44	32
Mean of the	16	40	5	35	60
Three Classes	40	73	19	54	27
	68	79	21	58	21

The numbers in this table are all reported as percentages.

Some additional experiments on verbal memory, imagination, etc., among children in the primary schools are underway. Some experiments are already finished, and we will very soon publish the results.

9

The Measurement of Visual Illusions in Children

I

It is well known that children are sensitive to sensory illusions. Child psychology books contain some observations and numerous anecdotes showing that children can deceive themselves about the form, size, and position of objects, but the question has not yet been systematically studied by means of controlled experiments.

This very broad subject might be approached from a number of different sides. I must say immediately what point of view I take. I have chosen a particular illusion which is easy to reproduce on a sheet of paper by means of some strokes of the pen, and I propose to investigate whether a child perceives it to the same extent as an adult. In other words, I seek to measure the child's illusion.

The illusion on which I have done the experiment is well known today. It was described two years ago by Brentano in an article which

Figure 1. The Mueller-Lyer illusion.

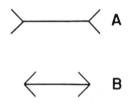

La mesure des illusions visuelles chez les enfants. *Revue philosophique*, 1895, 40, 11-25. The original translation of this article appeared under the co-authorship of R. H. Pollack and F. K. Zetland in *Perceptual and motor skills*, 1965, 20, 917-930.

has stirred up a large number of discussions and polemics. However, it was not Brentano who discovered and described it for the first time, but Mueller-Lyer, whose name it would not be fair to forget. The two figures [Figure 1] presented here show the illusion; Line B, although the same length as Line A, appears visibly shorter because of the position of the lines which intersect at its ends. In Figure A, the short lines form obtuse angles with the long one, and in Figure B, they form acute angles. Agreement has not been reached on the psychological cause of this illusion, and we will not speak of it here.

How do we measure a sensory illusion?[1] At first sight, it would seem impossible; one experiences the illusion or one does not. Let us suppose that a child is asked to tell which figure, A or B, appears longer to him. If he finds the two figures equal, then there is no illusion, no measurement. If he finds B shorter than A and therefore agrees with us who experience the same sensory impression, how can we know whether the child experiences it more or less than we?

Several procedures can be employed, but the most direct is one which Knox recently applied to another sensory illusion.[2] Two figures are to be compared. One of these, because of some complication, appears longer than it is in reality. Take, for example, Figure A, whose length appears augmented by the obliques which go off from its two ends; although A appears longer than B, these two figures are equal. We shall draw a series of figures similar to B but of different lengths and present them successively to the subject until he declares that one is equal to A. For this figure to appear equal to A, it will have to be longer; the difference between the two lengths will give the degree of the illusion. Such is the principle of the method which, as Knox notes, is a modification of the method of minimal changes.

This is how I applied Knox's procedure, and I shall enter here into some minute but important details.

We shall call A that figure whose obliques form obtuse angles with the principal line; B shall be any figure whose obliques form acute angles with the principal line. In all of our experiments, Figure

1 It is interesting to note that recent psychological investigations have extended measurement to a certain number of complex mental operations; one measures memory, one measures aesthetic feeling (Cohn, *Philosophical Studies*, X, 562-604) , one measures sensory illusions. In most of the cases, measurement is still only gross, but the attempt is nonetheless interesting.

2 *American journal of psychology*, June 1894, 413; work of the Cornell Laboratory, directed by Titchener.

A remains constant as we present to the subject a series of Figure B's of increasing size. These are compared to Figure A, which is considered the standard.

Figures of type B occupy the right-hand side of successive pages in a bound album. The single figure of type A occupies the outer half of the last page, which is 36 cm. wide. Since the other pages are only 18 cm., when the album is opened one can always see the outer half of the larger page. The distance between Figure A and the figures of type B is constant at 20 cm.

We made two albums of this kind in order to experiment on the Mueller-Lyer illusion with two different scales. The pages of the larger album are 32 cm. by 20 cm. One of the B figures is drawn in the middle of each of the pages. These figures, numbering seven, have the following dimensions: 9 cm., 10 cm., 11 cm., 12 cm., 13 cm., 14 cm., 15 cm. Figure A is constant at 10 cm. The obliques of Figure B form exactly a 45° angle with the principal line; the obliques of Figure A form a 135° angle. The length of the obliques in all the figures is 4 cm., and the thickness of the stroke is 0.1 cm. As these numbers indicate, all of the figures, even the largest, are in line with the breadth of the album. The largest figure, which is 15 cm. long, is separated from the edges of the page by 9 cm. on top as well as on bottom. These marginal distances are too great to serve as reference points for the eye in estimating the size of the figures. The obliques represent a uniform length which is not proportional to that of the total figure for the following reason: Auerbach[3] has shown that the length of the obliques influences the degree of the illusion—the longer the obliques, the stronger the illusion. If, in the series of B figures, we increased the length of the obliques at the same time as that of the principal line, we might not accomplish our goal of diminishing the illusory inequality between B and A by increasing the principal line of Figure B.

In the second album, we again bring together analogous figures, but on a more reduced scale. The pages of this little album are 22 cm. by 17 cm., and the figures are drawn with their long axis in the vertical direction. The principal line of the standard A is 2 cm. Among the 12 B figures, the principal lines are 1.8 cm., 2 cm., 2.2 cm., 2.4 cm., 2.6 cm., 2.8 cm., 3 cm., 3.2 cm., 3.4 cm., 3.6 cm., 3.8 cm., and 4 cm. The obliques in Figure A form an angle of 135° with the

[3] *Zeitschrift fuer Psychologie*, 1894, VII (2 and 3), 152-160.

principal line; in Figure B, they form an angle of 45°. The thickness of the stroke is 0.05 cm., and the length of the obliques is 0.8 cm. One can be sure that the different lengths were not chosen by chance. I must explain, and if possible, justify them.

At first, one may be astonished that in our series of B figures, the one which is equal to Figure A does not occupy the midpoint of the series. Symmetry doubtless would demand that when the standard is 2 cm., the figure which equals it would be situated between two points equidistant from A, for example, between 1 cm. and 3 cm. We thought, after mature consideration, that symmetry was not important here. We began by doing preliminary experiments on some 30 pupils, using the symmetrical B series where the shortest figure was 0.5 cm. and the longest 3.5 cm. These experiments showed us that, on the average, the B figure which was equated with A was a certain length, and it was this figure that we had occupy the middle of the B series. On this basis, then, we constructed the series which served in our definitive experiments.

For our little album, it is the sixth B figure, having a length of 2.8 cm., which is assigned the middle rank in the series. In this manner, the subject has, on the average, the chance to recognize quickly the B figure which appears to him equal to A as he runs through the B's in either increasing or decreasing order. Consequently, we succeed in rendering the increasing series comparable to a certain degree to the decreasing series. This is a precaution which Knox neglected. It is true, however, that this point is not of major importance.

Finally, we made the little standard of illusion comparable to the bigger one by establishing an exact proportion between them, as one may ascertain from reading the numbers given above. All elements of the big album are reduced to a fifth in the little one. There is an exception only in the distance at which the two figures are compared; in all cases, a white space of 20 cm. is interposed between the figures. We did not modify this distance, being unable to discover the correct modification.

II

Let us present first the results obtained with the oldest pupils. We did the experiments on a class of 40 pupils in an elementary school. This class bears the name "class of repeat," and it is composed solely of students who, provided with their certificate of studies, are seeking in school an extension of instruction, and who form, up to a certain degree, an elite. Of these 40 pupils, five are 11 years old, eighteen are 12 years old, twelve are 13 years old, two are 14 years old. Let us add —since we are concerned with experiments where sure-sightedness plays an important role—that all these pupils have been doing some exercises in manual art once a week for several years. To this class we add 20 pupils taken at random from the second class, of which two pupils are 10 years, ten are 11 years, two are 12 years, five are 13 years, and one is 14 years old.

The children were called into the principal's office in groups of five. Four of the children remained seated in the back of the room under the eye of the principal, who was almost always present. The fifth child remained close to us, separated from the other children by a rather high table and not at all distracted by the objects which surrounded him. I add that, having done numerous experiments in this school for three years, I know most of the pupils by sight, and my presence does not intimidate them as much as would that of someone unknown; besides, these pupils are not very timid.

We began by showing each child the large album, and we gave him the following explanation: "We are concerned here with comparing Figure A with Figure B. You are to tell me which one appears longer to you. Each figure is composed of a straight line (we pointed to it with our finger), at the end of which you will find oblique lines. These obliques do not count; you must compare only the length of the two straight lines. "See," we added, touching the ends of the lines with our thumb and index finger spread like two points of a compass, "this length is to be compared with that length."

Thanks to this procedure, we were quite certain that the children understood us. In cases where we had some doubt, we questioned the child and made him repeat our explanation, watching with great care that no confusion remained in his mind. We knew that this point was of great importance, and that it could not be insisted upon too much. A child is not like an adult who, when he does not understand, says so and asks for explanations. Often children, either from timidity or from a habit of understanding only half, go docilely through a very long series of experiments without informing the experimenter that they do not know what is expected of them.

In our experiment on the optical illusion, the child was standing before the table on which the album was opened, and he was placed equidistant (about 40 cm.) from the two figures to be compared. He was obliged, especially if he was tall, to make a slight movement of the head to see the two figures; in no case did he distinctly see the figures at the same time without eye movement. He ran over the figures from bottom to top or from top to bottom, and his eyes executed movements in the vertical direction.

We could, to a certain degree, take account of a child's attention by watching his eye movements. When the child made the comparison with great care, his glance went from Figure A to Figure B a great number of times—three or four times on the average. This transverse movement of the glance indicated that the attention was wide awake. It happened after some time, however, that the child had only to look once at the figure to make his comparison. For example, he had just seen B4 and had judged that this figure was smaller than A; he was presented with B3, which appeared smaller to him than B4, and he concluded by rapid reasoning that B3 was equally and *a fortiori* smaller than A.

We allowed the child sufficient time to make up his mind in each case. Although there was a slight delay during the "warming-up" period, one noticed that the responses were given quickly when the difference between the figures was very great, for example, at the beginning and end of the experiment. On the other hand, toward the middle of the experiment, when the differences between the two figures became smaller and passed through zero, there was a marked slowing of responses. We were not able to take exact measurements, being occupied with other matters. On the whole, however, our observations confirmed those recently published by Muensterberg.[4]

All 60 pupils were sensitive to the Mueller-Lyer illusion and believed that B was bigger than A in the case where the two principal

Table 1. Measurement of the Mueller-Lyer Illusion (in cm.)

	Large Standard					Small Standard				
	1	2	3	4	5	1	2	3	4	5
1st and 2nd Classes (60 pupils)	1.85	0.75	1.92	0.96	1.88	0.54	0.17	0.60	0.13	0.57
5th Class (45 pupils)	2.40	1.05	2.70	0.89	2.55	0.64	0.21	0.86	0.15	0.75

[4] A psychometric study of the psychophysical law, *Psychological review*, 1894, I (1) , 45.

lines were equal. The table [Table 1] gives the degree of illusion in these children.

Explanation of Table 1. All the figures are expressed in centimeters. Column 1 gives the mean degree of the illusion when series B is presented in the order of increasing size; Column 2 gives the mean variation of this measure; Column 3 gives the mean degree of the illusion when series B is presented in the order of decreasing size; Column 4 gives the mean variation of this measure; and finally, Column 5 is the mean of the numbers indicated in Columns 1 and 3. We recall that "degree of illusion" signifies the excess length in Figure B which makes it appear equal to Figure A.

This table [Table 1] shows that for pupils of the first and second class, the illusion produced by the large standard is $\frac{1.88}{10}$; the illusion produced by the small standard is $\frac{0.57}{2}$, or, reducing the two fractions to the same denominator, $\frac{2.85}{10}$. The illusion of the little standard is stronger by about a third. I suppose that this is the reason for the difference: When the line is very long, one can run over a sizable part of it without encountering the obliques and without constantly undergoing the illusory effect which they produce. I suppose, then, that this effect will be more considerable for a line of 2 cm., which one takes in at a single glance, and upon which the illusory effect of the obliques makes itself continuously felt.

It must be noted, in the second place, that the number measuring the error varies constantly, depending on whether the B series is run in decreasing or increasing order. In the increasing order, the number is constantly smaller. I imagine it is easy to explain this small fact. Let us suppose that one compares B3 to A, and finds B3 smaller than A. The comparison made, one casts one's eyes upon B4, which is bigger than B3. An abrupt effect of contrast is then produced; one is struck by the superiority of the length of B4 over B3 and thus tends to exaggerate the length of B4.[5] The effect of this contrast makes the line appear equal to A when, without this cir-

---

[5] It is well understood that this effect is not produced with the same vigor as our reasoning supposes; a distraction, a fortuitous circumstance, often makes one forget to compare B3 to B4 or erases the memory of B3 before one has looked at B4, and no contrast is manifested.

cumstance, it would have appeared smaller; consequently, the illusion is measured by an inferior number. In the inverse case, one follows the decreasing order, beginning with B6, which is bigger than A, and passing from B6 to B5, which is smaller. The contrast makes B5 appear smaller than it is in reality, and one may judge it equal to A; without this circumstance, it would have appeared smaller. As a result, one measures the illusion by the difference between the real length of B5 and A, that is, by an amount too great. The truth is probably found in the mean.

It is important to know exactly what value must be attached to a mean taken from 60 pupils. Is it a chance mean—a grouping of badly done observations from pupils who were not attentive or did not have analogous perceptions? We do not think so. Knox's procedure, by its very nature, protects us from this cause of error. The successive figures B1, . . . B5 vary regularly in length so that the child, if attentive, will make regular responses; he will find B1 smaller than A, he will judge B5 bigger, and he will find between these two extremes a Bx equal to A. If he is not attentive, or if for any other reason he responds by chance, his responses will not follow this regular order. Now, among the 60 pupils, we find that only 2 committed an irregularity in the order of response—what one might call a "disorder of comparison." Two out of 60 is obviously a negligible quantity; the other 58 pupils responded correctly.

On the other hand, we must take into account that the mean variation is considerable, which shows that important individual differences exist.

We thought it useful to determine the sure-sightedness of our subjects by making them compare straight lines of the same length as Figures A and B but without the obliques. We had them compare a line of 2 cm. to a series of lines equal to 1.8 cm., 2 cm., 2.2 cm., 2.4 cm., 2.6 cm., etc. The lines were 20 cm. apart, as were Figures A and B of our previous experiments. The mean error of comparison was very slight, $\frac{0.04}{2}$ cm.; the largest error was 0.2 cm. Consequently, this error of comparison can in no way explain the illusion produced by Figures A and B.

Breakdown of the Illusion. The Mueller-Lyer illusion is the result of a double illusion: in Figure A, the obliques produce an apparent increase in the principal line; in Figure B, they produce an apparent decrease in the line. It is possible to separate these two effects by having Figures A and B successively compared with straight lines, following Knox's method. We can then see what length, on the average, a straight line must be to appear equal to either of the two figures. We did the experiment on 14 pupils of the second class; this limited number of subjects seemed sufficient to us, given the great clarity and uniformity of the results. The experiments were done on the little standard. In a first series of trials, standard Figure A of 2 cm. was compared with a series of straight lines, first in ascending and then in descending order; we retained only the mean value obtained by the combination of the two experiments. In a second series, we had the series of straight lines compared with a figure of type B which appeared equal to Figure A, and which was in reality 2.6 cm. The experiment was done as before in ascending and descending order. The results are recorded in Table 2.

Table 2. Breakdown of the Mueller-Lyer Illusion (in cm.)

1	2	3	4	5
0.57	0.51	0.12	0.13	0.09

Incidentally, it is perhaps interesting to note that the preceding results resolve one of the numerous controversies which have taken place on the mechanism of the Mueller-Lyer illusion. Certain authors, Delboeuf[6] for example, maintain that the error comes from the attraction exerted on movements of the eye by the oblique lines placed at the extremity of the principal line. Others, Brunot[7] for example, think that when one judges the length of the two figures, the eye instinctively takes the distance from the centers of the two figures to the obliques which end each of the principal straight lines. This last explanation, if I understand it, does not explain why the illusion of Figure B is less strong than that of Figure A. On the contrary, if one brings in the movements of the eyes, one well understands that the eye, on following the principal line of Figure A, easily goes beyond the ends of the line to follow the obliques, which give the impression of a length of line greater than reality. One understands also that, for Figure B, this exaggerated movement of the eye is produced much less easily, because in this latter case the move-

---

6 Une nouvelle illusion d'optique, *Revue scientifique*, 1893, 51, 237-241.

7 Les illusions d'optique, *Revue scientifique*, 1893, 52, 210-212.

ment of the eye, in order to follow the obliques, must change direction sharply and thus does not continue with the acquired impetus.

Explanation of Table 2. Column 1 gives in centimeters the amount of error produced in children of the second class when the illusion is manifested in the comparison of Figures A and B; Column 2 gives the amount of illusion produced by the comparison of straight lines with Figure A; Column 3, the mean variation of this error; Column 4, the degree of illusion produced by the comparison of straight lines with Figure B; and Column 5, the mean variation of this error.

The table [Table 2] shows that the illusion of increasing size produced by the obliques which form obtuse angles with the principal line is much more considerable—about four times more—than the illusion of shortening produced by the obliques which form acute angles. In the first case, the illusion is $\dfrac{0.51}{2}$ cm. and in the second case, $\dfrac{0.13}{2.6}$ cm. Let us add that the illusion of shortening is not as general as that of elongation; among 14 children, 4 escaped it, while the illusion of elongation imposed itself, without exception, on the one hundred children who were tested in our experiments.

Another Method of Measuring the Illusion. We employed a second method which consists in making the child estimate in millimeters and in centimeters the apparent difference between A and B when the two figures are really equal. This method yields reliable results only among people who know precisely what a centimeter and a millimeter are. The pupils of the class of repeats fulfill this condition well, since they have been trained for several years in tasks of manual art—in making little things of cardboard and wood and thus in making continuous use of the centimeter. We endeavored to make them understand well what we were asking of them. At the moment when the child told us, in comparing B to A, that B was smaller, we asked him the question, "By how much?" If he did not appear to understand—which was rare in the class of repeats—we insisted, "What is the difference between the length of B and that of A?" In general, this measurement appeared difficult for the pupils, as shown by their attitude and slowness of response.

The mean of the estimated difference between A and B when the two lengths were really equal, each measuring 10 cm., was 1.44 cm.; when A and B were only 2 cm., the estimated difference was 0.50 cm.

It is seen that the extent of the illusion under this procedure gives an inferior number to that of Knox's method: 1.44 cm. instead of 1.88 cm., 0.50 cm. instead of 0.57 cm. Why the difference? And which should be believed—Knox's method or the estimation method? Without hesitation we say that Knox's method gives better results because the work imposed on the mind is simple; it consists in indicating whether there is an equality or a difference of length between two simultaneously seen figures. With our method, it is necessary to measure the difference, that is, to imagine what length added to B would equate it with A. It is a much more difficult, complicated operation and consequently more subject to error.

A careful examination of the distribution of responses with this latter method reveals that the majority were given with an important number—5 or multiples of 5. Thus, in estimating the apparent difference between lines A and B of the small standard (these lines being equal), the number 0.50 cm. was cited 20 times in 33 responses. In estimating the large standard, the responses were 1.50 cm. and 2 cm. Intermediary values were almost never given. This demonstrates to us a curious fact about the role of the *word* in designating sensations. We all possess a very complete nomenclature of lengths in our heads. We can indicate, according to our opinion, that a length is 1, 2, 3, . . . millimeters, just as we can trace these lengths with our hands. However, these different terms of nomenclature are not equally at our disposal; we do not have in our memory a series of words, all of which can be recalled with the same facility and have the same psychological importance. It seems that certain of these terms are awakened more easily than others; for example, 5 mm. is cited more often than 6 or 4 mm. For what reason? Probably because it is half of 10 and plays an important role in the decimal system. It is always cited more often. To use a comparison, it is as if certain numbers were written in our heads in larger characters than others. Thus, to employ a schema, the series with which one is concerned is not written 1, 2, 3, 4, 5, 6, 7, 8, 9, 10, but rather, 1, 2, 3, 4, **5**, 6, 7, 8, 9, **10**.

Awareness of Illusion. I wanted to determine whether the children were aware of the illusion without needing to measure the two figures, A and B, which they compare. When one is familiar with the illusion, one does not know whether the illusion is apparent or hidden. I thus put this question to the children at the conclusion of the experiment. I drew their attention for a last time to Figure A, and, pointing to the divergent obliques which bind the figure, I asked them what effect these obliques produced. Out of 30 pupils in the repeat class, one, understanding this vague question, answered at once that the obliques of Figure A made the line appear bigger; the other children appeared embarrassed. I then refined my question, having it take the following form: "Do these obliques appear to you to increase or diminish the length of the line, or do they produce no effect at all?" To this question, 18 pupils answered that the obliques increased the length of the line, 9 said that they knew nothing about it or that the obliques produced no apparent effect, and 2 made the rather bizarre response that the obliques of Figure A shortened the figure. From this, it must be concluded that the majority of pupils had a vague feeling of the effect produced by the obliques. I do not know to what degree this feeling intervened in the experiments; perhaps it was subconscious. I will readily admit that, in forming a precise question and in presenting an alternative to the pupils, I forced them to take account of the illusion. This is an illusion that one can get a clear idea of without tape measure and compass.

Importance of Individual Variations. From the first experiments, I was struck by the differences between children of the same age: for one child the illusion was very strong; for another, it was very weak, and so forth. This is what the rather high value of the mean variation shows [see Table 1]. The importance of this finding appears even greater when compared to what happens when one has the same children compare lines which are not bounded by obliques. In this latter case, individual differences are attenuated almost to the point of disappearing.

The considerable value of the mean variation in estimating the illusion is, then, a very characteristic phenomenon, and one can draw from it this practical conclusion: To obtain a stable mean which signifies something, one must perform numerous experiments. For example, if one wishes to know whether age influences the illusion, one must not restrict oneself to studying five or six children of different ages; one must experiment upon a very great number.

Exactly what is the significance of such a high mean variation? I do not know and am reduced to guessing about it. I suppose that individual differences in the degree of illusion are great because the operation, which consists in finding equality between two lines bounded by obliques of opposite directions, is a complicated and difficult one. The comparison is not the same as it is with simple lines. The illusion does not consist solely, as one is tempted to believe, in an apparent addition of so many centimeters, of 1.5 cm. for example, to one of the lines. If the elongation were clear and precise, it would be perceived with more uniformity. Further, there would be—and I continue the hypothesis—a tendency toward elongation, a subjective impression of elongation, which is difficult to define and to perceive exactly. We found instead that it was not a precise sensation, but rather a confused one.

III

The comparative experiments for making age differences conspicuous were done on 45 children of the fifth class. Previously, I had done a trial with 10 pupils of the sixth class who averaged 6 to 7 years of age, but had found that, at this age, attention was not sufficiently fixed for the experiments. I therefore restricted myself to pupils of the fifth class. Their ages were as follows: one of 7 years, thirteen of 8 years, ten of 9 years, thirteen of 10 years, three of 11 years, two of 12 years, with a mean of 9 years. The conditions of the experiment were identical to those for the older children. This time, however, I was even more insistent that the explanation of which lines were to be compared was clearly understood, and I often had my explanation repeated by the pupil. The attitude of the children of the fifth class was very different, in general, from that of their elders. They compared the two figures for a shorter time; one did not see them gaze from one to the other three or four times. They did not know how to look—after a simple glance, they indicated without hesitation which line appeared longer to them.

The results summarized in our table [Table 1] show more particularly that the illusion is stronger for them than for older children. While I was explaining the figures to the children, I had sort of expected this difference. I told them that, in their act of comparison, they must restrain themselves from taking account of the obliques and compare only the two lines in the middle. I understood then that this involves an act of dissociation which, whatever its nature, demands an effort of attention, and that since the younger children are less capable of this effort than their elders, they undergo the illusion more profoundly. Of the 45 pupils of the fifth class, there were 7 who showed what I had previously called disorders of comparison, due probably to a passing distraction. In the children of the first and second classes, hardly a case of disorder was found. Disregarding these pupils, the mean degree of illusion is, as shown in Table 1, more considerable in little children with a mean age of 9 than in those with a mean age of 11. Whether with respect to the large or small standard of the illusion or to the order of the trial, this difference does not flag. The mean variation is equally stronger. It must be noted that we obtain these differences by comparing 60 children on the one hand to 40 on the other. Among children of 9 years, it is very certain that several can be found who, by exception to the rule, are less sensitive to the illusion than certain older children. We are simply establishing a general rule.

To summarize our experiments on the Mueller-Lyer illusion:

1. The illusion is stronger for figures of the small standard than for the figures of the large standard.

2. The size of the illusion depends on the order in which the lines are compared.

3. The total illusion is the product of two illusions of opposite direction and unequal force.

4. The children have, in general, a vague awareness of the illusion.

5. The illusion is stronger in young children of 9 years (fifth class) than in those of 12 years (first and second class) .

On this last point, let me add a few words to serve as a conclusion. From recent investigations, Dressler[8] has shown that certain illusions of weight are stronger in adults than in children. The experiment was done in the following manner: Some objects of equal weight and of the same shape, but of different sizes, were presented to a person who was asked to lift them and to arrange them in order of weight. The adults arranged the objects in order of size, signifying that the larger objects appeared heavier to them. The children, on the other hand, made less regular arrangements. Dressler concluded that the illusion depends on associations established by experience in the minds of adults between the weight and the volume of objects: children, not yet having acquired these associations to the same degree, are by this fact less sensitive to the illusion.

These findings demonstrate that there are two kinds of sensory illusion. Illusions of the first kind are innate; those of the second

[8] *American journal of psychology,* June 1894, No. 3. See also Flournoy, *Année psychologique,* 1894, 1, 198.

kind are acquired. The first are experienced through the eyes of adults and of all children, the younger the better; the second are a fruit of experience and are manifested less profoundly in the child than in the adult. The Mueller-Lyer illusion belongs to the first category. The illusion studied by Dressler and Flournoy belongs to the second.

Section III

MISCELLANEOUS EXPERIMENTAL STUDIES

This group of papers clearly reflects Binet's unwillingness to be bound to a particular methodology. At times he was a precise experimentalist, at times a pure introspectionist, but the methodology he used was always the one dictated by the problem under study. Binet quantified his data whenever possible and relied upon careful qualitative description when he could not. As was the case with preceding selections, the procedures are described so carefully that each study is completely replicable.

These papers were chosen to illustrate something of the range of Binet's interests: perception, psychomotor functions, emotion, reaction time, and thought processes. Only three of the studies are concerned with children, but all five testify to Binet's intense interest in psychological development. Always implicit in his work are the questions of how a particular pattern of behavior developed and what internal processes produced it. Few psychologists of today consistently exhibit this kind of curiosity.

In many ways, the best chapter in this group is the one on the perception of extent by the eye. Binet began by posing the question of whether the perception of extent was due to the retinal image or to ocular muscle activity. To differentiate between retinal and muscular sensitivity, Binet sought to provide his subject with a stabilized image whose extent could be reported. He decided upon the use of that simple expedient—the afterimage. Through a series of simple demonstrations, he was able to show that eye movements and ocular muscle tension either distort the image or are irrelevant to the task of estimating extent. Thus the point was made with utmost clarity that it is the retinal image which inherently presents spatial relationships of position and extent.

Through the ingenious use of hypnosis, Binet again demonstrated

145

the role of the retina in estimating extent. The subject was given a post-hypnotic suggestion of blindness for a figure whose center was to be fixated upon. Following fixation, the subject accurately reported the afterimage, showing that form production is retinal and occurs without the intervention of consciousness or eye movement.

Such use of hypnosis, while rare in experimental psychology, is rarer still in studies of perception. Only recently, Parrish, Lundy, and Leibowitz (1968) created considerable stir with their demonstration of the effect of hypnotic age-regression on the magnitude of geometrical illusions. However inadvertently, these authors have taken a leaf from Binet's book.

It is surprising that, nine years after writing this paper, Binet felt compelled to propose an eye-movement explanation for the Mueller-Lyer illusion (see Chapter 9). He could have employed the same afterimage technique used in his study of the perception of extent. Had he measured the line length of the afterimage projections of the Mueller-Lyer figure, he would have found them to be distinctly unequal, despite the equality of those of the inspection figure. Sonoko Ohwaki published such a study in 1961.

The editors prefer to let the remaining papers speak for themselves about Binet's originality and versatility. As in earlier sections, some of the work is dated and very quaint, but the rest is surprisingly fresh and insightful.

REFERENCES

Ohwaki, S. On the afterimage of geometrical illusions. *Perceptual and motor skills,* 1961, 13, 326.

Parrish, M., Lundy, R. M., & Leibowitz, H. W. Hypnotic age-regression and magnitudes of the Ponzo and Poggendorff illusions. *Science,* 1968, 159, 1375-1376.

10

The Perception of Extent by the Eye

We wish to present some thoughts suggested by new experiments on a very complicated and controversial psychological question: the perception of extent by the eye.

The difficulty of this question is due in part to the fact that the eye is very experienced, and that it is impossible to distinguish its innate from its acquired perceptions. Physiologists are strongly divided on a theory of vision. Some—Mueller, Donders, Nagel, Panum, Hering—who belong to the nativistic school, tend to explain visual phenomena largely in terms of innateness. Others—Lotze, Wundt, Helmholtz—belong on the side of the empiricists, who, on the contrary, tend to explain such phenomena on the basis of experience and education of the eye. The English associationists should be consulted on this important question. Bain and Stuart Mill are empiricists. According to them, the knowledge of extent is not primitively furnished by the eye, but by the movement of members of the body; the sensation of unimpeded muscular movement constitutes the notion of empty space, and that of impeded muscular movement, the notion of occupied space. The perception of extent by the eye is a result of education, or, to speak more precisely, a result of the association of sight with touch and the motor apparatus. Sight reduced to itself is sensitive only to light and to color. The luminous impressions of objects are associated with the memory of the dimensions measured by touch and by movements of the body members; these impressions serve as indicators of the various dimensions, allow the mind to infer them, and finish by producing the illusion of a direct perception of extent.[1]

This opinion has not passed without opposition. In France,

La perception de l'étendue par l'oeil. *Revue philosophique*, 1886, 21, 113-121.

[1] Bain, *The Senses and the Intellect*, 1855, pp. 370-374. J. S. Mill, *Examination of Sir William Hamilton's Philosophy*, p. 427. — Taine, *De l'Intelligence*, II, p. 163.

classical philosophy has proposed an important distinction: depth perception is indirect, while surface perception is direct. This is a partial concession to the English opinion. But Janet, in a learned article published by *Revue philosophique,* returns to this problem and concludes that the eye directly perceives distance, as well as the other dimensions of extent, and that, after all, sight is not only the sense of color, but also that of space.

We will not discuss these three opinions; the experiments which we are going to report can serve neither to confirm them nor to destroy them. The point which we wish to study is distinct: Does the eye perceive extent, or only color and light? This problem is even more difficult to resolve since the retina and the eye muscles constantly function together during vision of an exterior object. In the perception of depth, intervening muscles produce convergence of the ocular axes and focal adaptation of the lenses. In the perception of surface extent, intervening eye movements describe the contour of the visible object or follow the distance of two points situated in the same plane. "There is no example," said Stuart Mill, "of a person born with the sense of sight, but without those of touch and of muscles; nothing more than this is needed to allow us to define with precision both the capabilities and limitations of the conceptions which sight is capable of giving, independent of associations which these impressions form with those of the muscle sense."

This being stated, how can one distinguish between the part due to the retina and that due to ocular muscles in the vision of exterior objects? How can one determine which of these elements has more importance for the perception of extent? Such is the question which we wish to examine.

To pose this question on its own terrain, we must put aside all the cases in which perception of extent is influenced by ideas already acquired relative to the real dimensions of the object. It is clear that when we have recognized the presence of a man in our visual field, we can evaluate his height on the basis of our knowledge of the human figure; we need not take account of all the elements of our optical impression, as we would be obliged to do if we wished to perceive the dimensions of an unknown object. Similarly, when an object partially hides another, we can conclude that the first body is closer to us than the second without needing to compare the distance of the two objects from our eyes by means of our two optical impressions. These are roundabout ways of perceiving extent—processes founded on memories and on special circumstances. We will eliminate them completely from our discussion.

It seems to us that it is possible to differentiate between retinal sensitivity and muscular sensitivity. The means of accomplishing this is furnished by the afterimage, which one can compare to a photograph of the luminous impression received by the retina. Let us follow this comparison and prove its exactitude.

First of all, to obtain a very clear afterimage, one must keep the eye completely immobile while looking at a colored object. Why is this immobility necessary? It is undoubtedly true that, for the length of the experiment, each part of the object makes only a single impression on the retina. This is the first relation between an afterimage and a photographic test; to obtain a photograph with clear contours, it is evident that the sensitive plate must remain as immobile as the object.

Let us now suppose that the eye executes small movements while watching the colored object whose afterimage one wishes to obtain. What effects would these movements have on the image? If our first comparison is correct, movements of the eye, far from being useful in the production of an afterimage, would destroy the clearness of the contours by causing the photograph on the retina to be displaced; in other words, such movements of the eye would be entirely comparable in their effect to jerks of the sensitive plate during posing time.

An experiment can confirm these predictions on all points. Try to obtain the afterimage of a triangle of red paper, not by fixedly looking at one point of the figure, but by following its contours with a continuous movement of the eye. You will obtain only a very pale green spot without appreciable contours.

One can vary the experiment. Instead of a triangle, use a small band of red paper 5 cm. long; place it vertically, and during two minutes, force your glance to follow it with a uniform movement from top to bottom and from bottom to top. At the end of this time you will obtain, as a consecutive image, a green band twice as long as the red band. This result, though different from the preceding one, is explained by the same cause: vertical movements of the eye have the effect of displacing, in this same direction, the image of the red band on the retina, and of making it successively occupy a larger space than it would have, had it remained immobile. A lengthening of the afterimage is then produced. One can see clearly from this experiment that the form of the afterimage is determined by the projection of the real image on the retina.

Movements of the eye determine the lengthening of the after-image in an indirect manner by displacing the real image. It must be noted, further, that movements of the eye are related to the actual length of the red band, and not to the length of the afterimage, which is twice as long. Eye movements, then, do not give the image its dimension and its form.

After eliminating, once and for all, movements of the eye, can one maintain that the muscle tension which keeps the eye in a fixed position intervenes in some way to produce the afterimage? Definitely not. Experiments which show the contrary are easy to imagine. While the eye is fixed, agitate a triangle of red paper in the field of vision. The afterimage will be deformed, which proves that the tension of ocular muscles is irrelevant. On the contrary, follow with the eye the triangle of paper which you gently displace with the hand, and you will obtain an afterimage as clear as if the object had remained immobile.

These insights on the production of afterimages enable us to explain in a satisfactory manner a curious experience in hypnotism. We inculcate in our somnambulistic subject the idea that, on awakening, he will not see the red cross of paper which we place on a white page in front of him. On awakening he sees nothing; we then beg him to stare fixedly at a point which we indicate and which corresponds to the center of the cross. At the end of some time, he is very surprised to perceive suddenly a green cross on the white paper. The experiment gives the same result regardless of the figure employed: the subject invariably sees the afterimage of the figure which had remained invisible when he looked at it directly.

In summary, when achromatopsia is produced by suggestion, the sight of color and form gives rise to the same afterimages that would have occurred had the achromatopsia not existed. This experience is explained by the hypothesis that it is the color of the object which produces the afterimage; it is understood that the red rays, although not felt, develop the same afterimage in the subject's brain as if they were perceived. Those who maintain that, in this case, the form of the image is due to a muscular effect, are forced to admit that the hypnotic who does not see the red cross nonetheless executes unconscious movements to follow the contour of this invisible figure with his glance. This hypothesis seems to us very unlikely.

We now have the means of determining the degree to which optical sensitivity contributes to the perception of extent. This problem is easily explored by discovering which dimensions of extent are furnished by the properties of the afterimage.

I

Surface perception

Fixate upon three red points placed at different distances from one another, and project the afterimage of three green points on a screen placed at the same distance from the eye as the red points. You will note that, under these conditions, the green points seem separated by intervals equal to those of the red points. Thus, the afterimage also reproduces form: a red cross produces consecutively the afterimage of a green cross, but the second is confused with the first, because the form of a plane figure is reducible to length and width. One can say, then, that the afterimage reproduces the perception of the surface space, and conclude from this that surface perception is furnished by the eye alone, without recourse to muscles.[2]

One remark must be added: The measure of the length and width of the afterimage is not reproduced in an absolute manner. For example, an image of three green points does not provide us with the number of centimeters which in reality separates them from one another. In fact, these distances are extremely variable. They increase when the screen on which the afterimage is projected is moved farther away, and they diminish when it is moved nearer. One also knows that the afterimage in the form of a cross increases and decreases under the same circumstances. The afterimage teaches us only a relationship: a relationship between two lengths, or between two widths, or between a length and a width. This relationship appears to be invariable for all the given positions of the screen. If, for example, the distance between the first green point and the second is a third of the distance between the second point and the third, the measures taken indicate that this ratio remains approximately the same whether or not the screen is moved closer or farther away.

---

[2] We could cite another fact to prove that the eye can comprehend the form of an object without executing movements: One perceives the form of entoptic images of the eye (opaque bodies of the cornea, of the lens, and of the vitreous humor) and of the vascular tree of Purkinje, even though these images, which are displaced with the movement of the eye, cannot be distorted by the glance. Proof of this was vaguely indicated by Helmholtz, who defends the same opinion as we do (*Optique Physiologique*, p. 687).

In the same way, if the length of one arm of the green cross is double that of the other, the ratio between them does not seem to change noticeably, despite changes in the size of the cross. The screen must be placed at the same distance as the first and must be equal to it rather than similar to it.

Consequently, one can say that the eye, as an optical organ, values only the relationship existing between the width and length of an object, and that it would not know how to measure these dimensions in an absolute manner unless the distance of the object from the eye were first determined.

This is a fact which recalls the solution of a rule of three. We know that the afterimage reproduces only the ratio between the length and width of an object; if, by the given position of the screen, one makes the length of the image equal to that of the object, one simultaneously makes the second dimension of the image, its width, equal to that of the object. It suffices merely to determine the value of the first to know the value of the second also. This is indeed a rule of three and it is not the first time that we have noticed our senses unconsciously resolving problems of mathematics.

All these experimental results are in formal contradiction to the ideas advanced by the English school, which, it seems to us, has too much reduced the role of the eye in the perception of extent. According to Bain and Stuart Mill, the distances in length and width would be given solely by the movements of the eye going from one point to another; the visible form would be provided by the eye's description of the contours of the object. It seems that, if this too absolute theory were correct, one would not find the form of the object inscribed in the afterimage. We do not maintain that movements of the eye never intervene in the perception of length and width. We believe, on the contrary, that measures made with the aid of eye movements are more exact than measures made with the immobile eye.[3]

II

Perception of depth

Does the afterimage give us an idea of extent in depth? This question is fairly difficult to resolve, and we propose, only with great reserva-

[3] Helmholtz, *Optique Physiologique*, p. 695.

tion, the following experiment, which seems to us to show that the afterimage can give the impression of a relief. Sketch on a piece of paper two stereoscopic images of a pyramid with four sections truncated at the top and seen from above [see Figure 1]; mark the lines of these figures with a fairly bright color, for example, a red crayon. Next, place the axes of your eyes parallel in such a way that each eye looks at the image which is designated for it. In doing this, you must accommodate your glance as if to see an object situated behind the images. Soon the two images become superimposed, and little by little give a vivid impression of a relief. This done, keep the glance

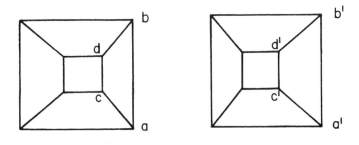

Figure 1. L.B. (242 reactions)

immobile, fixating upon some point of the figure, for example, one of its angles. After several minutes, turn your eyes upon an obscure background or close them gently; you will then see an image which differs from the first by the complementary color of its lines. The striking thing, however, is that this afterimage gives the impression of a relief as vivid as the stereoscopic fusion of the two figures. Such, in any case, is the result which we obtained on ourselves. In summary, this experience confirms that of the illustrious physicist Wheatstone, who first proved that it is the difference between the image perceived by the right eye and the left eye which constitutes the essential condition for the perception of a relief; from this conception came the beautiful invention of the stereoscope. Wheatstone's demonstration, however, was incomplete and left room for objection. One could question whether the convergence of the two eyes was not, in itself, an essential condition for the perception of a relief. In fact, when we look at the bases ab and a_1b_1 of the two pyramids, and then direct our glance along the lines cd and c_1d_1, which seem nearer to us, the line of sight of the right eye passes from a_1b_1 to c_1d_1, and the line of sight of the left eye from ab to cd. That is, it makes a shorter trip, and consequently the two visual axes become more convergent. Now, we have learned from the education of our senses that the closer an object is to us, the more the eyes must converge. One could thus maintain that the augmentation of convergence produced in stereoscopic vision is what causes us to believe that we have passed from the contemplation of a distant point to that of a nearer one,[4] from whence comes the impression of relief. The experiment with the afterimage answers this objection; it proves that the image of relief can be obtained by a simple optical sensation without movement of the eyes.

We do not mean to say that the eye can measure in an absolute manner the depth or the distance of a point; the eye does not truly perceive more than the relationship between two lengths or two widths. Finally, one can affirm that the afterimage, and consequently the eye, reproduces the extent of its three dimensions, and that it provides a measure of their relationship rather than an absolute measure of each of the dimensions.

In summary, the surface of the retina, except for some accessory differences, seems to us to be endowed with the same properties as the surface of the rest of the body; the retina is a piece of skin sensitive to light. This analogy is quite applicable to the perception of surface extent if one considers that the eye behaves very nearly like skin. It is known that when we excite two points of the skin with a compass, the subject perceives the distance without making any movement. It is also known that when we apply to a cutaneous region of delicate sensitivity a metallic tube with triangular or square edges, or large letters in relief, the subject recognizes the form of this body without making any movement. We have seen, similarly, that the retina perceives surface extent without any movement of the ocular muscles. From this point of view, the analogy between sight and touch is striking.

That which distinguishes these two senses is the property of perceiving the new dimension—extent in depth. We have shown that the eye can perceive a relief. It is evident that passive touch, deprived of the aid of movement, lets us know only the excitations which come in direct contact with the skin.[5] It is a more limited sense than sight. But one can add that that which touch loses in extent, it gains in

4 Bernheim, *Les Sens*, Bibliotheque Scientifique Internationale, p. 122.

precision. Touch not only allows us to know surface extent, it gives us its exact measure. If one excites two points of our skin, we can at least approximate the distance between them. This is not true for sight, which allows us to know only relationships. Sight does not perceive the absolute distance between two points situated in the same plane, because it perceives their distance from the eye at the same time. A separation on the retina between the images of the two points does not correspond to an invariable distance between these two points in space, but depends on their distance in relation to the eye, that is to say, on their depth.

At the beginning of this work, we were careful not to attempt to determine the proper object of vision, or to distinguish between that which the eye perceives directly because of its innate properties, and that which it perceives indirectly because of the effects of education and association with other senses. We expressly withheld this question, and in concluding, maintain the same reservation. For information's sake, we will simply say that it is our opinion that the eye perceives extent by virtue of acquired properties, among which the existence of local signs seems to hold an important position.[6]

Whatever solution one gives to this important problem, whether one is nativistic with Hering or empiricistic with Helmholtz, one must take account of the new element introduced in the debate by our study. In fact, the experiments made on the afterimage establish that the eye cannot perceive, either directly or indirectly, the absolute dimensions of surface extent, and perhaps also those of depth extent; the eye only grasps relationships. That is the conclusion which imposes itself with the same force to rival theories.

[5] Only one author maintained the contrary, namely Stumpf. According to him, the sense of touch perceives not only surface extent but depth extent. "In fact," he says, "the surface we feel when a contact is produced on some part of our body must be a plane or a curved surface; it is not possible to imagine others. Now these two types of surface imply the third dimension because they announce something which is related to depth: the presence or absence of an inclination to curve out toward depth." (*Über den psychologischen Ursprung der Raumvorstellung*, Leipzig, 1873; quoted by Ribot, *Psychologie Allemande*, p. 107).

[6] A. Binet, De la fusion des sensations semblables, *Revue philosophique*, Sept. 1880; reprinted in *Raisonnement inconscient*, I, Paris, 1886.

11

Studies on Movements in
Some Young Children

The general study of movements in young children has already been taken up by many authors, among whom I will name Preyer and Perez, whose works are frequently published and analyzed in this *Revue*. I do not intend to explore the question in its entirety; I am more interested in the investigation of some special points, which apparently have passed unnoticed among observers of childhood. I will therefore limit myself to expounding observations and experiments on the following topics:

1. The coordination of walking movements
2. Bilaterality of movements
3. Automatism
4. Physiological reaction times

1. *How the child learns to walk.* Authors who have studied walking in children are preoccupied with establishing the date at which this complex ensemble of movements first coordinates itself. Demme, who did observations of 50 children, found that 41 of them walked for the first time at 18 months; Preyer, from whom I borrowed this citation, places the first attempt to walk between the fourth and seventh trimester. The moment can vary according to a multitude of circumstances such as the child's health, the solidity of his bones, the strength of his muscles, and the habits of his family, which sometimes encourage his first steps and sometimes retard them, by a prudence which is never exaggerated. While studying two little sisters, I was able to convince myself that the psychical qualities of the child, no-

---

Recherches sur les mouvements chez quelques jeunes enfants. *Revue philosophique*, 1890, 29, 297-309.

tably the degree of its voluntary attention, can have a great influence on the success of its attempts to walk. The elder of the two little girls walked alone at 12 months, while the second succeeded only at 15 months. Although the elder was much more delicate, she did not have, like the second one, the advantage of being raised with another child who knew how to walk and whose example could excite and instruct her. I attribute this difference in the development of walking to the fact, repeatedly verified by the parents of the two children, that the older of the two girls paid a more consistent, more methodical attention to her first locomotive attempts. When she was standing on her feet, holding onto a solid object, a chair or a table, she risked abandoning that support only when she had visually selected another object a short distance away which would offer new support; she directed herself very slowly towards the second object, paying great attention to the movements of her legs. These movements were executed with great seriousness in perfect silence. The younger one, on the other hand, was a laughing, turbulent child; when put on her legs, she remained immobile for some moments and then was suddenly pushed forward by a desire to progress. It was evident that she never anticipated which object could furnish support, because she advanced without the least hesitation to the middle of an empty part of the room. She cried out, she gestured, she was very amusing to watch; she advanced staggering like a drunken man, and could not take four or five steps without falling. Thus, the beginning of walking was retarded; she could walk alone securely only at the age of 15 months.

The two children have grown, and the psychological differences we pointed out have not disappeared; on the contrary, they have imprinted a very clear character on their mental development. I will cite some examples in passing. The elder of the two little girls, the one who appeared capable of sustained attention, has a calm reserved character; the second has remained an open, vivacious personality. The first child has a much better memory than the second; she is more accurate in recalling the corrections made to her and consequently is easier to teach. Furthermore, as soon as her teething allowed her to eat solid foods, she ate at the table with her parents; the younger one was obliged to eat her meals alone, because she was so distracted by what she saw and heard when eating at the table with her parents that she ate much less. Moreover, this curious difference was noted in the two children when they still were at the breast. At the least noise, the younger one would stop sucking to turn her head and look at what was going on, whereas the elder would continue to suck. I am unaware of whether the state of attention can explain this last fact, very curious from several points of view: The older child sleeps less lightly than the younger; she is not awakened, like the latter, by a slight sound. It seems—if we may make this comparison—that she gives more sustained attention to whatever she is doing. From this point of view, awaking would be comparable to a distraction, and since she is less easily distracted than her sister, she is also less easily awakened. I do not insist upon this comparison which may be of no value; I am content to record a fact. Let us return now to our study of walking.

How do children learn to walk? Is walking an acquisition derived from imitation, or is it a result of a mechanism in great part inherited? Preyer inclines toward the second opinion: "The beginnings of the act of walking," he says, "are enigmatic, because there seems to be not the least reason for the alternate flexing and extending of the legs at the moment when the child stands for the first time."[1] In support, he reports an observation of Champneys', who saw a child of 19 weeks agitate his legs alternately while being held above the ground.

I willingly share Preyer's opinion on the instinctive character of walking. What convinced me above all was an accidental observation I made of one of the two young children I spoke of above. She was then about three weeks old. She had just been undressed. Her mother, who was lying in bed, lifted the child above her, holding her child under the arms. The child's bare feet touched her mother's stomach; under the influence of the contact, which was felt on the soles of the feet, the child very clearly sketched walking movements. When she was held up on one of her feet, the right one, she raised the other, bending her thigh toward her pelvis and her leg toward her thigh, placing it a little way in front. This foot pressed quite clearly on her mother's knees. Once it was in place, the right leg raised itself in turn, bent, advanced, and the child took a step. The alternation of the movement of the two legs was quite marked. Occasionally the angle of a foot was strongly directed inward. The child appeared to move her legs better when she was trying to climb an inclined plane than when one had her walk on a horizontal plane.

---

[1] *L'Ame de l'Enfant*, p. 225.

Given the age of the child, this fact seemed to me so remarkable that I repeated the experiment several times, always with the same result. I noted, further, that when one held the child too high above the ground and her feet were in the air, either both legs remained extended without executing any movements of locomotion, or the movements executed presented no alternation and did not have the character of walking. The excitation of the sole of the foot was necessary to produce the alternation of movements. This curious observation is not exceptional, because I could verify myself, or have verified by others, the execution of these same locomotive movements in even younger children of one or one and a half weeks old. In these latter also, the influence of the sensation of contact on the sole of the foot was clearly manifested. In another child of about the same age as the preceding ones, however, it was impossible to recognize these rudiments of walking movements.

The preceding observations, quite easily verified, demonstrate to us that walking may be a truly instinctive act in the child; this instinctive character is all the more striking since the child begins to walk alone fairly late. One sees that the slow development of a certain movement or function is not, as is sometimes thought, proof that the function is personally acquired by the individual. This is an illusion which must be guarded against.

Comparative psychology has shown us the importance of timing in the development of purely hereditary functions. The small chicken who has just come out of the egg by pecking the shell can walk alone and peck the grain given him. On the other hand, the young pigeon is incapable of walking and feeding himself. This does not prove that walking is instinctive in the chicken but acquired through experience in the pigeon. The difference between these two birds is due simply to the duration of the incubation period, which is 21 days for the chicken and 15 for the pigeon.

2. *Bilaterality of movements.* If one attentively follows the spontaneous arm movements of a one-week-old child as it is held in one's lap, one notes that these movements, which often have a sudden explosive character, and which are directed from the back to the front and from the outside to the inside, are executed by both arms simultaneously. When the child is undressed and extended comfortably on a rug, one sees that both legs together make similar, sudden movements of flection and extension. This fact is so extremely striking to me I am astonished that authors have not noted it. In this regard, it

is instructive to compare a child of a few weeks with a child of two to three years. One has little patience for counting all the movements executed by these two children spontaneously, but it will be easy to verify that, in the three-year-old child, almost all movements are unilateral, whereas in the few-weeks-old child, almost all are bilateral. Under the latter category I include alternate movements; it frequently happens, for example, that a small child makes a broad movement with his right arm which is followed by a similar movement with his left arm. There is an alternation of the two movements; but since the two are of the same type and succeed each other very rapidly, one can consider them as having a bilateral character.

Here, by way of example, are some of the numerous observations I made of a little six-day-old girl.

Table 1.

| | Movements | | |
	Bilateral	Alternative	Unilateral
Observations during a 5-min. period	5	—	4
Another 5-min. period	13	10	6
Another 5-min. period	4	14	1
While child's face is washed, and it exhibits defensive behavior.	3	9	2

The functional relationship between the two limbs in children explains the following observations I did on a 42-month-old little girl. In each of her hands, I placed an enclosed rubber tube, the two tubes being attached to a recording apparatus. It was agreed in advance that at a given signal, the child was to squeeze with only one hand. From the marks I obtained, I noted that the child would sometimes squeeze involuntarily with both hands; other times the pressure was unilateral. The child made this spontaneous reflection after the time, for example, she was supposed to squeeze only with her right hand: "I was going to squeeze with my left hand." We found the same thing with adults during periods of distraction.[2]

To conclude this point, I will note in passing the position of the hands of young children less than one year old. When one carries them and holds them upright, and they do not execute any arm

[2] Concurrence des etats intellectuels, *Revue philosophique*, February, 1890.

movements, their immobile hand maintains a position of pronation, that is, the palm is turned inward. I am unaware of the physiological conditions of this position which somehow is characteristic in the young child.

Related to the study of movement is the study of muscle sense. Charles Bell, one of the first—if not *the* first—to study muscle sense gives as an example the fact that a young child held in the arms perceives very correctly whether he is firmly held or runs the risk of falling. I had proof that this perception was already very clearly produced in a little girl during her third week. Each day the child was given a bath; she was carried nude into the bath, and held with one hand under her back and the other under her legs. The person who carried her held her close to the chest for more security. When the child was in this position, she remained quiet and let herself be carried to the bath without protest. It was otherwise, if, instead of holding her closely, one simply carried her on two extended arms; this, in fact, was slightly more dangerous, since the child, not being secured, could have slipped. As soon as this little being, hardly three weeks old, sensed that she was not being firmly held, she began to struggle and utter cries of fright. Because the origin of these cries could be interpreted incorrectly, I held the child before me a great number of times. The result was always the same: As soon as she was held lightly, the child's little face took on a very clear expression of fright and she uttered shrill cries. Her fright was all the more curious since she was hardly three weeks old, had never fallen—I can testify to that!—and consequently had no acquired experience on the dangers of a fall. It is difficult for me to interpret the case other than as the result of an inherited disposition. I have not yet had the occasion to compare the little girl with other children.

It is interesting that, while a child of three weeks can perceive by an inherited process that it is on the verge of falling, it cannot perceive, without personal experience, that fire burns or that such-and-such a substance is dangerous to touch.

3. *Automatism*. The studies of these last years on automatism and double consciousness permit us today to recognize in certain phenomena, which would pass almost unnoticed before the unbiased observer, a manifest proof of mental division. I will summarize in a few words what I was able to learn from the two little girls of whom I have spoken, and whose intellectual evolution I have followed step by step.

The first fact of automatism was observed in the older of the two little girls during her first six months; I have not found it in other children of the same age. When this little girl had her hand open, it sufficed to scratch her palm lightly for the extended fingers to bend and her hand to close. Conversely, when her hand was already closed, a light mechanical scratching on the dorsal face very rapidly resulted in the extension of the fingers. This little experiment succeeded under the most diverse conditions—while the child was asleep or awake, while she was attentive to what was happening in her hand, or while her attention was occupied elsewhere. I mentioned previously that I was unable to find this muscle phenomenon in other children, succeeding in provoking in them only general movements of defense, without precise character. Be that as it may, these reactions of the hand, determined by mechanical excitations external to the will of the child, can give us a first example, rare it is true, of automatic movements at a young age.

A second example of automatism is the ease with which one can arouse in a small child, when he is distracted, coordinated movements of which he is unconscious. I have seen this many times in many young girls. Here is one example among several. A little eight-month-old girl attentively watches a woman who smiles at her; her hand is open and in pronation. One slides a small object into the palm of her hand, a key, a ruler, etc. The child, occupied elsewhere, appears to notice nothing, but her little fingers fold around the object; they squeeze the object and hold it suspended for a certain time, sometimes for several minutes. Eventually the hand opens slowly or suddenly, and the object falls to the ground, sometimes without the child having suspected anything.

Finally, automatism can express itself not only by movements of a particular nature, but by the involuntary preservation of a fixed position. One day, when photographing a little child of 18 months, we removed a bouquet that she was holding in her hand. For a moment her fingers remained folded as if she were still holding the bouquet, and the preservation of this position was reproduced in the photograph. Another little girl of 30 months whom I was watching at the table heard an unusual sound as she extended her arm to reach for a glass. She listened a moment, her neck strained, her face curious, and she no longer thought of her hand, which stayed in the air, forgotten, her fingers directed toward the glass she was going to grab. Ordinarily, under similar circumstances, an adult would draw back his hand or take the glass and drink while listening.

The salient feature of all these muscular phenomena is their unconsciousness. Of course, I use the word "unconsciousness" in a very relative sense. I mean by it that the child, distracted by an interesting object, no longer perceives that the palm of its hand is excited and that its fingers are bent in order to close the hand or to hold an object. In the same way, it no longer knows—one could say it forgets—that its arm is stretched out to grasp an object, and so it holds that position unsuspectingly. Since the child continues to produce these movements after his intellect and will have stopped directing them, one must assume that they are maintained by muscular sensations or others of which the limb is the seat, following the schema given by Pierre Janet for analogous muscular phenomena in hysterics (for example, maintenance of a cataleptic stance). A small synthesis of movements and muscular sensations form temporarily and subsist without mingling with the large synthesis representing the intellectual personality of the child. It would be forcing the interpretation of these facts to see in them a regular division of the personality comparable to that of hysterics. Moreover, our observations are too few in number to lead to so serious a conclusion. What seems evident to us is that in the small children we studied, there is a tendency toward mental disaggregation, which proves simply that the systematization of intellectual elements which characterizes the healthy adult is not fully developed in the child.

Here are additional observations which will explain our interpretations. Everyone familiar with children knows how easy it is to distract them and to change the object of their attention. Indeed, this is a handy way of stopping tears if one does not wish to reprimand them. When a small child cries loudly for its absent mother, speak to him sweetly of something else, or surreptitiously attract his attention by executing a bizarre action like opening and closing a box, for example. It will produce a new group of representations and images in his mind, temporarily chasing away the first preoccupation by making him completely forget it. In an adult, one does not so easily obtain this change of mind, first of all, because it is more difficult to modify the center of attention, and secondly, because new ideas do not completely exclude old ideas; they can regroup themselves in a unique synthesis. Here is an observation I made on a little girl of three years and nine months; it would be difficult to find the analogue in an adult person: A little girl, having been scolded before strangers, cried freely, this being a situation to which she was particularly sensitive. Desiring to end this tremendous vexation, I tried to distract her; I sat the little girl on my knees and lit a match in front of her. Her cries suddenly stopped; she smiled; she looked at the flame with great curiosity and asked my permission to hold the end of the match. When it had burned up, the object of distraction was gone, and the child immediately resumed her crying. The tears lasted until I lit a second match, which produced the same result as the first: suppression of her sobs and smiling. After the extinction of the flame, her crying began again as it had the first time. Here we see two preoccupations succeeding each other or, more strictly speaking, two distinct mental syntheses mutually expelling each other and never mingling. It would probably be difficult to find such clear phenomena of mental disaggregation in adults (except in hysteria, of course, and other analogous conditions).

4. *Reaction time.* I am unaware of whether anyone has studied the reaction times of children from four to seven years to excitations of the senses. None of the authors I consulted have mentioned it. Experiments on reaction time are quite difficult to perform on young children; in fact, except under special circumstances, it seems almost impossible to work with children under three: the experiments are complicated and require the child's complete cooperation, which never lasts when performing such monotonous tasks. It is necessary, furthermore, for the child to understand that he must make a certain movement at a given signal, and that this movement must be carried out as quickly as possible.

I studied reaction time by using a recording apparatus, but it is possible to gain a rough idea of the slowness with which children voluntarily respond to an excitation without using such an apparatus. It suffices to put one's finger in the child's hand and ask him to squeeze it when he hears a signal agreed upon in advance, for example, when he is told, "Squeeze hard." In this manner, one can easily see that the child exerts pressure quite a long time after the signal is given, and that he has difficulty making a short squeeze. In general, he squeezes a very long time. The use of the graphic method allows us to arrive at a more exact idea of the reaction time and the form of the muscle contraction.

I used the following apparatus: The signal, always an auditory one, was given by a metronome which was put in motion by an assistant at the desired moment; thus, the signal consisted of the weak, short sound produced by the metronome. The precise moment at which the sound was heard was recorded on a revolving cylinder to which the metronome was attached. The subject's reaction, that is, the movement executed by the child as soon as he heard the auditory signal, did not consist, as is usually the case, in the interruption of an electric current. This mode of reaction, though frequently used, does not provide information on an especially interesting part of the experiment, particularly when one is observing young children. I am referring to the form of the muscle contraction. An experiment should be as complete and as comprehensive as possible and should illuminate the greatest possible number of phenomena. I therefore recorded the muscle contraction in a direct way, using the common graphic apparatus devised by Marey. For some experiments, a myograph was applied to the subject's arm, and he was asked to bend his arm when he heard the signal; for others, a simple rubber tube closed at one end was placed in the child's hand, and he was requested to squeeze the tube suddenly at the signal. In both cases, the devices were attached to the same recording cylinder as the metronome so that the interval between the signal and the child's response could be precisely measured on the tracing. Let me add, in conclusion, that the progress of the cylinder was controlled by the vibrations of a tuning-fork and, in some experiments, by the metronome itself.

Since certain experimental conditions are invariably difficult to control, and thus prevent one observer's experiment from being comparable to that of another, I was careful to record, with the same apparatus, the reaction times of some adults so that I would have a means of comparison. For reactions to auditory excitations, the mean reaction time was equal to .14 sec. This number does not differ appreciably from that given by other authors.

The reaction times of four children were recorded; the youngest was a little girl of 43 months; the oldest was 7½ years. Here are their mean reaction times:

Madeleine	(43 months)	.475 sec.
Adrienne	(4 years)	.66 sec.
Blanche	(7 years)	.58 sec.
Alexandre	(7 ½ years)	.44 sec.

The maximum times were:

Madeleine	.92 sec.
Adrienne	1.00 sec.
Blanche	1.30 sec.
Alexandre	.75 sec.

The length of the minimum times seems very characteristic; it would be unusual for an adult in good health to have such long reaction times. The minimum times were:

Madeleine	.19 sec.
Adrienne	.20 sec.
Blanche	.20 sec.
Alexandre	.20 sec.

I believe that the minimum reaction times are particularly important since they very likely correspond to the experiments during which the subject's attention was the best held. It is difficult to evaluate whether or not such a minimum time is due to a coincidence, that is to say, to chance; I took this factor into consideration only when an exceptional response was presented.

The variation in reaction times indicates, further, the difficulty we have in retaining the child's attention.

One sees that the minimum time in the children we have studied was always greater than the minimum time of a healthy adult.

Duration of the contraction. The use of graphic apparatus for recording reaction times has the advantage of showing us the duration and the form of the muscle contraction when the child has no other preoccupation than to give a signal as rapidly as possible. A single glance at the lines traced shows that the contraction signal is always longer in the child than in the adult.

In an adult, for example, the duration of a contraction signal is .34 sec. Here are some numbers for children:

Madeleine	.81 sec.
Adrienne	2.00 sec.
Blanche	.50 sec.
Alexandre	.45 sec.

In these experiments, the child, of course, was never asked to give a short or long contraction; it was left to his initiative.

In this regard, we studied the maximum number of times that a subject could press a rubber tube between his thumb and index finger during a limited period of time. Experiments on eight adults demonstrated that the greatest number of pressings that could be exerted in 4 seconds was about 18. Some people could exert up to 27 pressings during this interval; others did not go beyond 14.

When using children as subjects, the results are appreciably different. We obtained:

Madeleine	(46 months)	right hand	8	pressings
Adrienne	(4 years)	— —	8	—
Blanche	(7 years)	— —	8	—
Alexandre	(7 ½ years)	— —	12	—
*Charles	(8 ½ years)	— —	9	—
	(9 years)	{ right hand	11	—
		left hand	7	—

*Left-handed.

To conclude our discussion on the form of the muscle contraction, we saw in the experiments on reaction times that the lines for Madeleine and Adrienne ascended very gradually, and that the form of the contraction varied in each experiment. The line ascended slowly for Blanche as well, but her contractions took a more regular form. With Alexandre, the ascent was more sudden, and the form noticeably approached that of an adult.

In summary, we have observed in young children: the slowness of physiological reaction times, the importance of the variations, the length of the contraction signal, the slope of the ascending line, the variation in the form of the curve from one experiment to another.[3]

3 Herzen did some psychometric experiments on children from 4 to 15 years of age. He was struck by the slowness with which the children reacted, but he provided none of the figures he obtained. In particular, he studied subjects' reaction times in associating two movements which are not usually associated; for example, drawing back the hand and the foot on the same side at the same time. Under these conditions, the means from the experiments were as follows: 4- to 5-year-olds, 1.068 sec. for the foot and 1.003 sec. for the hand; 5- to 10-year-olds, 0.544 sec. and 0.532 sec. (Herzen, *Le Cerveau et l'Activité cérébrale*, p. 96) .

12

The Perception of Duration
in Simple Reactions

I propose to study, by way of a particular sensation whose conditions are easy to regulate, a much discussed problem of great interest: the relationship between the conscious and the unconscious. Many authors maintain that there is a precise limit for excitations, a threshold of consciousness, and that all excitations below this threshold are imperceptible. The limit would vary, of course, from one subject to another, and for any one individual it would vary according to the psychical conditions of the moment. If, hypothetically, these conditions were standardized, the perceptible minimum could be determined in such a way that any excitation equal to this minimum would produce a phenomenon of consciousness, whereas any excitation very near but a little below this minimum would produce no conscious phenomenon. Thus, suppose that the perceptible minimum for the odor of vanilla is, according to recent studies by M. J. Passy, .000005 mg. perfuming a litre of air; a quantity differing from the preceding only by the last digit of the number would give no olfactory sensation. Thus, the hypothesis is satisfied.

As reasonable as this hypothesis appears to be, it is not the only one that can be formed. It is permissible to suppose that, instead of a boundary sharply separating a perceived excitation from a non-perceived one, a zone of variable extent exists in which the excitation is neither absolutely conscious nor absolutely unconscious, but is accompanied by a weak consciousness. In other words, consciousness has degrees. This second hypothesis, frequently supported in

---

La perception de la durée dans les réactions simples. *Revue philosophique*, 1892, 33, 650-659.

the past, and more recently maintained by authors of great merit, appears to me to be in harmony with the results of hypnotic studies dealing with the subconscious.[1] I therefore feel it useful to look for experiments capable of throwing light on this important problem.

I would like it understood at the outset that we experience some difficulty in obtaining good experimental conditions. The question is simple only in appearance. What are we trying to demonstrate? That the perceptible minimum can vary during the course of the same experiment? This is a well-known fact. These variations follow the always unstable psychophysiological state of the subject; in particular, his degree of attention and state of fatigue. The variations of the minimum under the influence of these disturbances can cause a multitude of practical difficulties, but they will not offend the theory. Just because the limit of perceptibility can vary, it does not follow that there is no precise limit between consciousness and unconsciousness.

In our opinion, one does not overcome these difficulties by demonstrating the minimum variation for conscious perception; rather, one must demonstrate directly, if this is possible, that half-conscious perceptions can exist independently of conscious perceptions, and that they result from excitations which are inferior to the minimum of clear consciousness. The method of right and wrong cases seems to us quite adequate for this verification.

Here is the way the experiments are set up. I choose as the object of perception the length of a reaction executed by the subject himself; the reaction is uncomplicated, consisting solely of a movement executed by the subject as soon as he perceives a signal agreed upon in advance. For a practiced person, and with the apparatus we are going to describe, these reactions present a mean time of .12 sec. There are oscillations around this mean, and variations from one reaction to the next can be very short or very long, depending on the skill of the subject and his natural power of attention. The subject is asked to perceive these variations as precisely as possible and to indicate them by an exact number. It is clear that, when the variation is enormous, .5 sec. for example, all subjects can perceive it. If, however, the variation is small, it will require a more delicate perception, and if it is reduced to, say, .001 sec., few people will be capable of perceiving it. We have, then, on the one hand, perfectly conscious

---

[1] I refer to my book, *Altérations de la Personnalité*, p. 122 and following, on this point.

perceptions which always occur without error; these are the object variations of .5 sec. We have, on the other hand, a complete absence of perception for variations of .001 sec.; people who try to perceive this variation commit so many errors that the results are due to chance. What happens between these two extreme points? If, for the intermediary variations, we gather together all the subject's perceptions and compare the correct responses with the false ones, what will we get? If there is a clearly perceived variation, and the variation immediately below gives no precise perception (outside of that given by chance), then we can conclude that a threshold of consciousness exists, and that below that threshold nothing is conscious. But if, between variations always perceived and variations never perceived, a series of intermediaries exist which are perceived sometimes correctly, sometimes falsely, and if the relationship of these right and wrong cases between the two extreme points is regularly modified so that they are correlated with each other, we will conclude that there is no threshold of consciousness at a fixed position, but a zone in which all degrees of consciousness are present. I hope this will be clearly understood as we enter into the details of the experiments.[2]

The reaction times are measured with an Arsonval chronoscope; the signal is auditory (a sharp blow on a block of wood). The test trials are uniformly separated by a 10-sec. interval during which the subject rests. Each signal is preceded by a verbal warning. During a series of preparatory reactions, the experimenter loudly announces the subject's reaction times in hundredths of seconds in order to give him a notion of the time; after the subject has become familiar with the idea, he indicates, following each reaction, the time in hundredths of seconds he thought he perceived. This number is recorded without comment beside the real number, which he does not know. We give these details because they constitute the psychological milieu of the experiments.

In order to know to what extent a person realizes the length of his own reactions, we were led by our results to distinguish three distinct operations: 1) the perception of the direction of the variation; 2) the perception of the value of the variation; and 3) the perception of the absolute time. An example will clarify these distinctions. Say that there are two consecutive reactions, A and B, and that the first

---

[2] The question has a short history. To be brief, I cite only one author and refer simply to the *Psychology* of William James, Vol. I, p. 615.

one lasts .12 sec., the other .15 sec. In trying to estimate A, the subject says .20 sec.; for B, .25 sec. There are many ways of looking at these responses; if we compare the number said by the subject with the actual length of the reaction, we are studying the perception of absolute time. This would be done by comparing .12 to .20 for A and .15 to .25 for B. One can also see whether the subject, given two reactions of unequal length, will find the shorter one shorter. In reality, reaction A is shorter than the other; if the subject estimates it as shorter, then he correctly perceives the *direction* of the variation. Finally, one can state that the real difference between the two reactions is .03 sec., while the difference between the two estimations is .05 sec. There is reason, then, to study the perception of the *value* of the variation as well. Each of these points deserves a separate study.

Perception of the direction of the variation

Practiced subjects most frequently perceive the direction of the variation correctly, and consequently, do not say the numbers by chance. Thus, the numbers have a significance: they correspond to a very real perception of time. It is necessary to make this assumption, because if the number of incorrect responses were equal to, or higher than, the number of correct ones, nothing would be perceived and the results would be without value.

Besides the practiced subjects used in this study, we have experimented with many others who have given us as many wrong estimations as right ones. We do not know what conclusion to draw from these results. It may be that certain people, despite constant attention, cannot reflect on their reaction times; but then, we cannot be sure that they are always attentive. This problem dominates almost all psychological experiments. To be successful, these experiments need the complete cooperation of the subject, and we have no precise cues informing us on this delicate point.[3]

Be that as it may, we must remember that practiced subjects perceive variations in the reaction times. How does this perception occur? We willingly suppose that it is by memory; the reaction time is extremely short, and the entire operation is accompanied by little consciousness. It is, doubtless, by retrospective action, that is, by memory, that we come to estimate whether one reaction is shorter or longer than another.

[3] This is why psychological experiments on the insane are so difficult.

Let us add that this act of memory sometimes deserves the name of subconsciousness; I was able to verify this on myself with great clarity. The first time I subjected myself to the experiment, I was completely unaware of whether I had succeeded in sensing the variations. After giving the numbers in a long series, I stopped myself and withdrew from the experiment, not from fatigue, but because I was convinced that I said some numbers by chance. The following morning I did the calculations and was quite astonished to see that I was wrong only two times out of twenty. Other people, and myself under different circumstances, have the feeling that they estimate their reaction times according to concrete data. The act of memory, then, can be either conscious or unconscious; there is no point in giving a rule on this subject.

Since the psychological operation used in estimating reaction time is, most probably, subsequent to the reaction itself, it need not appreciably modify the characteristics of that reaction; in fact, I notice that there is no difference between a subject's reactions when he is consciously estimating his time and when he is not. At most, one can say that, in certain cases, the reactions with time estimation are a little shorter and more regular than the others, perhaps because the subject is more attentive. In obliging him to estimate very short times, one prevents him from falling into a state of distraction which would make his reactions irregular.

Let us examine more closely the perception of the direction of the variation by glancing at the graphic tables included here (Figures 1-7). These graphs are composed of a series of eight vertical lines placed above numbers ranging from .5 to 8.0. Each vertical line is double, being formed by a solid and a dotted line. These lines represent the proportion of right and wrong cases which occur in the perception of variations in time; the right cases are represented by the dotted line, the wrong cases by the solid line. The relationship between these two types of cases is expressed by the length of the two lines: when the subject has more incorrect perceptions than correct perceptions, the solid line is longer than the dotted line. All variations of time from .005 to .08 sec. are represented graphically; the numbers above the lines indicate the actual value of the variation. For simplicity, the absolute number of right and wrong cases is not given; instead, the numbers have been reduced to a common denominator to facilitate comparison, since the relationship between the two types of cases is more important than the numbers themselves.

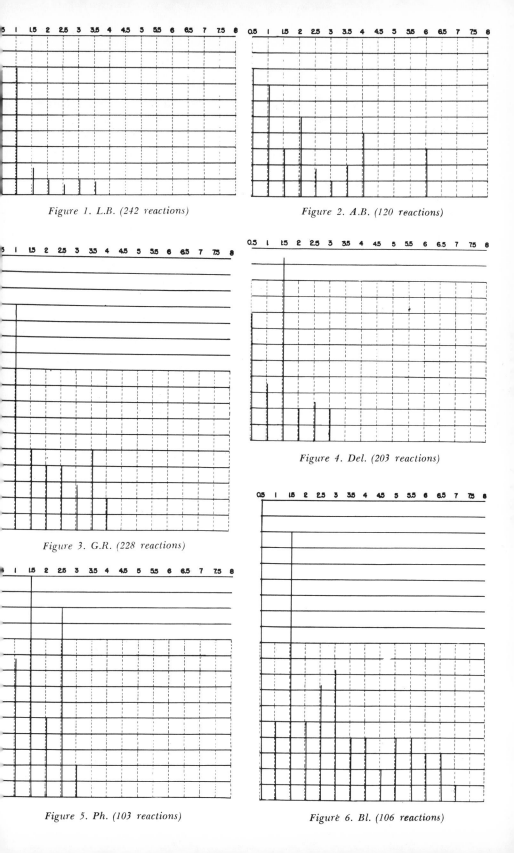

Figure 1. L.B. (242 reactions)

Figure 2. A.B. (120 reactions)

Figure 4. Del. (203 reactions)

Figure 3. G.R. (228 reactions)

Figure 5. Ph. (103 reactions)

Figure 6. Bl. (106 reactions)

The perception of the direction of the variation occurs better (in other words, more often correctly) for large variations than for small ones. With one of the subjects (L.B.) , no error was committed beyond a variation of .03 sec.; with another subject, the limit was .035 sec., and in two others, .04.

It is difficult to determine the smallest perceptible variation. In three of the subjects, there seemed to be a vague perception of a variation equal to .005;[4] in the fourth (G.R.) , this variation was not perceived at all.

The discrepancy among results is clearly indicated in Figure 7, which represents the mean of the first four graphs. According to this graph, there is no perception at all below .005 sec., and there is always correct perception above .04 sec.

What occurs between these two extreme limits? The problem arises that we indicated in the beginning of this article: Is there a precise boundary between perceived and non-perceived excitations? We do not intend to settle categorically a question whose complexity we do not hide; we give merely an interpretation of our experiments, and everyone is invited to test it.

It is certain that in all the graphs (excepting that of the mean [Figure 7]) , the relationship between right and wrong cases within the range of .04 and .005 sec. is extremely variable. For purposes of study, let us retain only the first four figures, since these are the most regular. One might wonder whether the relationship between right and wrong cases in these conditions was not simply the result of chance, the subject having perceived absolutely nothing. This inter- pretation does not appear correct. If we take the sum of both the right and the wrong perceptions for variations between .005 and .04 sec., we see that the first sum is higher than the second, and that in Figure 1, the ratio between right perceptions and wrong perceptions is 70:20; in Figure 2, 80:30; in Figure 3, 80:54; in Figure 4, 28:60. Thus, it appears well established that for variations lower than those which are always correctly perceived, the number of correct percep- tions is higher than that which would be given by chance.

What significance must be given to this result? The authors who maintain that a threshold of consciousness exists will admit that the limit of perceptibility can vary during the same experiment under

---

[4] For the first subject, L.B., the mean reaction time was .10 sec.; for the second, .12 sec.; for the third, .14 sec.; for the fourth, .12 sec. These four subjects have very regular reactions.

the influence of failure of attention or fatigue. One subject, Del . . . for example, committed a small number of errors beyond .015 sec.; had he been more attentive, this would not have been his limit of perceptibility. His errors were only failures of attention, and they had the effect of sometimes advancing, sometimes retarding, his threshold of consciousness. From these come the irregularities of the graph. While recognizing that this explanation contains a lot of truth, we think it is incomplete. It would satisfy us only if the errors committed within the range .005 to .03 or .04 sec. were distributed randomly. With a little attention, however, we discover that the number of errors decreases as .03 or .04 sec. is approached. It is true that the reduction is irregular, but this is due precisely to the influence of attention, distraction, fatigue, etc. The decrease in error nevertheless exists. To account for it, it suffices to divide the zone between .005 and .035 sec. into two parts and to compare the errors of the first zone (.005 to .02 sec.) with those of the second (.02 to .035) ; the errors of the second zone are always less. Now, failure of attention and fatigue do not explain why the number of errors is greater, in general, for the variations below .03 sec. or .04 sec. These disturbing influences explain only the irregularities of the curve. There is no reason why the subject should be more distracted or more fatigued when perceiving small variations than large ones. One cannot disregard the effect of the size of the variation.

In Figure 7, which represents the mean, all irregularities due to

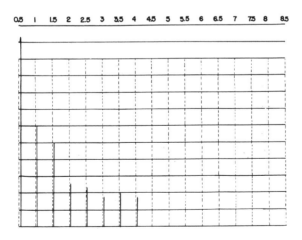

Figure 7. The mean of Figures 1, 2, 3, and 4.

individual differences disappear, and the reduction in errors appears with clarity. Consequently, we can summarize the preceding by saying that in certain subjects, if one considers smaller and smaller variations, the perception of the direction of the variation is not abolished at a fixed limit, but alters by degrees.

This conclusion does not have general significance; it does not apply in Figure 5. Studying this figure, we see that, prior to 3.0 sec., the variations were evaluated at random, because the number of incorrect cases is noticeably equal to that of correct cases. It follows that, for this particular subject, variations equal to 3.0 were perceived correctly, but that below this limit, nothing was perceived in a semiconscious form. This small fact shows how dangerous it would be to legislate on such delicate questions.

Value of the variations

By using the graphic method to visualize results contained in a considerable mass of numbers, we can dispense with having to insist at length on this last point. If we glance at Figure 8, in which the actual variations are represented by a solid line and the estimated variations

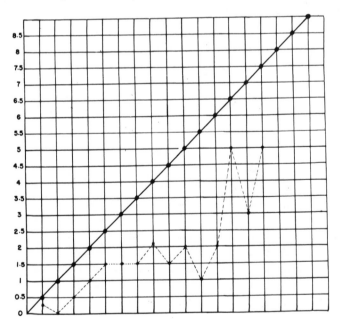

Figure 8. The perception of the value of the variation.

by a dotted line, we see immediately that the subjects generally underestimate the variations; in fact, the dotted line stays constantly below the solid line. A second fact, quite apparent from the graph, is that the extent of the variation is well perceived by the subject. In general, save some exceptions, a large variation is seen as a large variation. To take some examples from the graph, a variation of 2.0 is perceived as a variation of 1.0, and a variation of 4.0 is perceived as a variation of 2.5.

All the perceived variations were calculated by subtracting the value of the estimated variation from that of the actual variation, the former being considered as negative.

It is noteworthy that perception approaches reality chiefly for variations of small value; the dotted line representing the subjects' evaluations is much closer to the solid line for the variations lower than 2.0 than for those higher. It seems that one could draw the following conclusion from this observation: The perception of the value of the variation approaches reality more often for small variations than for large ones. Initially, this assumption appears to contradict the results expressed by the preceding figures, which indicate the direction of the variation. We saw, in fact, that it was easier to perceive the direction of a large variation than the direction of a small one.

Is this a contradiction? We do not think so. A somewhat complex point is involved here, but with a moment's attention, it is not difficult to understand why the estimation of the value of the variation approaches reality, especially for small variations. In this latter case, the subject's choice is restricted within quite narrow limits. But suppose that the subject has perceived a large variation; how will he estimate it? He can draw from numbers going from 3.0 to 4.0 to 15.0, to 20.0, and on. Consequently, he is exposed to committing important errors of estimation. On the contrary, if he judges that the variation is weak, his choice is between numbers going only from 0.5 to 2.0, and thus there is less chance of his estimate being wrong.

In summary, we have arrived at the following conclusions:

1. A person can estimate the duration of his reactions.

2. The direction of the variation is generally estimated without error for variations from .03 or .04 sec. and above.

3. Some people never perceive variations less than .03 or .04 sec. correctly; others perceive them, but err increasingly as the variations become smaller.

4. These results confirm that, in certain people, consciousness does not have a threshold, a fixed limit, separating it from the unconscious, but rather develops by degrees.

5. The value of the variation is generally underestimated.

6. The most correct estimation of the value occurs for the smaller variations.

13

Fear in Children

Several methods were used in our study of fear in children: 1) Questionnaires were distributed to about 100 teachers. 2) Questions were addressed to adults, to persons whom we know personally and who seem to us to be trustworthy and capable of self-analysis. 3) Personal observations were made on our own children and our acquaintances' children.[1]

Questionnaires were distributed among the teachers with questions printed in the margin of a large white page; the questions, which were reduced to a minimum, were as follows:

1. In what form and under what circumstances have you observed the sentiment of fear in some of your students? (Kindly relate your observations.)

2. What physical signs of fear have you noticed?

3. What is the proportion of fearful children? (For example, how many are there in a class of 30 students?)

4. What is their health? (Physical development, weight, height, muscular strength, sex, age?)

5. What is their intelligence? Their rank in class?

6. What is their character?

7. Have you observed the influences which cause fear in children? Does it come from their parents? Do contagion by example, frightening stories, etc., play some role? What are the influences of age, religious education, and environment (city or country)?

8. Can one cure a frightened child, and how should it be done?

9. Name and address of the correspondent.

[1] We do not intend to present a bibliography of the question. We will refer only to recent semi-popular articles by James Sully in *Popular science monthly*, 1895; the author described many details of fear in children and discussed the mechanism of the fear of darkness.

La peur chez les enfants. *Année psychologique*, 1895, 2, 223-254.

Approximately 250 copies of the questionnaire were distributed. They were not given indiscriminately to all teachers, but only to an elite. The supervisors of the academy were willing to select from among the teachers in their departments the most intelligent and the most zealous. Without a great effort on our part, we collected 110 completed questionnaires. We limited our inquiry to six departments; we certainly could have collected a larger number of documents, but thought that these would suffice.

The obliging intervention of the supervisors assured the success of our inquiry. Reduced to our own resources, we could not have gathered more than 10 responses. It is a curious fact that people who, by profession and by taste, are interested in these questions show an extreme indolence in filling out and returning the questionnaire. Approximately 50 teachers wrote spontaneously to us for questionnaires; of this number of volunteers, only two returned their answers.

The questionnaires intrusted to academic authorities were distributed among the teachers of elementary schools, and a small number were sent to the principals of nursery schools. Some of the replies were, in a polite form, simple refusals to answer; they were generally worded in the following manner: "No circumstances have permitted me to verify feelings of fear in the children intrusted to my care." Or again: "The principal of the school and her assistants, after having deliberated on the question, agree in affirming that they have never noticed the slightest indication of fear in the students."

Another teacher made the same declaration in terms which deserve to be reproduced: "I never noticed fear in my students. For that matter, of what would they be afraid? Of their teacher? That is outdated. Of the school? It is made as agreeable as possible for them. Of the work? They are instructed while being amused. Of punishments? These are so gentle, so infrequent. No. Right or wrong, the children of today are not afraid; at least, the feeling of fear does not have the chance to manifest itself during school time." Let us salute this happy school and pass on to others.

Several correspondents, without using this as an excuse for not answering, noted with reason that the school, where children are secure and surrounded by their comrades, is not a favorable milieu for the observation of fear. Incontestably, the fathers of these children know more on this point than the teachers, but if one directed a questionnaire on psychology to the fathers, they would not answer it. Furthermore, several of the teachers have families of their own and can note observations made in the home. Others know the parents of the students, receive their confidence, witness intimate scenes, and consequently have all the necessary information; a questionnaire addressed to cooperative teachers is thus not useless. Several, in fact, provided us with observations made outside the school. We received veritable memoirs composed of 10 or 12 pages, written with the calligraphic care which is generally characteristic of teachers. On the average, however, the answers were half a page of printed text in length. It seemed to us that the answers from female teachers were often more detailed, more carefully prepared, if not more intelligent, than those from male teachers. But their reports lacked precision; for the weight and height of the child, the female teacher would be satisfied with saying, "Ordinary weight, very tall," and similar expressions, whereas their male counterparts would generally send us a precise measure in kilograms and centimeters.

Above all, our questionnaire requested the correspondents to send us facts of observation. The majority sent us precise facts, detailed information about children on whom we were given short biographies; some gave us only diffuse observations without adequate specifications. Five or six teachers questioned their students. There were even some who had their children write compositions on the feeling of fear and requested them to describe the conditions under which the sentiment was most strongly felt. These are the best observations. We will contrast them with the answers of correspondents who, not understanding the exact object of our inquiry, sent us a series of moral reflections or a veritable homily more edifying than instructive.

I

Definition of fear

Some correspondents began by remarking, with reason, that before making observations on fear in children, one must define the feeling of fear because it is exemplified in many quite different varieties. A legitimate fear is manifested in the presence or the idea of a real danger, possible or only probable, which permits us to act with prudence. We are not speaking about this natural sentiment, at once reasonable and useful, when we question teachers about fear in children. The concept of fear, as we understand it, is an unreasonable sentiment in the sense that it is applied either to an entirely imaginary danger, such as darkness or phantoms, or to a real but absolutely improbable danger. We recall that, in mental alienation, there is a large category of individuals who are victims of phobias, that is to say, victims of exaggerated fears and repulsions produced by the most varied of objects. One fears being poisoned by the contact of an unclean object, another fears being bitten in the heel by a dog, and a third dares not cross a large deserted square alone. Some of these fears are inspired by completely imaginary dangers. Others represent a potential danger: it is possible to be bitten by a dog, contaminated by the contact of an object, killed in the theater by a falling chandelier, or asphyxiated in a fire. The morbid character of the feeling of fear, in these last cases, is the result of individuals considering as probable, and even imminent, dangers which occur so rarely that a wise and prudent man would not preoccupy himself with them.

The fear that one must seek to correct and to cure in children is thus not a sentiment of legitimate fear. It is an anguish disproportionate to the danger, both when it is a question of an imaginary danger or when it is a question of a possible event, the probability of which is almost nil.

As another approach, one can distinguish between fear and legitimate fearfulness. The latter stimulates the intelligence and augments one's physical strength: one sees the danger, finds a means of protecting oneself, and acts rapidly upon this reflection. Very different are the consequences of fear which depress the individual, temporarily remove from him the faculty of speaking and acting, trouble his mind and memory, and in a word, deprive him of all means of defense.

In children, one must thus develop prudence, an apprehension of legitimate danger, and the presence of mind and judgment to avoid a mishap; but one must also act against fear and attempt to suppress it as much as possible. This is a differentiation upon which everybody will be in agreement.

II

Subjects of fear

A list of objects capable of frightening children would be unending, and we cannot conceive of making a complete enumeration of all the facts presented to us. Some overall views must suffice.

1. One must rank in first place the fear of night or of darkness; the two are almost identical except that night results in both darkness and isolation. The fear of darkness is the typical fear in children. First, it is, so to speak, general, and, if I believe the documents which I have before me, very few children escape it; secondly, the fear of darkness presents a quality of mystery, of the unknown, which gives its own character to the sentiment of fear. How many times has one said to a child who refuses to enter a dark room: "Of what are you afraid?" The child does not know, or rather, he finds it difficult to define clearly what he feels; several of our correspondents noticed this. A child's fear is directed toward things which are poorly understood, ill defined, and mysterious; in one form or another, it is invariably a fear of the unknown. For this reason, perhaps, the fear of darkness is very general. The darkness suppresses the control of visual perceptions and opens the field to the imagination; one can then imagine a crowd of terrible beings since the eyes are unable to contradict these idle fancies.[2]

The fear of darkness is manifested in children in a number of circumstances: When night has fallen, they refuse to leave the house and go into the street or to the country. They refuse to enter the basement without light, or even with light. They refuse to sleep alone, far from their parents. In their beds, they hold their breath and hide entirely under the eiderdown or under the covers.

A large number of other fears, which are really no different from fears of the unknown or the mysterious, must also be placed in the same category as the fear of night. To express the fact that these are produced by imaginary objects, our correspondents refer to them as psychic fears. They are, for example, the fear of masks, of solitude, of phantoms, of the chimney sweep, of the coalman, of wolves (which are the topic of so many children's conversations, without the latter having ever seen any).

2. The second group of fears forms an obvious contrast with the preceding one. These are fears produced by violent noises such as the detonation of firearms, the sound of a firecracker, the cracking of thunder, the opening of a bottle of lemon soda or champagne.

---

[2] A little girl who is in the habit of telling stories to her sister at night after the lights are out, said spontaneously to me that, in the darkness, she imagines she sees the things she is describing. This is certainly an excellent example of the clarity which the imagination acquires in the dark.

Although these fears are frequent among girls, small boys are not exempt from them. Their fright is of a peculiar nature; it is produced by the idea of a detonation, which, in itself, causes only a slightly disagreeable sensation of trembling and a short inhalation. When one prepares to fire a pistol in front of a child, he will plug his ears with fright, but most often he knows that he is not in any danger. In any case, he would experience only a slight jolt; his fear is as devoid as possible of any frightening physical consequences. It is clearly distinguished from the fear of darkness and fear of the unknown.

3. Fears in which the dominant sentiment is that of disgust or repulsion, such as fear of small animals, of rats, of caterpillars, of spiders, of blood, of corpses, etc.

Example: "I have seen a small girl who, up to the age of nine years, cried out with fright and trembled with her entire body whenever she saw a mouse. The cover of a notebook engraved with a mouse would produce almost the same effect."

A second observation can further serve as a typical example: "One of my own daughters, who is now 17 years old, evidenced from her youngest childhood great fright at the sight of a snail. The sight of the shell, even empty, or the sight of any other mollusk made such an impression on her that her mother and I were forced to take many precautions to avoid a nervous crisis which might lead to convulsions. As the child grew up, the intensity of her fright remained constant. We appealed to her judgment in trying to persuade her that a snail is in no way horrible. Nothing helped; she could not even glance through the pages of a book in which there were sketches for fear of encountering a snail. Today, through a great effort of will, she is able to view a picture of the animal or the animal itself, but she remains unable to touch one. By contrast, she was hardly ever afraid of the dark as a certain number of children are."

4. An exaggerated fear of possible danger; these fears, on the whole, are the most reasonable of all. For example, fear of encountering a drunken man or a beggar or an individual with a questionable demeanor along the road; fear of being attacked by a dog; fear at night of thieves hidden under the bed, behind the curtains, or in the closets. These fears are produced by the imagination, but they are not entirely imaginary fears. The following case can also be placed in this category:

"A child, aged 10, suddenly left his seat during a reading lesson and ran to the teacher, crying in a frightened voice, 'I'm going to die! I'm going to die!' He could barely hold himself up and his face expressed great terror. He had eaten some hot bread and was simply experiencing the discomfort which accompanies indigestion. Some months later, the situation recurred under these circumstances: I had just recommended to the children that they refrain from going into a neighboring village where diphtheria had appeared. Again, the same child suddenly left his seat, brought his hand to his throat, and cried, 'I'm going to die!' He imagined having the disease we had just spoken of. The first time the other students had been frightened; this time, however, they responded to their comrade's cry with a burst of laughter, instantly curing the fearful one of his malady. The child's parents noted the same thing happening, especially at night. Whenever the child was somewhat indisposed, a fear of darkness or of death was often manifested." The fear of dying seems rare in children; it was only noted three times in our inquiries.

5. Fears which result from the memory of a terrible accident. One child becomes fearful following a deep cut; another, having missed being knocked down by a bicycle, trembles when crossing a busy street and wants to be held by the hand; another, having narrowly missed drowning in a river, is afraid of water and manages never to pass near the river; another, aged two, is surprised by a dog who puts its paws on his shoulders, and from that day on, has an extraordinary fear of dogs. Certainly, many fears or instinctive repugnances found in certain adults come from such childhood impressions.

To evaluate the relative importance of these different types of fears, one can consult the results of a school experiment. As a composition topic, a class of 28 students was asked to relate the strongest fear they had ever experienced. The teacher who read the papers sent us the following conclusions:

"Seven recounted fears caused during the night or during the day by a more or less real danger such as a dog, a bull, a drunken man who followed them; or else by an accident, a fall into water, a persistent nose bleed.

"Thirteen were afraid of a supposed danger: an unexpected encounter, the night, the rustling of branches, a shadow mistaken for a criminal, the clap of thunder, surprise caused by a practical joker.

"Only four found the subject of fright within their imaginations: one was afraid of the bogeyman, another of Father Fouettard accompanying St. Nicholas, the third was frightened by a wolf, and the fourth was frightened simply by spending the night near a fir plantation.

"Two confused fear with the anxiety they experienced when they were lost.

"Finally, two others confused it with the fear of a merited punishment."

If one adds up the fears of the imagination, one can see that there are 17 of these and consequently a majority.

III

Signs of fear

Even though the observations are numerous, I do not think that they add anything essential to what is already known about signs of fear. I have just read Darwin's book on the expression of emotion in which he enumerates all the effects indicated by our correspondents. These effects can be divided into three groups:

1. *Means of defense*. Flight in great haste, flight toward the person capable of defending the child, gestures and attitudes taken to avoid a blow or a threat. It is worth noting that observations on these different points are very scanty, which seems to indicate that when the child's fear becomes extreme, it removes from him the faculty of defending himself and of protecting himself by adaptive acts.

2. *Expressive signs of fear*. Crying and trembling throughout the body are the two signs most often indicated; next in order of frequency come paleness of the face, alteration of facial traits, dilation of the eyes, suspension of breathing, palpitations, crying. None of this, we repeat, is either new or interesting; the only fact worth noting is the order of importance of these phenomena, which comes from the fact that the signs indicated most often are crying, trembling, and paling.

3. *Phenomena of paralysis*. These are noted almost as often as signs of expression. In the most simple form, they are reflected in immobility. The frightened child remains immobile. In the evening, when somebody tells a frightening story, he does not dare to budge from his chair. If he is surprised by some phenomenon which frightens him, he remains glued to the spot. A child sent to the school play-

ground at night sees two men; struck by terror, he remains standing in the middle of the court, incapable of taking a step. A five-year-old child is surprised by a tramway in the middle of the road; neither the cries of the passengers nor those of the coachman can move him away; he remains glued to the spot until a passerby grabs him. Not only do the children lose their ability to walk, they become speechless as well. They cannot pronounce a single word, and there is even a momentary loss of memory; the confusion comes from their perceptions. This mutism is observed during the examinations of some very timid children. Finally, the extreme form is fainting, which was observed several times during anguish over the fear of an operation, for example, revaccination.

"For two hours, a nine-year-old child remained like a wet cloth, almost speechless, her eyes haggard, after her companions recounted the story of a severe wound to the wrist."

In a large number of observations, we saw convulsions, aggression, fainting, at times even rather lengthy illnesses, come after fear. For example:

"A child, having learned that someone was hung in the woods near the village, wished to see this person. He became very frightened and returned to the class trembling. For the remainder of the day, he retained the impression of this fright and was unable to attend to his work. The following day he appeared calmer, and there was no external sign to indicate that his fright would have any disturbing consequences.

"Nonetheless, a short time later he cried out suddenly in class and was seized by convulsions. After a few minutes, he regained his composure but was trembling so violently that he could no longer stand up. Another day he complained quite suddenly of severe pains in his thumb and hand; he then became weak and for several minutes cried and rolled about as he had done the first time. Fear had caused a nervous reaction; prior to this time, he had never experienced anything similar. His parents have taken care of him, and since then (this was eight years ago) he has not undergone another crisis. He remains intelligent and has enjoyed excellent health."

I will also quote, as a singular fact, the following example of mutism produced by fear. It should be noted that fear can produce either mutism—observed often during examinations—or excessive loquacity, just as it produces either paling or reddening. Here is a fairly rare case of mutism:

"A 12-year-old and his younger brother had walked to school each day for a year. The older child talked along the way, but became completely mute when he approached the school; he could not be made to say a word or even to accept a gift. All day he remained stationary with his arms folded and refused to do any work. The only thing he enjoyed was gymnastics. He did not participate during recreation nor speak to anyone; and when it was time to go home, he hurried to get his basket and overcoat."

IV

State of health of fearful children

As to the state of health of fearful children, our correspondents gave us precise information only rarely because they lacked medical knowledge; their responses, nevertheless, contain some useful suggestions. We will divide these into three principal categories:

1. Some teachers told us of tragic accidents in which children were the victims (an accident in a car, peril at sea, etc.) and reported that, following the terror, these children became seriously ill. Many were required to rest in bed for several days and even months; others manifested nervous illnesses, those most often cited being chorea and epilepsy.

2. The teachers described in their own words the state of health of the most fearful children. Some of them presented no notable characteristic; some were even robust in appearance; most often, however, they were of an inferior muscular strength as compared with the average and had a nervous temperament. Here are some random descriptions: small and delicate; good health but delicate complexion; sickly and nervous; delicate, nervous, impressionable, muscle strength below average, anemic; not good in gymnastics; etc. Certainly the repetition contained in these descriptions is significant, and until we receive information to the contrary, we will assume that the particularly frightened child is a debilitated child. Teachers often use the word "nervous" without specifying precisely what they mean. But a nervous child, most probably, is one with a mobile physiognomy, one who is easily fatigued and easily excited, one whose mood fluctuates, and one who is incapable of long and sustained effort.

According to several teachers, fear is related to the physical constitution of the child in two ways: First, fear is a consequence of a weak nervous system; and second, the child who is conscious of his physical weakness loses confidence in himself and thus becomes more susceptible to a variety of fears.

Here is one observation among many which indicates the influence of illness:

"A child of 11 had typhoid fever. Before his illness, he was decisive and courageous; afterwards, he became timid and fearful. Fear had made him so sensitive and unlike his former self that, whether or not his teacher threatened him with a slight punishment, he would attempt to save himself by running headlong from the school and remaining in the fields until forced to come back."

V

Intellectual characteristics of fearful children

Two propositions summarize the responses collected on this subject: First, there is no correlation between fear and intelligence; and second, children with vivid imaginations are predisposed to fear. It should be noted that these two conclusions were not given in response to a precise question; the question was broadly stated as simply, "What is the character of fearful children?"

1. A sufficiently precise indicator of a child's intelligence is provided by his rank in class. On this point, the child's teacher is better informed that his father, first, because he has a broader basis of comparison, and second, because he is not biased by his affection. It is evident that if fathers had answered our questionnaire, they would have had a tendency to place the intelligence of their children above the average; we have several example of this. It is true that rank in class perhaps does not give an exact measure of intelligence, since it is obtained not only by intelligence but by work, that is, by willingness; the approximation, however, is sufficient to satisfy us.

One could suppose a priori that fear, being an unreasonable sentiment, must be manifested above all in children who lack good sense and judgment. The one or two teachers who suggested this deduction presented it, furthermore, as a deduction rather than as an observation. Generally speaking, the teachers were not in agreement on this point. Some said that the fearful children they observed belonged in the second half of the class; others placed them among their best students. It was not rare for a teacher to write: "The best student in my class is the most fearful." Others, finally, ranked the fearful children among those of average intelligence. Some of these different responses were given in general terms; others were more precise, providing the child's initials and some special information. In compiling the responses, I was unable to verify any one trend. In two of the departments, the observations on fearful children were divided as follows: 30 children of above average intelligence, 23 of average intelligence, and 24 of below average intelligence.

These figures indicate that children subject to fear are not distinguished from others on the basis of intelligence. Approximately 15 teachers came to the same conclusion after fairly extensive observation. "I have courageous children in the lowest ranks," said one teacher, "and I have fearful children in the highest." Said another, "Nothing marked nor general as to rank." "I have fearful children who are intelligent and others who are idiots," said another, with this use of the personal pronoun which is so frequent among teachers and leaders.

This negative conclusion is in agreement with my personal observations. I have known quick-witted, alert young girls with a good deal of common sense who are tormented by ridiculous fears; they are the first ones to laugh at them while continuing to tremble. These facts, taken in their generality, show us that intelligence and emotions can be independent of one another. Evidently, this independence is not a general and absolute law, since some individuals, thanks to their intelligence, can dominate their emotions. In others, there are a number of subtle and complex reactions between emotion and thought. We are not trying to cast doubt upon this order of phenomena, the analysis of which has often tempted moralists. What we wish to affirm is that fear is not exclusive to unintelligent children; it is not proof of intellectual mediocrity: intelligence and fear are independently developed in children.[3]

2. In regard to the intelligence of fearful children, teachers often remarked that it is a vivid and precocious intelligence; furthermore, a large number affirmed, without being prompted by any precise question from us, that fearful children have a vivid imagination, making them appear to have an intelligence above the average.

This affirmation emerges from the overall observations with startling clarity, but it is really no surprise. Upon reflection, we can see

---

[3] The popular opinion reflected here was found to be in disagreement with the results of our inquiry. One often hears of fearful ones being accused of stupidity.

that feelings of fear are above all excited by imaginary dangers; even when they arise out of real, impending dangers, like falling from a precipice or being crushed on the road, imagination plays a part in depicting the consequences of the accident, the pain, the blood. As a result, children who have a vivid and prompt imagination are prone to fear because they are better able to picture the real or imaginary objects capable of frightening them. There seems to be a direct relation here—an interdependence between an intellectual function and a state of feeling.

Making use of my personal observations, I will now permit myself to correct this proposition somewhat. I studied at length two little sisters who, even though raised in the same environment, present some curious differences of character. One, the younger, has a more vivid imagination than the other. This is not a subjective, false impression; it is a fact of observation. Every night for years, when the two children were settled in their twin beds, the younger would recount the continuation of an unending story which she invented as she went along and which the older one listened to religiously. I have often encouraged the older child to tell stories, but her inventions are dry, short, without conviction. Her mind has developed in another direction; she is serious, reasonable, with considerable power of attention. Here, then, are two children whose imaginative capacities are quite different. Finally, a very instructive fact, attested by daily observation: the younger is bolder and more courageous than the elder.

I do not think that this is an isolated case; I collected another observation of the same type. Since I attach great importance to facts that I am able to verify with my own eyes, I am led to doubt that there is a constant relationship between the development of imagination and the feeling of fear. One might interpret the almost unanimous responses of our correspondents in the following manner: A child is not fearful solely because he is highly imaginative; imagination is not the direct cause, but rather plays the role of a resonance box. It amplifies the feeling of fear and feeds it with all the terrible objects a vivid imagination can so easily represent. A fearful child whose imagination is poor and limited would have less occasion to be frightened: he would be less easily taken by the contagion of example. In any case, fear is a sentiment which originates elsewhere, in an ill-defined, or perhaps undefinable, physiological weakness.

We will say, in summary, that 1) fear in children is not related to the development of intelligence, and 2) it is augmented by a vivid imagination.

VI

Moral character of fearful children

This question provoked no precise responses, or rather, it provoked such a large number of different responses that it is impossible for us to discover the slightest unity amid this diversity. If we use only the documents we now have in our hands, we will be unable to trace the moral character of the fearful child. Here, as an example, are some of the teachers' evaluations of the fearful children they studied: sweet and timid character; fearful, timid, yet violent and obstinate; sweet character, lacks initiative, is easily led; sad and taciturn character; suspicious, cowardly, sometimes cruel; credulous; imaginative; emotional; inconsistent, passing from laughter to tears; proud, irritable; reserved; timid; indecisive; sweet, good, compassionate; good; indecisive, very irritable character.

If one considers that each of these epithets was carefully thought out and accurately describes each child, then one must conclude that all fearful children do not have the same moral character; nor is there anything characteristic of this range of ideas. At the very most, one could remark that sweetness and timidity are the two traits which appear most frequently in these observations.

VII

What is the proportion of fearful children?

If a question were badly posed, it must truly be this one; our correspondents did not fail to notice it. They were quite right. It is impossible to determine the proportion of fearful children since this number would vary according to certain influences one cannot measure: education, environment, ambient ideas, and especially the moral character of the observer. The latter cannot fathom the extent of the child's fear except in relation to his own ideas and temperament; a teacher who is strong and courageous to the point of indifference would not make the same judgment as one of his more gentle and sensitive colleagues. Let us hasten to add, however, that we should not carry this scruple too far. Our question, such as it is, can give useful information. In everyday practice, an inspector asks a teacher, "Do your students work? Are you satisfied with your class?" No matter how the personality of the teacher affects his answer, the inspector can be certain that it is not totally erroneous and contains some worthwhile information. There is a high probability that a class of dunces will not satisfy any teacher and that a class of model students will satisfy almost all of them.

Let us note, first of all, that according to unanimous opinion, all the children know fear to some degree; all children, regardless of their health and physical constitution, are afraid of something. The feeling of fear is a normal part of the psychology of a child and in some way expresses the weakness of his body. It should be remarked that a child resembles a woman more than an adult man by the graceful form of his body, by his voice, by the partial development of his hair, etc., and that he resembles her equally in emotional aspects, being inclined toward fear. Thus, all children are fearful. Those who are sickly and are gifted with vivid imaginations, have more difficulty dispelling these feelings, which is a sign of weakness; in others, fear gradually fades with age, with acquired experience, and with the development of physical strength. Aging, in many cases, constitutes the best treatment of fear—the most simple and the most natural.

Some teachers tried to determine the exact beginning and end of childhood fears. Several school principals thought that two-year-old children were not fearful and that this feeling did not develop until about age three. I am quoting averages here, because the ages which were indicated varied a little. Furthermore, fear begins to decrease fairly rapidly between the ninth and twelfth years.

I think that one can make some remarks relative to the first appearance of fear. It does not seem definite to me that children are never accessible to fear before the age of two. Furthermore, one must agree that the fear of danger generally remains undeveloped until the child has experienced such danger and can forsee it and represent it to himself. Many young children remain insensitive to danger through ignorance or through insufficient mental development.

We must still describe the direct response we received to our question: What is the proportion of fearful children? Our correspondents provided two types of answers. Sometimes they indicated only a number without other commentary; sometimes they replied in detail.

The proportion of fearful children varied from 1 in 30 to 10 in 30. This variation, in itself, is sufficient to show that our question lacked precision. Maintaining the most frequent response,[4] the proportion of 3 in 30 indicates the number of fearful children, that is, those who are so fearful that they constitute exceptional cases, that they are, as one teacher says, "true martyrs." Other teachers, as we said, made slightly more precise answers. "Ten children in 30 (from 8 to 13 years) admit that they are afraid to go out at night for fear of encountering thieves." "More than 40 students out of 56 say that they won't go to a cemetery at night for fear of ghosts and phantoms." "Out of 30 students, 9 will not leave their homes at night and do not dare to sleep without their parents beside them." "Only 5 out of 150 can go to a cemetery or to any isolated place during the night. One child cannot spend the night alone in a room," etc.

Although these different responses are more interesting than a simple proportion, they have the fault of containing evaluations which do not rest upon direct observation. Seemingly, the teacher was satisfied with questioning the students and did not subject them to a test. Is there possibly some test, some experience free of serious danger, which would measure the students' courage in some way? M. Thamin was kind enough to suggest one to me which he was going to use on his own children: Have them jump from the top of a flight of stairs; the number of steps, or the height of the jump, varies with the age of the child, his height, and also shows his bravery.

The study of the proportion of fearful children permits a comparison between the sexes. Comparing the responses of male and female teachers, one finds a most curious difference.[5] The proportion of 3 in 30 indicated above refers to boys; the average proportion for girls is much higher, 10 in 30. If we are to believe these figures, there are about three times as many fearful girls as boys.[6]

To end this section, let me reiterate that the information we have just summarized lacks precision and consists simply of ideas for further study.

---

[4] I use the most frequent answer rather than the mean, because the latter is too much influenced by the divergence of opinion.

[5] [In France, the men teach boys and the women, girls.]

[6] The most important difference between the two sexes is not the degree of fear, but rather the fact that men are ashamed of being fearful whereas women acknowledge it openly—a circumstance which must influence the development of this feeling.

VIII

Causes of fear

Contagion. Of all the observations we received, the fact of capital importance is that fear is one of the most contagious of feelings; fear, a teacher says, is as contagious as laughter or giggling. In these studies, fear and laughter offer great analogies. Several principals of primary and nursery schools gave almost identical descriptions of their students' state of mind during a violent storm; this little scene, which we will now summarize, shows the influence of contagion.

At a girls school, one day during class, lightning struck very near the buildings and a furious rain invaded the court. Instinctively, all the pupils turned toward the teacher and fixed their eyes upon her, not only to ask for help and protection, but in some fashion to consult her about whether they should be frightened. At this moment, the teacher was clearly aware of the fact that her attitude would determine the feelings of her students. If she succeeded in maintaining her composure, the children would quickly become confident and once again be calm.

At a nursery school, workers were looking for a gas leak; about 50 students watched quietly as they worked. A small explosion occurred. The children looked at the teacher, who very calmly ordered a servicewoman to close the gas outlet. The latter cried out in fright and gave all indications of genuine fear, which all the children immediately shared.

Two types of contagion are exerted upon a child. One is contagion in the presence of danger. It is communicated by gestures, by expressions of the physiognomy; it is a sudden contagion which produces, by direct imitation, an epidemic of fear comparable to epidemics of nervous illness, chorea, and convulsions. There is also the slow, secret, sly contagion from everyday conversation and examples. When one is not yet 10 years old, said one teacher, one cannot see people being frightened without becoming frightened oneself. Children, these young logicians, must think: "My parents are afraid, therefore there is some danger to be feared." Of this last type of contagion, we could cite many examples which are of a curious uniformity. Here is an extremely frequent example of contagion from one child to another: A small girl, living for only 15 days with a friend who was afraid of the dark, soon experienced this same fear, although she had not known it beforehand. Here is another observation:

"A child of four had never paid attention to the darkness and remained alone when she was put to bed (without light). While spending a month's vacation in the country, she saw girls of 12 and 14 years refuse to go to bed alone or to walk in the garden at night. On returning to Paris, she demanded that the door be left open onto a lighted room and was unwilling to go on an errand in the next room under the pretext that she could not find anything without light, etc. Without ever admitting that she was afraid, she showed it. She had not heard fear spoken about, but she had seen it."

Young girls who have brothers are much braver than those who do not have any.

Some correspondents thought that the least endowed children were the ones most susceptible to contagion by example.

Overexcited imagination. The recounting of a frightening or dramatic story maintains fear and predisposes one to it. Here are some observations:

"I have seen my own children (two girls of 7 and 9 years), after telling of sad or tragic events, dream with cries, tears, painful oppression, etc., during the night. To restore tranquility to their sleep, I was forced to stop reading them stories (with somewhat gloomy episodes) before sending these two little scatterbrains with too vivid imaginations to bed. Thanks to my efforts, the dreams disappeared, but a relapse would occur if a suggestive question was raised during the evening. A final example: The theatrical performance of *Michel Strogoff* unnerved my children to the greatest possible extent."

From another correspondent:

"A five-year-old child, who, up to that time, was not easily frightened, became fearful following a story told at nursery school in which monsters and especially men with horses' heads appeared; it took several years to free her from the idea of these monsters, which obsessed her even during the day and which gave her nightmares each night."

Here is another observation of exactly the same type—a type of observation which is extremely frequent:

"I was able to verify fear in my little girl—at the time she was seven—following a story about ghosts told in class in a township I used to live in. That night, about one hour after going to bed, she called out for me. She was the victim of convulsive trembling, her eyes were haggard, and she did not want me to leave her, as she was afraid that someone would come and take her away. She finally went to sleep again, but several times during the night let out sharp cries occasioned by the vision of the ghosts who wanted to capture her. In the days that followed, she did not cry anymore at night, but she refused to go into the next room or into the dark courtyard alone."

Heredity. The influence of heredity on the development of fear, like all questions relative to psychological heredity, can give rise to numerous discussions, and it is difficult to arrive at any conclusion. I gave up the idea of dealing with the subject in its entirety, and I will be satisfied with extracting from our documents some propositions which appear to be very well demonstrated.

The first of these propositions is the following: Of two brothers from the same family and with similar upbringing, one was courageous, the other fearful. At least 20 observers affirmed this. If the environment in which the children were raised is visibly the same, then the difference must be innate. Thus, there is a predisposition acquired by the child at birth. Where does this predisposition come from? It might be the result of an influence exercised on the child by its mother or by exterior agents during pregnancy. Then it is not a question of heredity. It might also be that certain ways of feeling and reacting have been transmitted to the child by his ancestors.

We have found several instances where calm, courageous parents were distressed to find that they had fearful children. But this does not disprove hereditary transmission for several easily understood reasons. A child does not necessarily summarize the dispositions of all his ancestors, but only those of a few. It can happen that a child inherits certain moral dispositions from a distant relative in the same way that he sometimes inherits facial features or certain bad habits.

On the other hand, several examples of fearful parents having equally fearful children were reported to us. Due to the lack of close observation, these facts do not prove very much because it is possible that the parents have transmitted their dispositions by other than hereditary means—by education and by example.

One can see how many difficulties are raised by the question of psychological heredity. The negative cases do not prove anything; the positive cases can often be explained by influences other than heredity.

Bad treatment. Our correspondents report that several children are daily witnesses to the mistreatment of their mother by a brutal father; these children carry the marks of sadness and especially of fright on their faces.

"I have a child who is frequently beaten by his family; no teacher can approach him without his raising his arms as if to protect himself, instinctively moved by his fear of mistreatment. Others are frightened at home by threats of police, prison, wolves, bogeymen, etc.; their fear shows as soon as these words are pronounced in front of them, even in the form of a simple explanation."

Another observation:

"When I began at Chateau-Landon, some of the children raised their hands when I came upon them quickly to see if they were doing the work I had assigned. These fearful movements did not last more than a short time, the children recognizing rapidly that I did not make use of corporal punishment."

Here is another entirely typical observation:

"I have known only one truly fearful child. She lived with her parents in an isolated house near the woods. The father, whimsical and brutal—and certainly not the least bit fearful—had terrorized his daughter to the extent that she fled every human being, probably thinking that everyone wished to hurt her. Even the seamstress had a great deal of difficulty when the child was trying on a dress.

"When she was taken to school for the first time, Jeannett was nine years old. At first, I could not get anything out of her; when I approached her, she withdrew. She did not flee from her new companions, but as to drawing one word out of her? Impossible, to such an extent that she appeared dumb.

"I observed her a great deal, but without her noticing so that I wouldn't frighten her. I saw immediately that the child was not without intelligence, but that her ideas about people led her to keep herself apart. Her sad air, her large eyes which spoke very well indeed, indicated the road to be followed.

"Initially, I pretended to pay no attention to her; I even avoided approaching her. On the third day, her eyes, which at first fled mine, began to search for them and the first crossing of our glances indicated that I had won her. It is useless to relate all the phases of this battle against an aversion occasioned by fright. I will say only that a short time later the young girl spoke to me, sat on my lap, caressed me spontaneously, and even played a little with her companions. To her parents and to many others, this indeed seemed prodigious: the child who otherwise did not open her mouth at home spoke often of her teacher and companions. Nonetheless, it was quite simple: One draws more flies with honey than with vinegar. What is more surprising, in my opinion, is that a father can raise his child in such a fashion.

"Seeing the result, he began to understand; but the child did not always allow him to caress her. What grief for a father! But he wished it so.

"This child had at least ordinary intelligence and was very careful. Four or five months later, she knew her phonics and didn't write too badly.

"Moved at that time; I could not continue the experiment." (Madame Dubreuil)

IX

Treatment of fear[7]

Our question on the treatment of fear, primarily a pedagogical question, inspired the greatest number of judicious remarks and useful advice from the teachers. A very small number refused to answer, supplying only such vague information as: "One must speak to the child's reason, to its good sense," or "Science will destroy our superstitions."

First, is it practically possible to cure all fearful children? No one dares to suppose this. One must make distinctions among children. Teachers agree that the treatment is very long and very difficult, and to be successful one must have the simultaneous cooperation of both the teacher and the parents; the role of the latter is most important since the parents are constantly with the children. With a great amount of energy and perseverance, it is possible in most cases to diminish the feeling of fear. As to suppressing it completely, this is rather rare. Many teachers have remarked that fear differs from one child to the next not only in degree but in nature. Three principal cases have been distinguished:

1. In certain children, fear is the expression of a state of weakness of the nervous system; these children need not only the help of the teacher but the opinion of a doctor.

---

[7] Rousseau, l'Emile, (11th ed.). Several teachers have probably been inspired by this book.

2. In other children, fear, even though it is produced by a natural predisposition, is precipitated by external causes such as a terrible accident or mistreatment, and most often by stories, by fantastic or frightening fables. These children will more easily be cured by a purely mental treatment than the first kind.

3. A certain degree of fear is encountered in almost all young children and is a normal part of child psychology; it is not necessary to deal with it seriously. The majority of these childhood fears disappear with age; it has been remarked that time, in certain cases, is a more effective cure than all others.

Without attaching a great importance to these distinctions, which were formulated more clearly by us than by the teachers, we think, nevertheless, that they correspond to the practical realities of daily life.

The mental treatment of fear must be both preventative and curative. The preventative treatment includes a collection of ways to prohibit the development of fear. The curative treatment opposes a declared and admitted fear.

One rule dominates the entire question: The methods of treatment vary with the child and with the environment. We will be content with general reflections, which will have to be adapted to the particular circumstance being dealt with.

What I find striking about the treatment of fear is that absolutely *all* the teachers are in agreement in condemning those remedies which come naturally to the mind of one who has not thought sufficiently about them. It is quite probable that this negative treatment is the most important of all, and that it is very useful to know what one must not do. Hasn't it been noted that the most effective role of medicine consists in discarding all harmful techniques?

Never employ corporal punishment, threats, or mockery. One must inflexibly proscribe violence against fearful children—violence in all its forms, both mental and physical. Does a child refuse to go into a dark place, to go down the basement, or to run an errand in the garden? One must not, at any price, coerce him with threats, much less strike him for his disobedience. Such brutal punishments are used by the majority of parents, who too often have a tendency to strike a child that resists them or to force him to perform an act which he refuses to do.

I see two principal reasons which might explain these deplorable habits: 1) Physical punishment can be given without taking the trouble to think. A child has lied, been lazy, stolen, or been rude, and one strikes him. Instead of considering what provoked him, instead of seeking the motive powers which should be used on him, one employs an expedient which requires no effort of reasoning. It is by laziness of the mind that one is brutal, unless it is by default of intelligence, as with the inferiors, the domestics. 2) There is a second reason, perhaps even less admitted to than the first: One is brutal because one is addressing a defenseless being. Every day we experience certain feelings of anger and indignation toward our equals which prudence compels us to repress, because we have before us individuals capable of returning material acts for material acts. We do not go to the limit of these violent feelings, the evident and logical consequences of which are to strike, as various photographs expressing emotion can show us. However, when it is a child who has aroused our anger, we do not view him as an individual to be feared, capable of returning pain for pain. In many cases, then, a parent strikes a child out of a feeling of impunity and security.

To prove that corporal punishment is not a good remedy against fear, it suffices to recall that children mistreated by their parents live in continual terror, and that those accustomed to being struck by their teachers raise their hands above their heads as soon as they are approached a little brusquely.

Violence should not be used against fear, nor should one respond to it with laughter or mockery. This, again, is one of the points on which all teachers without exception are in agreement. The reasons for these prohibitions seem to be the following: Fear is a depressive feeling which develops especially in puny, weak children and which expresses either an overexcited imagination or a weak will, and often both at once. The fearful child is one who lacks mental strength. Now, the purpose of a thorough education is to augment the child's strength as much as possible, to make him more powerful, and consequently, to develop in him potent sentiments with which he can fight against fear and counterbalance its effects. Can corporal punishment, threats, mockery, produce these modifications of character? It is quite evident that they cannot; they are, to the highest degree, depressive measures which only diminish the mental energy of a weak child. If absolutely necessary, one could say that in some cases, especially with well-fed, healthy children, corporal punishment can awaken strong feelings of anger, rebellion, and hatred; similarly, mockery, by exciting one's self-respect, awakens it and gives it a surplus of force. This psychological reaction, however, will not occur in a weak child, and thus one must not provoke him at random.

Suppress the circumstances which cause fear in the child. If there is a rule of good sense, it is clearly this one: One should always attempt to lessen the child's fear. It is necessary, first, to suppress its habitual causes so that the child may lose the habit of fear. To this end, one must first direct one's thoughts to contagion by example. Contagion is one of the most widespread and potent causes; fear, one correspondent remarked, is as contagious as laughter, and these two studies have many points in common.

We have read and quoted several examples of courageous children, who, after visiting with fearful comrades or witnessing their terrors, are overcome by panic and manifest the same feelings. The cowardice of parents has the same effect. In such cases, a change of environment is imperative. The teachers think that fear by contagion is not as lasting or as deep as spontaneous fear, and that it is easily dismissed. One should see to it that the child is not terrified at a young age by fantastic or superstitious stories, the tradition of which is unfortunately not yet lost; domestics, friends, and grandparents should be sharply warned against this. One should not take children to wakes. One should proscribe not only the telling of detailed stories, but also threats of imaginary danger (wolves, police chiefs, etc.) —threats which are so often used to obtain obedience and peace. In a word, one should attempt to suppress all fears by suggestion.

This is not yet sufficient. Measures should be taken so that the child will not have the opportunity to be frightened rightly or wrongly. One should prohibit those games which consist of hiding behind a door and appearing suddenly to surprise the child who passes—small mockeries which at school are exercised most often against children of known cowardice. Similarly, one should avoid sending the child on roads where he might encounter drunkards or into a basement where there are rats. During the duration of the treatment, fear should be avoided; as with a nervous illness, all excitement which might lead to a crisis is avoided.

Do not overexcite the imagination. Many terrors have children's imaginations as their unique source; to avoid these terrors, one must give no fuel to the imagination, but on the contrary, control it by placing the child in a tranquil atmosphere and by avoiding excitement through stories, read or told, or theatrical representations.

"It was observed," wrote one of our correspondents, "that the fearful, when they are secure, take delight in the most frightening details. One should refrain from telling stories which might stimulate their nervousness, whether these be fictitious (fairy tales, ghost stories) or historic (stories about martyrs, tortures during the Middle Ages, etc.) or real (accidents on the railroad, explosions in the mines). If these facts are mentioned, all details should be omitted." (Fontaine) In two little girls, aged 7 and 9, a bedtime story about sad or tragic events resulted in a night of bad dreams; the suppression of these stories brought back calm.

Thus, through patience and daily study, one must eliminate from the child's experiences anything which might create feelings of fear, either directly or indirectly; one's objective is to help the child lose the habit of fear.

Restore the child's self-confidence. This is simply a complement of the ideas we just developed. One not only removes all occasions which might prompt fear, but one prevents it from existing in the child's mind in the form of a memory and a judgment; one should see to it that the child is unaware of his cowardice. At the moment when the child first manifests fear, one should neither comment upon his attitude nor, above all, bring it to his attention; if he is being watched, he should not perceive that his cowardice has been recognized and judged. His confidences should neither be accepted nor provoked, and one should never force the child to admit that he has been frightened or to recount the impressions he may have experienced. In all cases, it is necessary to prevent the child's attention from becoming fixed on states of consciousness which one is attempting to eliminate. One would commit a major error in having him admit that he was trembling, that he lacked presence of mind, etc.

We are obviously far from the practice of confession. Confession, which is a grave and solemn form of confidence and which was imposed by certain religions as a form of expiation, may have certain advantages in circumstances we have not examined; but according to the responses of the teachers, it seems established that as far as fear is concerned, confession should be rejected.

One should, on the contrary, tactfully try to persuade the child that he is not afraid and to put him above himself by evidencing confidence in him. With a little skill, one should be able to convince him that he is brave in circumstances arranged without his knowledge. He will be made to feel that he is considered a courageous child and his self-esteem will thus be elevated. One correspondent advised making the child fight with stronger comrades who were ordered to allow themselves to be beaten.

Progressive training in courageous acts.[8] This is the main aspect of the treatment. Before, we were talking about treatment through words and advice; now it is a question of practical experiments, of acts the child is led to execute. A difficult job, a job requiring tact, moderation, gentleness; in the hands of an unskilled person, the treatment could aggravate the malady instead of curing it.

Our objective is to familiarize the child with the thing he is afraid of. At the moment of crisis, when his terror is at its peak, the time is not right for intervention. It is best to wait for calm to be restored and to proceed always with extreme gentleness. The treatment must be confined to a person who has been able to inspire the child's absolute confidence.

How can this person lead the child to accomplish some act which he is afraid of? First, by appealing to his common sense, by instructing him, by forcing him to get a clear idea of things. When the danger is real, one explains to the child that fear paralyzes his resources, reduces him to a state of weakness, and consequently prevents him fighting against the danger. When the danger is imaginary, it should be explained to him with calm and assurance. One tries to convince him of his error, to help him put his finger on the cause of the delusion. Most often, however, addressing oneself to the child's reason is not enough; one must use all of his strong feelings, self-esteem, emulation, by mentioning his comrades and by never seeming to doubt him. The educator should reflect an absolute calm, not only in his words, but especially in his tranquil and natural attitude. He must practice what he preaches; what one does speaks louder than what one says. For this reason, at school and at parties, one must flee the company of fearful children so that the child is not affected by the contagion of example. Fearful children should be surrounded by troops of children who have given proof of their courage.

The educator should govern the child in somewhat the same manner that one would break a young colt who was afraid of everything—

[8] On this point, consult *l'Emile* by Rousseau.

that is, by soothing him and by leading him toward that which frightens him. If a child is afraid of a mask, show it to him, make him touch it, put it on his face, have him look in a mirror. If he is afraid of a small, inoffensive animal, a slug, mouse, or worm, place it in front of him, hold it a moment in the hand, explain the nature and habits of the animal, and then bring the child, without rushing him, to look closely at the small animal. On another occasion, have him touch the object, and he will eventually hold it himself, yielding to the example set by his teachers, his comrades, or his parents. One of our correspondents suggests that the child should be amused with small toys representing these animals and giving the illusion of the living animal.

The fear which occurs during physical exercises can be efficiently defeated by graduated exercises in gymnastics. The children must also be encouraged to participate in games in order to develop their nimbleness and their will.

"At Marcilly-sur-Seine, the children, accustomed to traveling through the woods and riding on boats, are generally less fearful than children of other villages who have neither woods nor river."

We have spoken at length of fears produced in children when no real danger threatens; these are caused by silence, darkness, isolation. The fear of darkness, above all, seems to be almost universal in young children.[9] It should be fought chiefly through practical experience. You do not reason with the the child who is afraid of the dark; you take him into it often, but you proceed carefully, one step at a time, guarding against the remedy itself producing a wild terror. Go into the room first at twilight, holding the child by the hand; have him notice that despite the decrease in light, all objects remain in place and no important changes have occurred. Then, sometime later, still holding him by the hand, lead the child into a darker room, into a corridor, or into the basement. Go to the country after dark, or else remain outside long enough to be caught by nightfall during a walk. One should attempt to distract the child, to speak about other things so that he does not think of being afraid. Little by little, after he becomes accustomed to the darkness and a germ of habit develops, send him alone on small errands to the basement, to the attic, or into the garden, and accompany him only part of the way. He will go alone the rest of the way, but one must talk aloud

9 Some authors have wondered whether the fear of darkness is learned or spontaneous.

to him so that he understands someone is there and awaits him.

Finally, for the detonation of firearms, the same method is always used. Have the noise heard several times, first with the child at a distance, then with him approaching by small steps. Repetition of the sound in itself will attenuate the effect. A child has been cured of the fear of thunder because, by chance, he has been exposed to a violent storm.

Supposed dangers also deserve mention. "In the case of an assumed danger—a sudden noise at night, the apparition of an object with a bizarre shape," wrote one correspondent, "any person with the child, instead of increasing his fear by words and acts of imprudence or weakness, should require the child to be calm and reasonable, and to approach and listen without fear or prejudice and to take account of what caused the trouble in his imagination." (M. Meline)

The central theme of this part of the treatment seems, again, to be the graduation of exercises. There is no child, no matter how cowardly, who cannot exercise some act demonstrating a little will power; the art of education consists in finding small, well-graduated tasks which shape the character of the child and progressively give him the habit of courage.

It is dangerous to proceed too quickly, reawakening fear instead of inciting courage. During the course of the treatment, one should, obviously, prevent the child from experiencing a genuine fear before he is sufficiently cured to fight against the feeling.

In ending this small resume, I think it entirely useless to add that I do not feel that I have investigated the psychological mechanism of fear. To understand this mechanism, one must conduct an experimental and physiological investigation of capillary circulation and respiration, the nature of which occupies me at the moment. The present study, using questionnaires, had the object of serving as an introduction to the study of fear by collecting some facts of current observation. All, or almost all, tend to show, by a great number of harmonious details, that fear is a depressive emotion.

14

Imageless Thought

To profit from the practice in introspection which two children had received during the psychological experiments (part of which I published here),[1] I asked them for information on the role which images play in ideation. This is a fairly subtle question, and it is surprising to study it in collaboration with persons who are strangers to psychological treatises. The principal difficulty is to distinguish between thought and its representation or image, between ideation and imagery;[2] and it is to this point that I will now direct my investigation. I aim to determine what relationships exist between what one thinks and what one pictures, and of what help the image is for thought. Thought will be taken as the departure point of this study, and I will define it according to all that I can learn from my subjects. Once thought is defined, I will assess the extent to which images help in its formation. Going immediately to extremes, I will ask: Can one think without images? This concise question is subdivided into two secondary questions: either thought is *not* accompanied by any appreciable type of image, or else thought *is* accompanied by certain images, but they are insufficient to illustrate it completely.

[1] See *Revue philosophique*, October 1902, Le Vocabulaire et l'Idéation. All these questions and many others relative to ideation, to abstract thought, and to individual psychology will be taken up in a collective study soon to appear under the title, *Etude expérimentale de l'Intelligence*.

[2] I intentionally oppose the two words ideation and imagery, which so many authors have confused. By ideation, I mean all phenomena of thought in a broad sense. Imagery has a more restricted meaning; it is a sensitive representation either of an object or of a word. In the text, I speak exclusively of sensory imagery and leave verbal imagery aside.

La pensée sans images. *Revue philosophique*, 1903, 55, 138-152.

Images that follow the hearing of a word

It is possible that, after hearing a word, a precise thought is formed without its being accompanied by any appreciable image; several times my two subjects declared this to me spontaneously and without hesitation. To understand fully the importance of their assertion, certain explanations must be given. We have seen from other experiments that, when a person hears a word, there is a short moment during which the word is understood without an image arising. In the same way, we can understand the meaning of words like "house," "deer," or "horse," without applying them to precise objects or imagining them. These are thoughts without images. In the experiments and observations I will now describe, the situation is different and much more interesting. We no longer have a vague and undetermined thought as we had before; the word is not only understood, it is applied to a definite object. This object is as if designated by a mental gesture; it is such-and-such a man, or the coachman of such-and-such a village. We contemplate the object and sometimes attempt to form an image of it, but the image does not come.

Let me cite an example provided by Armande, one of my two little subjects, who, more often than her sister, has this sterility of images after a voluntary search. I say the name "Firol," a well-known person whom we had as a servant for six or seven years and whom we now see occasionally five or six times a year. Armande, after some effort to picture Firol, abandons the attempt and replies: "They are only thoughts; I cannot picture anything at all to myself. I think that Firol was here (living in our house) and that she is now in Val d'Avon (where she and her husband have just rented a house), but I have no images. I thought about having an image, but none came to me." Let me repeat that this was a specific, highly individualized thought; it was fixed on a known person and on certain details of the existence of that person (her change of habitation and condition), but no images appeared.

Other examples from Armande: "Tempest." "Oh, I cannot picture anything. This time I tried, but I could not." "Favorite." "Oh, that doesn't mean anything at all. I don't picture anything to myself. I cannot picture words which have different meanings, and I sometimes think it means one thing, sometimes another. Then while I am thinking . . . no image comes."

These examples are from Marguerite. I say the word "Bouguin," which is the name of a former coachman of S . . ., a small village in Seine-et-Marne. After a few seconds of thought, she replies: "I said nothing to myself. I saw your books (this takes place in my study). My thoughts were very vague, because the name of the carriage keeper of S . . . was repeated very low. Above all, I thought about the sound of his name; it seemed darker to me than those volumes over there." "Did you have any thoughts about the coachman?" "I had the vague impression that he lived in a house set back from the street and that it was dark there." Marguerite had a thought specific to a known person; while she pictured his home as being dark and off the street, she did not picture the person himself, and thus it was a thought without sensory image.

Marguerite sometimes has a delayed image. I say the word "belfry" to her, and she replies that she thinks of the belfry of the church at M. . . . Did she envision it? Yes, but this occurred an appreciable time after she thought about the word. "I eventually saw it," she said, "because I thought so much about it."

In the preceding examples, we wanted to show above all that thought without images is possible, but that, in our two little girls, the complete absence of images is rare, especially when it is the overt goal of our experiment to provoke images. Frequently, we have a lack of agreement between thought and image. Examples of this abound and are extremely varied. Ordinarily the thought is wider, more comprehensive; one thinks of the whole, only a part of which is represented by the image. While this part can be important, it is sometimes only an accessory.

An example given by Marguerite: I say the word "string." "First, I vaguely saw a piece of yellow string, then I said to myself, 'a person of string.' Madame X is very stringy . . . , and I saw Madame X." Question: "Did you say the word before seeing it?" Answer: "I don't know." In this example, she thought of a character trait—the "stringy character"—but there was no image. The thought was more complete than the image.

Here is another example of the thought exceeding the image: I say the word "Cerberus." "First," answers Marguerite, "I saw the word on a golden background. . . . I repeated it very low, and then I had a glimpse of the form of the fat lady David Copperfield spoke about in the scene with Stefford and the little dwarf (memory of a novel by Dickens)." Question: "Did you picture the novel, the little dwarf, etc.?" "No, not at all. This must be the thought. I saw a fat lady, and I knew she was in the novel. I didn't actually say to myself in words that it was the novel about David Copperfield; I knew it without saying it."

With Armande in particular, one often encounters cases in which the imagery is not adequate for the ideation. Without going so far as to say that Armande thinks of one thing and pictures something else, one can cite numerous thoughts for which images were developed quite extraneously. For example, I pronounce the word "elephant"; she visualizes the mounting platform where children in the Jardin d' Acclimation climb on the elephant, but the pachyderm is absent. It is represented by its name, which Armande sees in writing (typographical visual image). Another time I tell her the name "Clau," a maid she knows well. She says: "I pictured to myself the door of the dining room of B.M.'s apartment (where this person is), but I didn't picture Clau. I thought of her without picturing her." The accessory is visualized, the main object is not. I tell her the word "cutlet." She pictures a bicycle trip to get cutlets for lunch. It is a memory in which she envisions the angle of a street and the red wall of the butcher's shop, but not the cutlets. Another time she is led to think of our neighbors who live on property with a large garden, but she does not picture them. She pictures only their garden, and they are not in it. One out of four times, Armande has these unsuccessful images. It is like someone who, firing at a target, strikes to the side. This strange fact is also encountered in Marguerite, but much more rarely, and it is undoubtedly due to the fact that the sensory imagery of Armande evolves very rapidly, almost independently of her will. We have seen, moreover, that Armande complains of being unceasingly obliged to fight against distractions, whereas Marguerite is much more skillful at directing the image. Sometimes the very nature of the image differs from that of the thought, although the difference is not large enough to be absurd. This type of case is a bit more complicated. When I say "Cerberus" to Armande, she replies, "I picture the stories of Greek history, or rather, I think of them." Question: "What were you thinking of?" Answer: "I pictured Hell, and I saw a dog who was probably Cerberus in front of the entrance to a grotto." Question: "Why did you have this image?" Answer: "Because Hell is guarded by a dog with 20 heads who is called Cerberus." Question: "Did you see the 20 heads?" Answer: "No, I didn't even see one; the image was too vague. I don't remember seeing any heads." One will note with interest the difference between the image and the memory of the education which prompted it. Hell became a grotto, and Cerberus assumed the more modest appearance of a dog without a head.

The discrepancy between ideation and imagery is even more striking in this other example. I say the word "string." After a moment, Armande answers, "I don't know why, but I picture the road to F . . . ; it has no relationship. First I think a little about the word 'string,' and I get used to it. An image (the road) appears, but it is then driven away by other thoughts. . . . I am quite surprised to see it." Another time the dictum, "A light rain weakens strong winds," lends itself to the image of the road to F . . . , but without rain. In these last two cases, the disparity is so great that a new thought is brought into being.

It goes without saying that, to demonstrate the possibility of an independence between thought and imagery, I have selected somewhat exceptional examples; the general rule is not the incoherence of the image, but rather its agreement with the thought.

We have just studied incoherent imagery. Authors have published some singularities of imagery which are similar to the preceding ones without being absolutely equivalent. These are cases of symbolic imagery. I give them this name because there is a constant association between a particular thought and a disparate image. Incoherent imagery becomes symbolic when it takes a constant form. Let us cite several examples:

Sidgwick, quoted by Ribot (*Évolution des Idées générales*, p. 143), assures us that when he reasons on political economy, the general terms often have as concomitants very bizarre images like the following: "Value" equals the vague and partial image of a man who weighs something on a scale. A lady I know admitted to me with some restraint that she associates two proper names with rather bizarre images. In one instance, the name Alfred is indisolubly linked to the idea of a cold, muddy, grayish body, and in the other, the name Duval recalls the image of a windmill. The origin of these images could not be found, nor could any explanation be given; she knew only that these representations were of very long standing. I will add that this lady has traces of colored hearing and an exceptional ability to memorize numbers (dates, addresses, etc.) . Recently, the American author Bailey, after studying several persons, described numerous examples of similar cases (*American Journal of Psychology*, 1901, 12, 80-130) . For one individual, the word "above" invariably gave the visual image of a chasm. For another, the word "cold" recalled the memory of a painting of an arctic scene in his geography class. These representations are not without analogy to those described under the name of schema or personifications, a large number of which are cited in the remarkable work of Flournoy on the synopsies[3] and in the more recent book by Lemaître.[4] The latter demonstrates numerous examples of graphic symbols corresponding to the idea of towns or waterflows.

This type of imagery is perhaps more frequent than one realizes; many persons unsuspectingly possess it because they have not recognized its true nature. The represented events are a part of their private life, and so they have little occasion to discuss them due to their lack of practical interest. The case here is similar to that of colored hearing, for example. The principal characteristic of these representations is that they are involuntary. Either they follow us constantly, as do obsessions, or they surge up at our call when we need them. In either case, we have the vague feeling that they are constructed outside our world and that we cannot modify them.

Images that follow the hearing of a phrase

I have already remarked that, if one requests the subject to form an image after hearing a word, one places him under conditions favorable to the development of images; we have no evidence that images play as important a role in thoughts which develop naturally without special emphasis on introspection—when reading a book, for example, or listening to a conversation. This is the first objection to the experimental study of ideation through the use of words.

Another objection is much more serious: One does not know precisely how the subject has understood the words said by the experimenter, or whether he has understood them at all. Take, for example, experiments in which the subject is given some general terms and then questioned about the idea which formed after hearing each word. One implicitly admits, without even asking the question, that the subject has a broad thought in mind when he receives the word. This is in no way proven, but it is possible. It is also possible that the subject may fail to fix his attention on the word or to

---

[3] Flournoy, *Des Phénomènes de Synopsie*, Paris, 1893.

[4] Lemaître, *Audition colorée et Phénomènes analogues observés chez des Ecoliers*, Paris, 1901.

penetrate its meaning; passing rapidly over the word, he may go directly to the image, since it is the image which he is asked to explain. To guard against this objection, which seems to me fairly serious theoretically—I cannot estimate its value practically—one should conduct the experiment in such a way that no one knows it is an experiment: Form words in a natural tone and wait for them to be understood; immediately thereafter, direct questions to the subject about his images. If it is possible to combine these conditions, one can be assured that the subject is not preoccupied with pursuing images, and that he is taking the time to comprehend what is being said to him. This is an experiment with two sides: from the subject's viewpoint, it is the observation of a spontaneous phenomenon developing with a natural freedom of pace; from the experimenter's viewpoint, it has the merit of precision and of answering an important question. One cannot, however, pronounce isolated words, as we have done until now, without warning people. I succeed in not putting them on their guard by addressing some simple questions or a few words to them about the affairs of their current and private life. As soon as I perceive that the sentence, always very simple, has been understood, I rapidly ask the important question point-blank: "Did you have an image, and what was it?" Great skill is required not to alert them to my intention; generally, it is during the course of another experiment that I will present the evocative sentence in a natural tone and without hurrying.

Many sentences, although understood, produce no appreciable images; others give rise to incomplete or fragmentary images which illustrate only a part of the sentence, for example, the name of a familiar object. None arouses an image sufficiently complete for the meaning of the entire sentence to be understood. This is perhaps one of the experiments which best shows the contrast between richness of thought and poverty of imagery.

Let us first cite thoughts without images. At the end of a random conversation, I say to Armande, "Soon we are going to leave for S . . . ," and I add, "What image?" Armande replies: "I simply hear the sound; I don't picture anything. There must be nothing else to think about before I picture images to myself." Nonetheless, she understands perfectly well what I have just said. Here is another example. I address this sentence to her after leading up to it by other reflections: "Have you made much progress in German this year?" Armande replies laughingly, "At least more than with Ber,"—an answer which implies a comparison with the progress made the preceding year by an entirely different method. I ask for images. Armande replies, "It was too short; I only had time to think. No images came." Sentences without images are frequent with Armande. Almost all happen under these circumstances, and she invariably gives the same explanation: When she limits herself to understanding the meaning of the sentence, she does not have the time to form images. Nonetheless, she has had a few sentences with complete images. When I say, "I will give the lesson tomorrow at about 10 o'clock," the image she forms is this one: "I pictured the dining room; Julie was sewing near the window, because she will be there Wednesday." To understand this very precise answer, it must be mentioned that the lesson is habitually given in the dining room and that Julie, a seamstress, is supposed to come to work the day after tomorrow. It is this picture which is visualized; the lesson does not enter into it. Furthermore, the visualization often pertains only to the scenery; this is easily understood since the scenery is material, immobile, stable, and thus easier to visualize than action.

It sometimes happens that Marguerite, listening to the sentence I address to her, fails to form any image; or rather, she is unable to tell me what image she has had, because she did not pay attention and does not know precisely whether or not she has had one. Even in its negative form, this answer is interesting, because it is a question of sentences which Marguerite has thought about only two or three seconds earlier when questioned about the image. Thus, if she really forgets the image, it is due to the fact that it is by nature very fleeting; besides, Armande has already warned us that she forgets images very quickly—much more quickly than reflections. As a rule, Marguerite's images correspond to only a part of the sentence. One day, after speaking about the death of our dog, I say with conviction, "It's sad, all animals die, all without exception." I let ten seconds elapse, then ask suddenly, "What images?" Marguerite jumps, declares that she has not imagined anything. This is her initial answer; after thinking it over, however, she discovers a small, insignificant image—a black, immobile, withered insect.

Another day I say to her, "Have you made a great deal of progress in German this year?" She answers, "Oh, we know how to construct sentences now. Much better!" I ask for images. "I don't think I had any. Wait . . . Perhaps I saw our German teacher, but I'm not sure . . . I thought of some sentences . . . I saw some letters, I think, but it is quite vague." If we combine the image of the letters and the image of the teacher, we have not restored the meaning of my original sentence. There is no continuity to these images, nothing which even resembles a complete thought. Another time, thinking correctly that it will recall a very agreeable idea, I say to her, "Departure in 15 days for S . . . !" I ask for images. She answers: "I saw the months and all the series of days in numbers. They had the shape of a serpent: from 1 to 20 in a straight vertical line and then going out toward the left to 30 or 31. The right half of the column was gray, and for some reason it was June." Question: "You did not see S . . . ?" Answer: "No, not at all." Thus, she understands that the sentence signifies a coming trip to S. . . . By means of a schema—this was the first time I discovered that she had one—she visualizes the approximate date of departure for the country, but she does not picture the trip, the country, or the abstract thought of departure. If, as documents, one had only images, it would indeed be impossible to ascertain the meaning of the sentence.

One time I caught Marguerite looking at the clock and crying with some anxiety, "Oh, my God! There's a lesson at 11:00!" This is certainly a natural remark and entirely felt. I suddenly ask her what images she has had. She tells me, and I note her exact words: "I thought of the *Misanthrope;* I saw the word vaguely in a grayish tint . . ., and I saw a page of the physics book, a small paragraph with a number . . . indistinct. . . . I saw a little of the dining room; I saw Armande at her desk; then I saw a little of the small sitting room."

To explain these images, I must briefly add that there is a lesson in physics and a passage from the *Misanthrope* in this day's program, and that the lesson is usually given in the dining room or the small sitting room. Afterward, I ask Marguerite to tell me all the thoughts she has just had. Easily distinguishing between her thoughts and the images, she answers without hesitation, "I thought of asking you to send me away (from the room where she had been called for the experiment) so that I could go over my homework, because I was afraid that I was unprepared for the lesson. Then I thought of Armande, who had said to me, 'My God! Is there a lesson this morning?' As for the *Misanthrope,* I felt that I didn't know it, not at all. And the physics? I'm not certain what I thought. I did know that I had very little time."

These words, as one can see, translate the thought much better than the fragmentary images of the *Misanthrope* and the page of physics.

When the subject knows in advance that the sentence he hears will have to be translated into images, his images are more abundant and more precise. Armande, for example, does not spontaneously have many images, but is provided with them in this way. Having warned her that she must describe her images, I repeat the following sentence: "A blast of wind carried off the roof of the house." At the end of seven seconds she answers, "I see as an image the corner of Fouquet and National Street, only it's not the roof that's being blown away, it's the railing." An inexact image, mistakenly drawn. Another example is curious in its implication. After ten seconds of meditation, the phrase, "His goatee was dark yellow," results in the following reply from Armande: "I picture a forest with a small cabin in it; it's a scene from *Gil Blas*." Surprised by the comic discordance between what I suggest and what she answers, I ask, "Where's the goatee?" Answer: "There isn't one, but an old beggar with a yellow beard lived in the cabin in the woods." Question: "Did you actually see him?" Answer: "No." Note how much of this thought failed to appear in image form! The memory of the novel *Gil Blas,* the memory of a certain description, of a beggar with a yellow beard, which was incorrect, etc. These images are only a small part of the entire thought—and not the most important part, at that.

The images of a spontaneous story

I ask my two subjects to tell me what they would do if left alone in S . . . for three hours with complete freedom of action. This question interests them a little. I ask it of them during an experiment. They are well aware that it is an experiment, but do not suspect that I am going to ask for images; the story is thus invented without an appreciable concern for subsequent introspection. Armande, somewhat weary from a long, unpleasant errand which took half the day, portrays a fairly brief account. Here is what she says, and I write it down as fast as I can while she dictates (June 3, 1902).

Armande's spoken story. "First, we'd visit the house of Bre . . .; we could stay at least half an hour. Then we would go to the house of M . . . to get a bicycle so that we could take a trip in the country, in S . . .; we would follow the path to Fontainebleau."

Immediately thereafter I asked her for images. They appear to be very simple and refer only to scenes in which the story takes place. It is a visualization of the scenery, nothing more: "I had an image of our garden, then Fouquet Street, and we were on our bicycles. Then S . . ., National Street, the forest, the guardian's house, the Madeleine, then near the little bridge." It seems to me that this series of images illustrates the thought about as summarily as five images in a book illustrate twenty pages of travel stories. I cannot be certain of Armande's exact thoughts, however, because I did not ask enough minute questions.

Here is the experiment with Marguerite; it is much better done (June 4, 1902). I will present, first, Marguerite's spoken story; next, the spoken description of her images; and finally, the enumeration of her thoughts. This is the order in which the study was made.

Marguerite's spoken story. "Upon arriving, we would get dressed in our bicycling clothes, and if we were free to go where we wanted, we would take a trip. Three hours, one cannot do very much . . .; we would go to see A . . . (a friend) at M. . . ."

Marguerite's images. "I'll tell them in a general way because I was not forewarned. I pictured Fouquet Street, then the road to F. . . . When I said that we would put on our bicycling costumes, I saw our dresses and our belts, as if we were wearing them already. I pictured them on Armande. Then I saw the village as a whole, and I pictured places rather than people. I saw the road from the Table du Roi to M . . . , but it's funny, I hardly pictured the bicycles at all. I caught sight of the village of M . . . , and of Irma (a friend), a young girl in black, not very distinctly. . . . I saw a small shaded street with a grayish building . . . , and then I saw the figure of A . . . (a friend). Again I had the image of Fontaine-le-Port as one sees it when one is on the bridge looking up the road."

Marguerite's thoughts and reflections. "I said to myself: Perhaps I could get my machine fixed at Cavagnac's (a bicycle renter), only this would not be a pleasurable trip. Perhaps we could go see Madame Lelu, Madame Lecuyer, and Madame Brunet, but I said to myself that this would not be a very interesting way to use the day. I was always thinking of a bicycle trip. I said to myself again: Perhaps we could go to B . . . or to N . . . , but it would be a little too far for so short a time. Then I thought of M . . . and of Irma, because I know that she lives there . . . , and then I said that to go see Irma at M . . . would not be very pleasant. Next I thought of A . . . in her boarding school . . . ,and I even thought that we would have to go on a day when we could see her. That bothered me a little, but I skipped over it. I said to myself: We are not allowed to go out alone in the forest. In connection with N . . . , I remembered that Armande was not with us on our last excursion and that it would be amusing to show it to her.''

This example of a bicycle trip lends itself very well to the development of images, for there is much to see on a trip and the images especially recall visual perceptions. Nonetheless, one can notice what a considerable number of reflections are without images.

Conclusions and hypotheses

I forced myself, in all that preceded, to suppress theoretical considerations and to expose only the precise, detailed experiments. Regarding these matters, there has been much too much theorizing and schematizing, and I now think that it would be useful to substitute some pure and simple observations for complicated reasoning and over-worked theory; even naive observations, given without affection, have the merit of being made naturally. That which stands out clearly from these observations is that, in subjects such as ours, the image does not have the primordial role it is often assumed to have. Our subjects do not seem to me to be exceptional persons deprived of images. If Armande, as we will see later, has fairly vague images (and again, I believe them to be clearer than mine) , to compensate, Marguerite visualizes with a great deal of clarity, and she assures us that some of her representations are as intense as reality. For imaginative ability, I think that she is above the median and represents fairly well what must go on in the mind of a good visualizer.

We can conclude, therefore, that the image is only a small part of the complex phenomenon to which we give the name thought. The ease with which one describes mental images, and undoubtedly, understands them by the rather gross comparison that has been made with an illuminated image of Epinal, is what has fostered the illusion of the importance of images.[5] It was the psychology of Taine, so beautiful in its extremes, which popularized among us this idea that the image is a repetition of the sensation and that one thinks with images. Then there were the remarkable clinical studies of Charcot

---

5 [Epinal, a town in northeastern France, was famous at the end of the eighteenth century for the production of printed images, viz., lithographs and engravings of saints and famous people, or religious, historical, and romantic scenes.]

on aphasia, which showed the distinctions to be made between visual, auditory, and motor images, and further contributed to the importance of the image in psychology.

The study of images has become one of the most perfected in French science. Taine and those who followed him were correct in acknowledging the sensory element of thought, because this element does indeed exist. Similarly, Charcot, in showing the multiplicity of varieties of mental images, rendered a service which advanced the paths of individual psychology.

If I may cite myself after such great names, I will recall that in my *Psychologie du Raisonnement*, I tried to show that reasoning leads to an internal vision of the things about which one reasons—a vision constructed from the inherent properties of mental images. I am far from being hostile to theories which accord importance to mental images, but it seems to me that one should not go too far.

To overly materialize thought is to render it unintelligible. To think is not the same thing as contemplating Epinal. Strictly speaking, the mind is not a "polyp of images," except perhaps in dreams or day-dreams. The laws of ideas are not necessarily the laws of images; to think does not consist solely of becoming conscious of images; to be attentive does not mean that one image is simply more intense than another. We have verified—and I think this is a question of facts which cannot be doubted—that certain concrete thoughts[6] occur without images, that in other thoughts the image illustrates only a small part of the phenomenon, and that the image is often incongruous with the thought; one thinks to oneself of one thing but pictures another.

This is our precise and demonstrated conclusion. I hope I may be allowed to go a little further and end this article with a hypothesis. I gave myself an explanation of the mechanism of thought; I would now like to summarize it, separating it very clearly from what preceded.

It seems difficult to me to suppose that the image—I mean the sensory image derived from perceptions of the senses—can always be coextensive with thought. Thought is composed not only of contemplation but of reflection, and I do not clearly see how reflection can be translated into images, other than in a symbolic manner. In our preceding observations, the image was almost always visual. It

6 At another time, I will examine the relationship between image and abstract thought.

almost always reflected material objects; it never represented a relationship. I find it difficult to understand how one finds mental images which are equivalent to this very simple thought expressed by Marguerite: "I'm going to be late for the lesson!" I willingly imagine to myself someone who runs or a busy student who looks forlornly at her book, but that is only symbolism. To understand, to compare, to relate, to deny—all, properly speaking, are intellectual acts and not images.

It is, above all, internal language which expresses the course of our thought. In a certain sense, words are inferior to images as well as to perceptions because the nuances cannot all be expressed; that is to say, the most precise description of a stone will never completely exhaust all that can be said about it. In return, words, with all the resources of syntax, are much better at expressing the associations of our ideas.[7]

Consequently, one can assume that in the parts of thought which are imageless, thought is composed essentially of internal language; it is a monologue. William James, the great intuitive psychologist who so profoundly studied the mechanism of thought, made this supposition as if in passing. He was also surprised when he verified what a small role images play in thought,[8] even though his conclusions were arrived at primarily through theoretical reasoning and rarely through observation; this is the only criticism I can make of his beautiful chapter, "The Stream of Thought." James made a curious observation: One of his friends was able to recount the menu of his meal and what was on the table without visualizing the table or the plates. He assumed that the description was made solely of words and that, in this particular case, they represented a substitute for the absence of images.[9] This was the interpretation he provided, but he did not insist upon it. If James had examined the question a little more thoroughly, with a mind as cunning as his, he would surely have perceived that this explanation was simply impossible. Unless it is supposed that the diner learned the menu of the meal by heart and recited it mentally from memory, one must admit that he thought about each plate before thinking of the word; of necessity,

[7] The image, like the sensation, is what best reflects the external world; language, on the contrary, is what best reflects the logic of thought. I think that it would be useful to make this distinction when one studies the function of the word in thought.

[8] W. James, *Principles of Psychology*, Vol. I, p. 472.

[9] *Ibid.*, Vol. I, p. 265, and Vol. II, p. 58.

the thought precedes the word. The same comment can be made about many of the observations we have collected.

Let us recall some examples. When I say the name Firol to Armande, she thinks of this person; she remembers that this person is no longer here (at our house), but has changed homes. She then has a fairly complex thought related to Firol, to her home, to her existence. Of what nature is this thought? On the one hand, it is lacking in sensory images—Armande claims that she pictures nothing to herself. On the other, if, in reality, she expresses herself through words, which supposes verbal images, it is very certain that the verbal images are only an expression of the thought which has already been called. The thought precedes. For Armande to say to me or to herself, "Firol is no longer here, but elsewhere," for her to compose this sentence, means that she has to have the corresponding thought beforehand, no matter how attenuated the thought may be. Thus, it is a thought formed without images—even without verbal images. This is the important point. In the same way, we must admit that many spontaneous reflections suppose a thought preceding the words which express it—a thought directing and organizing the words. This is said without in any way diminishing the importance of the word, which must greatly influence the nature of the thought by a counter-effect. I suppose that the word, like the sensory image, gives precision to the thought which, without these two aids—that of the word and that of the image—would remain very vague.

I even presume that it is the word and the image which contribute the most to making us conscious of our thoughts. Thought is an unconscious act of the mind which, to become fully conscious, necessitates words and images. No matter what difficulty we have in depicting a thought which is imageless—and it is only for this reason that I say thought is unconscious—it nevertheless exists. Thought constitutes, if one wishes to define it by its function, a directing organizing force which I would willingly compare (this is probably only a metaphor) to the vital force which, directing the physical-chemical properties, models the shape of beings and leads to their evolution, an invisible worker detected only through material works.

Bibliography of Binet's Writings

The following chronologically arranged bibliography includes all of Alfred Binet's writings. Translations, where available, have been cited, with their year of publication, along with their French counterparts. Those works that have been translated by the editors for the present volume are indicated by the notation: (P & B, 1969).

Binet's principal works are denoted by an asterisk.

1880   De la fusion des sensations semblables. *Revue philosophique, 10,* 284-294. On the fusion of similar sensations. (P & B, 1969).

1883   Du raisonnement dans les perceptions. *Revue philosophique, 15,* 406-432.

1884   La rectification des illusions par l'appel aux sens. *Mind, 9,* 206-222.
        L'hallucination: Recherches expérimentales. *Revue philosophique, 17,* 473-502.
        L'hallucination: Recherches théoriques. *Revue philosophique, 17,* 377-412.
        Visual hallucination in hypnotism. *Mind, 9,* 413-415.
        With Féré, C. Les paralysies par suggestion. *Revue scientifique, 34* (2), 45-49.
        With Féré, C. Note sur le somnambulisme partiel et les localisations cérébrales. *Comptes Rendus [hebdomadaires] des Séances et Mémoires de la Société de Biologie, 36,* 491-492.

1885   La polarisation psychique. *Revue philosophique, 19,* 369-402.
        L'image consécutive et le souvenir visuel. *Revue scientifique, 35* (2), 805.
        With Féré, C. Hypnotisme et résponsabilité. *Revue philosophique, 19,* 265-272.
        With Féré, C. La théorie physiologique de l'hallucination. *Revue scientifique, 35* (1), 49-53.
        With Féré, C. L'hypnotisme chez les hystériques: Le transfert. *Revue philosophique, 19,* 1-25.

1886   La perception de l'étendue par l'oeil. *Revue philosophique, 21,* 113-121. The perception of extent by the eye. (P & B, 1969).
        With Delboeuf, J. L. R. Les diverses écoles hypnotiques. *Revue philosophique, 22,* 532.
        With Féré, C. Expériences sur les images associées. *Revue philosophique, 21,* 159-163.
        With Féré, C. Hypnotisme et résponsabilité. *Revue scientifique, 38* (2), 626-629.
    * With Féré, C. *La psychologie du raisonnement.* Paris: Alcan. Translated by A. G. Whyte, *The psychology of reasoning.* Chicago: Open Court, 1886. London: Kegan Paul, 1901.

1887 * La vie psychique des micro-organismes. *Revue philosophique, 24,* 449-489; 582-611. Translated by T. McCormack, *The psychic life of micro-organisms.* London: Longmans, 1889.
        Le fétichisme dans l'amour. *Revue philosophique, 24,* 142-167; 252-275.
        L'intensité des images mentales. *Revue philosophique, 23,* 472-497.
        Note sur l'écriture hystérique. *Revue philosophique, 23,* 467-707.
    * With Féré, C. *Le magnétisme animal.* Paris: Alcan. *Animal magnetism.* New York: Appleton, 1892.

With Féré, C. Recherches expérimentales sur la physiologie des mouvements chez les hystériques. *Archives de Physiologie, 10,* 320-373.

1888   *Etudes de psychologie expérimentale.* Paris: O. Doin.
    Sur les illusions de mouvement. *Revue philosophique, 25,* 335. Note on illusions of movement. (P & B, 1969).
    La résponsabilité morale. *Revue philosophique, 26,* 217-231.
    Le probléme du sense musculaire d'après les travaux récents sur l'hystérie. *Revue philosophique, 25,* 335.
    Recherches sur l'anesthésie hystérique. *Comptes Rendus hebdomadaires des Séances de l'Académie des Sciences, 107,* 1008-1010.
    Sur les rapports entre l'hémainopsie et la mémoire visuelle. *Revue philosophique, 26,* 481-488.

1889   Contribution a l'étude de la douleur chez les hystériques. *Revue philosophique, 28,* 169-174.
    La vision mentale. *Revue philosophique, 27,* 337-373.
    Les perceptions in conscientes de l'hypnotisme. *Revue scientifique, 43* (1), 241-242.
    Note sur l'enregistrement des excitations portées sur une région anesthésique du corps ches les hystériques. *Comptes Rendus [hebdomadaires] des Séances et Mémoires de la Société de Biologie, 41,* 27-29.
*   *On double consciousness.* Chicago: Open Court.
    Quelques observations sur la sensibilité tactile, rétinienne et auditive chez les hystériques. *Comptes Rendus [hebdomadaires] des Séances et Mémoires de la Société de Biologie, 41,* 487-488.
    Recherches sur les mouvements volontaires dans l'anesthésie hystérique. *Revue philosophique, 28,* 470-500.
    Sur les altérations de la conscience chez les hystériques. *Revue philosophique, 27,* 135-170.
    With Henri, V. La simulation de la mémoire des chiffres. *Revue philosophique, 27,* 114-119.

1890   La concurrence des états psychologiques. *Revue philosophique, 29,* 138-155.
    La double conscience dans la santé. *Revue philosophique, 29,* 103-114. Double consciousness in health. *Mind,* 1890, *10,* 46-57.
    La perception des longueurs et des nombres ches quelques petits enfants. *Revue philosophique, 30,* 68-81. The perception of lengths and numbers in some small children. (P & B, 1969).
    L'inhibition dans les phénomènes de conscience. *Revue philosophique, 30,* 136-156.
    Recherches sur les mouvements chez quelques jeunes enfants. *Revue philosophique, 29,* 297-309. Studies on movements in some young children. (P & B, 1969).
    Perceptions d'enfants. *Revue philosophique, 30,* 582-611. Children's perceptions. (P & B, 1969).

1891   La disposition des connectifs dans la chaîne nerveuse sous-intestinal des hanneton (Melolantha vulgaris). *Comptes Rendus [hebdomadaires] des Séances et Mémoires de la Société de Biologie, 43,* 556-558.
    Organisation d'un ganglion thoracique chez quelques Coléoptères de la tribu des Mélolonthiens. *Comptes Rendus [hebdomadaires] des Séances et Mémoires de la Société de Biologie, 43,* 757-759.
    Sur la chaîne nerveuse sous-intestinal du hanneton (Melolantha vulgaris). *Comptes Rendus [hebdomadaires] des Séances et Mémoires de la Société de Biologie, 43,* 489-490.

Sur un cas d'inhibition psychique. *Revue philosophique, 32,* 622-625.

1892   La nerf alaire chez quelques Coléoptères aprésiques. *Comptes Rendes [hebdomadaires] des Séances et Mémoires de la Société de Biologie, 44,* 257-258.

La nerf du balanciar chez quelques Deptères. *Comptes Rendes [hebdomadaires] des Séances et Mémoires de la Société de Biologie, 44,* 358-359.

   *   *Les altérations de la personnalité.* Paris: Alcan, 1892. Translated by H. G. Baldwin, *Alterations of personality.* New York: Appleton, 1896.

Les mouvements de manége chez les insectes. *Revue philosophique, 33,* 113-135.

La perception de la durée dans les réactions simples. *Revue philosophique, 33,* 650-659. The perception of duration in simple reactions. (P & B, 1969).

Les racines du nerf alaire chez les Coléoptères. *Comptes Rendus hebdomadaires des Séances de l'Académie des Sciences, 114,* 1130-1132. The nervous centre of flight in coleopitera. *Monist,* 1893, ___, 65-67.

Structure d'un ganglion abdominal de Mélolonthien. *Comptes Rendes [hebdomadaires] des Séances et Mémoires de la Société de Biologie, 44,* 166-168.

Sur la structure d'un ganglion nerveux d'insecte. *Annales de la Société entomologique de France, 61,* clxxii-clxxv.

Sur la structure interne des ganglions sous-intestinaux des Coléoptères Mélolonthiens. *Bulletin de la Société philomathique de Paris, 4,* 2.

The nervous ganglia of insects. *Monist,* ___, 35-50.

With Beaunis, H. Recherches expérimentales sur deux cas d'audition colorée. *Revue philosophique, 33,* 448-461.

With Henneguy, L. Contribution à l'étude microscopique de système nerveux larvaire de Stratiomys longicorns. *Annales de la Société entomologique de France, 61,* 309-316.

With Henneguy, L. Observations et expériences sur le calculateur J. Inaudi. *Revue philosophique, 34,* 204-220.

With Henneguy, L. Structure de système nerveux larvaire de la Stratiomys strigosa. *Comptes Rendus hebdomadaires des Séances de l'Académie des Sciences, 114,* 430-432.

With Philippe. Etude sur un nouveau cas d'audition colorée. *Revue philosophique, 33,* 461-464.

With Philippe. Notes sur quelques calculateurs de profession. *Revue philosophique, 34,* 221-223.

1893   Application de la psychométrie à l'étude de l'audition colorée. *Revue philosophique, 36,* 334-336.

La psychologie expérimentale d'après les travaux du congrès de Londres. *Revue des Deux Mondes, 117,* ___.

Les grandes mémoires: Résumé d'une enquête sur les joueurs d'échecs. *Revue des Deux Mondes, 117,* 826-859. Translated by M. L. Simmel & S. B. Barron, Mnemonic virtuosity: A study of chess players. *Genetic Psychology Monographs,* 1966, *74,* 127-162.

Note Complémentaire sur le calculateur Inaudi. *Revue philosophique, 35,* 106-112.

Note sur la mémoire visuelle géométrique. *Revue philosophique, 35,* 104-106.

With Charcot, J. M. Un calculateur de type visuel. *Revue philosophique, 35,* 590-594.

With Courtier. Note sur la mesure de la vitesse des mouvements graphiques. *Comptes Rendus [hebdomadaires] des Séances et Mémoires de la Société de Biologie, 45,* 219-220.

With Courtier. Sur la vitesse des mouvements graphiques. *Revue philosophique, 35,* 664-671.

With Henri, V. La simulation de la mémoire des chiffres. *Revue scientifique, 51* (1), 711-722.

1894   Expériences sur M. Périclês Diamandi, calculateur mentale. *Revue philosophique, 37*, 113-119.

* Contribution à l'étude de système nerveux sous-intestinal des insectes. (Thesis at the Sorbonne) *Journal de l'Anatomie et de la Physiologie normales et pathologiques de l'Homme et des Animaux, 30*, 449-580.

* *Introduction à la psychologie expérimentale.* Paris: Alcan.

La mémoire des joueurs d'échecs qui jouent sans voir. *Revue philosophique, 37*, 222-228.

La psychologie de la prestidigitation. *Revue des Deux Mondes, 125*, 903-922. The psychology of prestidigitation. In the *Smithsonian Institute Annual Report.* Washington, D.C.: Smithsonian Institute, 1894. Pp. 555-571.

Le renversement de l'orientation. (Author's manuscript) Translated by J. N. Dodd, Reverse illusions of orientation. *Psychological Review,* 1 (4), 337-350.

Note sur la structure fibrillaire des cellules nerveuses de quelques Crustacés Décapades. *Comptes Rendus [hebdomadaires] des Séances et Mémoires de la Société de Biologie, 46,* 162.

With Courtier. Expériences sur la vitesse des mouvements graphiques. *Revue philosophique, 37*, 111-112.

With Courtier. Le criterium musical. *Année psychologique, 1*, 529-530.

With de Curel, F. M. Francois de Curel notes psychologiques. *Année psychologique, 1*, 119-173.

* With Henneguy, L. *La psychologie des grands calculateurs et joueurs d'échecs.* Paris: Hachette.

With Henri V. Recherches sur le développement de la mémoire visuelle des enfants. *Revue philosophique, 37*, 348-350. Investigations on the development of visual memory in children. (P & B, 1969) .

With Henri, V. De la suggestibilité naturelle chez les enfants. *Revue philosophique, 38*, 337-347.

With Henri, V. Les actions d'arrêt dans les phénomènes de la parole. *Revue philosophique, 37*, 608-620.

With Henri, V. Mémoire des mots. *Année psychologique, 1*, 1-23.

With Henri, V. Mémoire des phrases. *Année psychologique, 1*, 24-59.

With Passy, J. Etudes de psychologie sur les auteurs dramatiques. *Année psychologique, 1*, 60-118.

With Passy, J. La psychologie des auteurs dramatiques. *Revue philosophique, 37*, 228-240.

1895   Contribution à l'étude de la télépathie. *Annals des Sciences psychologiques, 5,* ――.

La mesure des illusions visuelles chez les enfants. *Revue philosophique, 40*, 11-25. The measurement of visual illusions in children. Translated by R. H. Pollack & F. K. Zetland in *Perception and motor skills,* 1965, *20*, 917-930.

La peur chez les enfants. *Année psychologique, 2*, 223-254. Fear in children. (P & B, 1969) .

Psychologie des grande calculateurs et jouers d'échecs. *Revue philosophique, 39*, 328.

Sur les illusions d'orientation. *Revue philosophique, 39*, 229.

The mechanism of thought. *Fortnightly Review,* (approximate date) , *55*, 785-799.

Travaux de laboratoire de psychologie physiologique des hautes études. *Revue philosophique, 40*, 671-672.

With Courtier. Application nouvelle de la méthode graphique à la musique.

Comptes Rendus hebdomadaires des Séances de l'Académie des Sciences, 120, 646-647.

With Courtier. Influence de la respiration sur le tracé volumétrique des membres. *Comptes Rendus hebdomadaires des Séances de l'Académie des Sciences, 121,* 219-220.

With Courtier. La circulation capillaire dans ses rapports avec la respiration et les phénomènes psychologiques. *Année psychologique, 2,* 87-157.

With Courtier. Note sur l'influence que la travail intellectual exerce sur la respiration, le pouls capillaire de la main. *Comptes Rendus [hebdomadaires] des Séances et Mémoires de la Société de Biologie, 47,* 806.

With Courtier. Note sur un dispositif permettant d'éviter la projection et les vibrations du stylet inscripteur dans l'enregistrement graphique desphénomènes rapides. *Comptes Rendus [hebdomadaires] des Séances et Mémoires de la Société de Biologie, 47,* 212-213.

With Courtier. Note sur une application nouvelle de la méthode graphique au piano. *Comptes Rendus [hebdomadaires] des Séances et Mémoires de la Société de Biologie, 47,* 212.

With Courtier. Note sur un stylet à encre d'un modèle graphique. *Comptes Rendus [hebdomadaires] des Séances et Mémoires de la Société de Biologie, 47,* 212.

With Courtier. Recherches graphiques sur la musique. *Année psychologique, 2,* 201-222.

With Courtier. Seconde note sur la correction des tracés au moyen d'un orifice capillaire. *Comptes Rendus [hebdomadaires] des Séances et Mémoires de la Société de Biologie, 47,* 296-298.

With Courtier. Un régulateur graphique. *Comptes Rendus [hebdomadaires] des Séances et Mémoires de la Société de Biologie, 47,* 320-322.

With Henri, V. Psychologie individuelle. *Année psychologique, 2,* 411-465.

With Passy, J. Contribution de l'étude de l'olfaction chez le chien. *Association Francaise pour l'Advancement des Sciences,* __, 659-661.

With Rebatel. Un cas d'affection mentale quéri par la trépanation. *Lyon médicale,* No. 19.

1896 Connais toi-même. *Revue des Revues, 19,* 419-424.

Les temps de réaction. *Presse médicale,* __, 51; 55; 80; 303; 327.

Psychologie individuelle: La description d'un objet. *Année psychologique, 3,* 296-332.

Réflexions sur le paradoxe de Diderot. *Année psychologique, 3,* 279-295. The paradox of Diderot. *Popular Science Monthly,* 1899, 51, 539-543.

Review of recent French works on psychology. *Psychological Review, 3,* 551-556.

With Courtier. Signification des diverses formes du pouls capillaire étudié chez l'homme adulte. *Comptes Rendus [hebdomadaires] des Séances et Mémoires de la Société de Biologie, 48,* 279-282.

With Courtier. Influence de la vie émotionelle sur le coeur, la respiration, et la circulation capillaire. *Année psychologique, 3,* 65-126.

With Courtier. Influence des repas, de l'exercice physique, du travail intellectuel et des émotions sur la circulation capillaire de l'homme. *Comptes Rendus hebdomadaires des Séances de l'Académie des Sciences, 123,* 505-508.

With Courtier. Les changements de forme du pouls capillaire aux différentes heures. *Année psychologique, 3,* 10-29.

With Courtier. Les effets du travail intellectuel sur la circulation capillaire. *Année psychologique, 3,* 42-64.

With Courtier. Les effets du travail musculaire sur la circulation capillaire. *Année psychologique, 3,* 30-41.

With Vaschide, N. Influence du travail intellectuel des émotions et du travail physique sur la pression du sang. *Année psychologique, 3,* 127-183.

1897   La consummation du pain pendant une année scolaire. *Année psychologique, 4,* 337-355.

La description d'une cigarette. *Revue de Psychiatrie,* ___, 235-243.

La Dantec's work on biological determinism and conscious personality. *Psychological Review, 4,* 516-522.

La psychologie moderne et ses récents progrés. *Année biologie, 1,* 593-620.

Les récentes recherches de psychologie physiologique sur la circulation capillaire et les phénomènes vasometeurs. *Revue générale des Sciences, 8,* 60-65.

Notes on the experimental study of memory. Translated by H. C. Warren, *American Naturalist, 31,* 912-916.

Plural states of being. *Popular Science Monthly, 50,* 539-543.

Quelques réflexions et une hypothèse sur la forme du pouls capillaire. *Année psychologique, 4,* 327-336.

With Courtier, Influence de la musique sur la circulation le coeur et la circulation capillaire. *Revue scientifique, 4,* (7), 257-263.

With Vaschide, N. Critique du dynamomètre ordinaire. *Année psychologique, 4,* 245-252.

With Vaschide, N. Corrélation des tests de force physique. *Année psychologique, 4,* 236-244.

With Vaschide, N. Données anatomiques, capacité vitale et vitesse du coeur chez 40 jeunes gens. *Année psychologique, 4,* 225-232.

With Vaschide, N. Echelle des indications données par les différents tests. *Année psychologique, 4,* 137-141.

With Vaschide, N. Echelle des indications données par les test. *Année psychologique, 4,* 223-225.

With Vaschide, N. Expériences de force musculaire et de fond chez les jeunes garcons. *Année psychologique, 4,* 15-63.

With Vaschide, N. Expériences de vitesse chez les jeunes garcons. *Année psychologique, 4,* 64-98; 200-224.

With Vaschide, N. Expériences sur la respiration et la circulation du sang chez les jeunes garcons. *Année psychologique, 4,* 99-132.

With Vaschide, N. Examen-critique de l'ergographe de Mosso. *Année psychologique, 4,* 253-266.

With Vaschide, N. Influence des différents processus psychiques sur la pression du sang chez l'homme. *Comptes Rendus hebdomadaires des Séances de l'Académie des Sciences, 124,* 44-46.

With Vaschide, N. La mesure de la force musculaire chez les jeunes garcons: La force dépression de la main, la traction, la corde lisse, le saut. *Année psychologique, 4,* 173-199.

With Vaschide, N. La physiologie du muscle dans les expériences de vitesse. *Année psychologique, 4,* 267-279.

With Vaschide, N. La psychologie à l'école primaire. *Année psychologique, 4,* 1-14.

With Vaschide, N. L'effort respiratoire pendant les expériences à l'ergographe. *Année psychologique, 4,* 280-294.

With Vaschide, N. Les temps de réaction du coeur, des nerfs vaso-moteurs et de la pression sanguine. *Année psychologique, 4,* 316-326.

With Vaschide, N. Mesures anatomiques chez 40 jeunes garcons. *Année psychologique, 4,* 113-136.

With Vaschide, N. Réparation de la fatigue musculaire. *Année psychologique, 4,* 295-302.

With Vaschide, N. Sur un ergographe à ressort. *Comptes Rendus hebdomadaires des Séances de l'Académie des Sciences, 125,* 1161-1163.

With Vaschide, N. The influence of intellectual work upon the blood-pressure in man. *Psychological Review, 4,* 54-66.

With Vaschide, N. Un nouvel ergographe (à ressort). *Année psychologique, 4,* 303-315.

1898 La mesure en psychologie individuelle. *Revue philosophique, 46,* 113-123.

La question des études classiques d'après la psychologie expérimentale. *Revue des Revues, 26,* 461-470.

La suggestibilité au point de vue de la psychologie individuelle. *Année psychologique, 5,* 82-152.

Note relative à l'influence du travail intellectuel sur la consommation du pain dans les écoles. *Année psychologique, 5,* 332-336.

Revue générale sur la graphologie. *Année psychologique, 4,* 598-616.

Un projet d'expérience sur le sens de l'orientation chez le chien. *Intermédiare des Biologistes, 1,* 251.

With Henri, V. Courbe de vitesse du coeur. *Intermédiare des Biologistes, 1,* 384-389.

* With Henri, V. *La fatigue intellectuelle.* Paris: Schleicher Frères.

1899 La pédagogie scientifique: L'enseignement mathématique. *Revue internationale, 1,* 29-38.

* Attention et adaptation. *Année psychologique, 6,* 246-404.

Le premier devoir de l'education physique. *Revue des Revues, 28,* 597-609.

Nouvelles recherches sur la consommation du pain dans ses rapports avec le travail intellectuel. *Année psychologique, 6,* 1-73.

Recherches sur la sensibilité tactile pendant l'état de distraction. *Année psychologique, 6,* 405-440.

1900 Est-il possible de mesures la sensibilité tactile au moyen de la méthode de Weber? *Bulletin de l'Institute Psychologique internationale, ——,* 145-150.

* *La suggestibilité.* Paris: Schleicher Frères.

L'observateur et l'imaginatif. *Année psychologique, 7,* 519-523.

Recherches complémentaires de céphalométrie sur 50 enfants d'élite et arriérés des écoles de Seine-et-Marne. *Année psychologique, 7,* 403-411.

Recherches complémentaires de céphalométrie sur 100 enfants d'intelligence inégale choises dans les écoles primaires de Seine-et-Marne. *Année psychologique, 7,* 375-402.

Recherches de céphalométrie sur 60 enfants d'élite et arriérés des écoles primaires de Paris. *Année psychologique, 7,* 412-429.

Recherches préliminaires de céphalométrie sur 59 enfants d'intelligence inégale choises dans les écoles primaires de ville de Paris. *Année psychologique, 7,* 369-374.

Recherches sur la technique de la mesure de la tête vivante. *Année psychologique, 7,* 314-368.

Revue générale sur la pédagogie expérimentale en France. *Année psychologique, 7,* 594-606.

Technique de l'esthésiométre. *Année psychologique, 7,* 240-248.

Un nouvel appareil pour la mesure de la suggestibilité. *Année psychologique, 7,* 524-536.

Un nouvel esthésiométre. *Année psychologique, 7,* 231-239.

1901 Correlation des mesures céphaliques. *Année psychologique, 8*, 363-368.
La croissance du crâne et de la face chez les normaux entre 4 et 18 ans. *Année psychologique, 8*, 345-362.
Les proportions du crâne chez les aveugles. *Année psychologique, 8*, 369-384.
Les proportions du crâne chez les sourds-muets. *Année psychologique, 8*, 385-389.
Nouvelles recherches de céphalométrie. *Année psychologique, 8*, 341-344.
Quelques réflexions sur l'application de la méthode expérimentale à la pédagogie. *Bulletin de la Société Libre pour l'Etude Psychologique de l'Enfant, 2*, 41-43.

1902 Appareils dynamométrique. In Richet (Ed.), *Dictionnaire de Physiologie.* Tome V. Paris: Alcan. Pp. 196-198.
Influence de l'exercice et de la suggestion sur la position du seuil. *Année psychologique, 9*, 235-248. The influence of exercise and suggestion on the position of the threshold. (P & B, 1969).
La mesure de la sensibilité. *Année psychologique, 9*, 79-128.
L'écriture pendant les états d'excitation artificielle. *Année psychologique, 9*, 57-78.
Le seuil de la sensation double ne peut pas être fixé scientifiquement. *Année psychologique, 9*, 248-252. The threshold of a double sensation cannot be scientifically determined. (P & B, 1969).
Les distraits. *Année psychologique, 9*, 169-198.
Les interprétateurs. *Année psychologique, 9*, 199-234.
Les simplistes enfants d'école et adultes. *Année psychologique, 9*, 129-168.
Le vocabulaire et l'idéation. *Revue philosophique, 54*, 359-366.

1903 Avis à nos collègues nouveau plan de travail. *Bulletin de la Société Libre pour l'Etude Psychologique de l'Enfant, 11*, 258.
Compte rendu sur l'étude expérimentale de l'intelligence. *Année psychologique, 10*, 546.
La pensée sans images. *Revue philosophique, 55*, 138-152. Imageless thought. (P & B, 1969).
De la sensation a l'intelligence. *Revue philosophique, 55*, 449-467, 592-618. From sensation to intelligence. (P & B, 1969).
La création littéraire: Portrait psychologique de M. Paul Hervieu. *Année psychologique, 10*, 1-62.
La graphologie et ses révélations sur le sexe, l'âge et l'intelligence. *Année psychologique, 10*, 179-211.
Le sexe de l'écriture. *La Revue, 1*, 17-34.
* *L'étude expérimentale de l'intelligence.* Paris: Schleicher Frères. A. Costes, 1922.
Note sur l'appréciation du temps. *Archives de Psychologie, 2*, 20-21.
Questions de technique céphalométrique. *Année psychologique, 10*, 139-178.
Revue annuelle des erreurs de psychologie. *Année psychologique, 10*, 396-400.
Sommaire des travaux en cours à la société de psychologie de l'enfant. *Année psychologique, 10*, 116-130.

1904 Addition à un article de Boyer sur un essai de céphalométrie chez des enfants idiots. *Bulletin de la Société Libre pour l'Etude Psychologique de l'Enfant, 15*, 412.
Addition au rapport de la commission sur la mémoire. *Bulletin de la Société Libre pour l'Etude Psychologique de l'Enfant, 17*, 499.
Avis au grand public. *Bulletin de la Société Libre pour l'Etude Psychologique de l'Enfant, 15*, 385.
Commission ministerielle pour les anormaux. *Bulletin de la Société Libre pour l'Etude Psychologique de l'Enfant, 18*, 504.

Expériences sur les relations entre l'écriture et l'intelligence. *Bulletin de la Société Libre pour l'Etude Psychologique de l'Enfant, 15,* 385.

La passé et l'avenir de notre société. *Bulletin de la Société Libre pour l'Etude Psychologique de l'Enfant, 19,* 547-555.

Les frontières anthropométriques des anormaux. *Bulletin de la Société Libre pour l'Etude Psychologique de l'Enfant, 16,* 430.

Les petits problèmes moraux: A propos d'un article de M. Flamand. *Revue pédagogique, 45,* 65-70.

Nos commissions de travail. *Bulletin de la Société Libre pour l'Etude Psychologique de l'Enfant, 14,* 337-346.

Sur une commission de sociologie scolaire. *Bulletin de la Société Libre pour l'Etude Psychologique de l'Enfant, 15,* 414.

With Boitel. Lettre aux directeurs de Directrices d'Ecoles normales. *Bulletin de la Société Libre pour l'Etude Psychologique de l'Enfant, 19,* 529.

With Trérouenne. Ressemblance de deux jumelles. *Bulletin de la Société Libre pour l'Etude Psychologique de l'Enfant, 19,* 522.

1905 Allocution de M. Binet. *Bulletin de la Société Libre pour l'Etude Psychologique de l'Enfant, 27,* 21-27.

A nos collègues. *Bulletin de la Société Libre pour l'Etude Psychologique de l'Enfant, 21,* 589.

A propos de la mesure de l'intelligence. *Année psychologique, 11,* 69-82.

Etude de métaphysique sur la sensation et l'image. *Année psychologique, 11,* 94-115.

Expériences sur la mesure de la fatigue intellectuelle scolaire au moyen du sens du toucher. *Bulletin de la Société Libre pour l'Etude Psychologique de l'Enfant, 22,* 628.

* *L'âme et le corps.* Paris: E. Flammarion. Translated by F. Legge, *The mind and the brain.* London: Kegan Paul, 1907.

La science du témoignage. *Année psychologique, 11,* 128-136.

Le grossissement provoqué de l'écriture. *Archives de Psychologie, 4,* 81-82.

L'enseignement artistique par la craûte. *Rapports (du) Premier Congrès International d'Education,* Section I, 4-9.

Le problème des enfants anormaux. *Revue des Revues, 54,* 308-322.

Les mensurations corporelles dans les écoles. *Bulletin de la Société Libre pour l'Etude Psychologique de l'Enfant, 21,* 590.

Même titre (suite et fin). *Bulletin de la Société Libre pour l'Etude Psychologique de l'Enfant, 23,* 644-652.

Nos commissions d'études. *Bulletin de la Société Libre pour l'Etude Psychologique de l'Enfant, 20,* 557-559.

Nos nouvelles commissions de pédagogie. *Bulletin de la Société Libre pour l'Etude Psychologique de l'Enfant, 22,* 613-615.

Note sur le travail de M. Vaney: "Nouvelles méthodes de mesure applicables au degré d'instruction des élèves." *Bulletin de la Société Libre pour l'Etude Psychologique de l'Enfant, 23,* 653.

Note sur l'étude de Mme Rousson: "Verbes connus par deux enfants de cinq ans." *Bulletin de la Société Libre pour l'Etude Psychologique de l'Enfant, 25,* 700.

Recherches sur la fatigue intellectuelle scolaire et la mesure qui peut en être faite au moyen du dynamomètre. *Année psychologique, 11,* 1-37.

Réflexions sur les communications de Mme Meusy: "Enfants arriérés de la Salpêtrière" et de M. Boyer, "Lecture et écriture chez les enfants anormaux." *Bulletin de la Société Libre pour l'Etude Psychologique de l'Enfant, 20,* 563.

Société pour l'instruction et la protection des enfants sourds-muets ou arriérés

Bulletin de la Société Libre pour l'Etude Psychologique de l'Enfant, 24, 664.

Sur la nécessité d'établir un diagnostic scientifique des états inférieurs de l'intelligence. *Année psychologique, 11*, 162-190.

Un laboratoire de pédagogie normale. *Revue générale des Sciences, 16*, 1069.

With Simon, T. Application des méthodes nouvelles au diagnostic du niveau intellectuel chez des enfants normaux et anormaux d'hospice et d'école primaire. *Année psychologique, 11*, 245-336.

With Simon, T. Enquête sur le mode d'existence des sujets sortis d'une école arriérés. *Année psychologique, 11*, 163-190.

* With Simon, T. Méthodes nouvelles pour le diagnostic du niveau intellectuel des anormaux. *Année psychologique, 11*, 191-244.

1906   A propos de la communication de M. Vaney sur les degrès de la lecture. *Bulletin de la Société Libre pour l'Etude Psychologique de l'Enfant, 37*, 82-83.

Avis. *Bulletin de la Société Libre pour l'Etude Psychologique de l'Enfant, 37*, 73.

Cerveau et pensée. *Archives de Psychologique, 6*, 1-26.

Comité international de pédagogie. *Bulletin de la Société Libre pour l'Etude Psychologique de l'Enfant, 28*, 50-53.

Commission des sentiments moraux. *Bulletin de la Société Libre pour l'Etude Psychologique de l'Enfant, 28*, 53-57.

Examen pédagogique de l'état de la vision chez les élèves. *Bulletin de la Société Libre pour l'Etude Psychologique de l'Enfant, 29*, 66-79.

L'attitude de l'enfant qui écrit. *Bulletin de la Société Libre pour l'Etude Psychologique de l'Enfant, 31*, 132-143.

Les premiers mots de la thèse idéaliste. *Revue philosophique, 61*, 599-618.

Les révélations de l'écriture. *Bulletin de la Société Libre pour l'Etude Psychologique de l'Enfant, 33*, 185.

* *Les révélations de l'écriture d'après un contrôle scientifique.* Paris: Alcan.

Même titre (discussion avec M. Tissié). *Bulletin de la Société Libre pour l'Etude Psychologique de l'Enfant, 32*, 163.

Pour la philosophie de la conscience. *Année psychologique, 12*, 113-136.

Quelques réflexions sur la traitement de bégaiement. *Bulletin de la Société Libre pour l'Etude Psychologique de l'Enfant, 37*, 86.

Résponse à M. Tissié à propos des photographies d'attitude. *Bulletin de la Société Libre pour l'Etude Psychologique de l'Enfant, 32*, 170-175.

With Simon, T. Misère physiologique et misère sociale. *Année psychologique, 12*, 1-24.

With Simon, T., & Vaney. Le laboratoire de la rue Grange-aux-Belles. *Bulletin de la Société Libre pour l'Etude Psychologique de l'Enfant, 34*, 10-24.

With Simon, T., & Vaney. Recherches de pédagogie scientifique. *Année psychologique, 12*, 233-274.

1907   A propos d'expériences sur l'ápellation et des critiques de M. Payot. *Bulletin de la Société Libre pour l'Etude Psychologique de l'Enfant, 38*, 101-105.

Cerveau et pensée. *Archives de Psychologie, 6*, 1-26.

Encore la controverse sur les deux photographies. *Bulletin de la Société Libre pour l'Etude Psychologique de l'Enfant, 36*, 67-70.

Epilogue d'une discussion sur l'attitude d'un enfant qui écrit. *Bulletin de la Société Libre pour l'Etude Psychologique de l'Enfant, 35*, 43-48.

La valeur médicale de l'examen de la vision par les instituteurs. *Bulletin de la Société Libre pour l'Etude Psychologique de l'Enfant, 40*, 145-159.

Les nouvelles classes de perfectionnement. *Bulletin de la Société Libre pour l'Etude Psychologique de l'Enfant, 41*, 170-183.

Quelques réflexions au sujet de la conférence de M. Lévy (L'air insalubre dans les écoles). *Bulletin de la Société Libre pour l'Etude Psychologique de l'Enfant, 39,* 119.

Une expérience cruciale en graphologie. *Revue philosophique, 64,* 24-40.

With Simon, T. Le carnet sanitaire des écoliers. *Revue scientifique,* ___, 97-103.

* With Simon, T. *Les enfants anormaux: Guide pour l'admission des enfants anormaux dans les classes de perfectionnement.* Paris: A. Colin.

1908 Allocution de président sur les enfants anormaux. *Bulletin de la Société Libre pour l'Etude Psychologique de l'Enfant, 44,* 59-60.

A propos de récentes expériences de psychologie sur la mémoire de l'orthographe. *Bulletin de la Société Libre pour l'Etude Psychologique de l'Enfant, 46,* 104-108.

Causerie pédagogique. *Année psychologique, 14,* 405-431.

Essai sur la chiromancie expérimentale. *Année psychologique, 14* 390-404.

L'âge de la lecture (à propos de la communication de Mlle Brès sur l'écolier de 2 à 6 ans). *Bulletin de la Société Libre pour l'Etude Psychologique de l'Enfant, 46,* 98-100.

Les méthodes permettant de contrôler le rendement scolaire d'un enseignement d'une classe ou d'une école: Application à une classe d'enfants anormaux. *Bulletin de la Société Libre pour l'Etude Psychologique de l'Enfant, 48,* 145-152.

L'évolution de l'enseignement philosophique. *Année psychologique, 14,* 152-231.

Nos nouvelles commissions. *Bulletin de la Société Libre pour l'Etude Psychologique de l'Enfant, 45,* 82-85.

Petites nouvelles pédagogiques (Prusse et Allemagne). *Bulletin de la Société Libre pour l'Etude Psychologique de l'Enfant, 49,* 182-184.

Réflexions sur quelques problèmes qui ont été étudiés à la société. *Bulletin de la Société Libre pour l'Etude Psychologique de l'Enfant, 43,* 37-52.

Un livre récent de William James sur l'éducation. *Bulletin de la Société Libre pour l'Etude Psychologique de l'Enfant, 46,* 114; 167.

* With Simon, T. Le développement de l'intelligence chez les enfants. *Année psychologique, 14,* 1-94. Translated by E. S. Kite, *The development of intelligence in children.* Baltimore: Williams & Wilkins, 1916.

With Simon, T. Langage et pensée. *Année psychologique, 14,* 284-339. Translated by E. S. Kite, in *The intelligence of the feeble-minded.* Baltimore: Williams & Wilkins, 1916.

1909 A propos de l'enquête sur les enfants paresseux. *Bulletin de la Société Libre pour l'Etude Psychologique de l'Enfant, 56,* 154-157.

A propos des applications de la psychologie à la pédagogie. *Annales pédagogiques, 1,* 11-15.

A propos du conflit entre les sourds-muets et les professeurs de sourds-muets. *Bulletin de la Société Libre pour l'Etude Psychologique de l'Enfant, 58,* 32-33.

Bibliographie (E. Claparède. Psychologie de l'enfant et pédagogie expérimentale). *Bulletin de la Société Libre pour l'Etude Psychologique de l'Enfant, 55,* 144.

Ce que vaut l'école primaire comme préparation à la vie (enquête de Sannois). *Bulletin de la Société Libre pour l'Etude Psychologique de l'Enfant, 52,* 58-66.

L'âge de la lecture. *Bulletin de la Société Libre pour l'Etude Psychologique de l'Enfant, 54,* 112-114.

La pédagogie expérimentale d'après la littérature allemande (travail de M. Piat avec annotations de Binet). *Bulletin de la Société Libre pour l'Etude Psychologique de l'Enfant, 52,* 67-71.

Le bilan de la psychologie en 1908. *Année psychologique, 15,* v-xii.

L'école primaire comme préparation à la vie. *Bulletin de la Société Libre pour l'Etude Psychologique de l'Enfant, 54,* 112-114.

Le mystère de la peinture. *Année psychologique, 15,* 300-315.

* *Les idées sur les enfants.* Paris: E. Flammarion. Translated by G. Anschuetz and W. J. Ruttmann, *Die neuen Gedanken ueber das Schulkind.* Leipzig: Wunderlich, 1912.

Notre première filiale. *Bulletin de la Société Libre pour l'Etude Psychologique de l'Enfant, 53,* 73.

Petites nouvelles. *Bulletin de la Société Libre pour l'Etude Psychologique de l'Enfant, 52,* 71.

Psychologisme et sociologisme. *Année psychologique, 15,* 357-372.

With Binet, Alice. La psychologie artistique de Tade Styka. *Année psychologique, 15,* 316-356.

With Lorde, A. *Théâtre d'épouvante.* Paris: Librairie théâtrale.

With Simon, T. Etude sur l'art d'enseigner la parole aux sourds-muets. *Année psychologique, 15,* 373-396.

With Simon, T. L'intelligence des imbéciles. *Année psychologique, 15,* 1-147. Translated by E. S. Kite, in *The intelligence of the feeble-minded.* Baltimore: Williams & Wilkins, 1916.

With Simon, T. Nouvelle théorie psychologique et clinique de la démence. *Année psychologique, 15,* 168-272. Translated by E. S. Kite, in *The intelligence of the feeble-minded.* Baltimore: Williams & Wilkins, 1916.

1910 Comment les instituteurs jugent-ils l'intelligence d'un écolier. *Bulletin de la Société Libre pour l'Etude Psychologique de l'Enfant, 64,* 172-182.

Correspondence. *Bulletin de la Société Libre pour l'Etude Psychologique de l'Enfant, 60,* 89.

Deux mots au sujet de la communication de M. Boquet. *Bulletin de la Société Libre pour l'Etude Psychologique de l'Enfant, 63,* 166.

Expériences sur le self-government à l'école. *Bulletin de la Société Libre pour l'Etude Psychologique de l'Enfant, 60,* 82.

La bilan de la psychologie en 1909. *Année psychologique, 16,* i-ix.

La neutralité scolaire. *Bulletin de la Société Libre pour l'Etude Psychologique de l'Enfant, 60,* 87-89.

Le diagnostic judiciare sur la méthode des associations. *Année psychologique, 16,* 372-383.

Les signes physiques de l'intelligence chez les enfants. *Année psychologique, 16,* 1-30.

Réflexions sur la contribution de M. Martin a l'étude du travail scolaire. *Bulletin de la Société Libre pour l'Etude Psychologique de l'Enfant, 61,* 117-118.

Rembrandt: D'après un nouveau mode de critique d'arts. *Année psychologique, 16,* 31-50.

With Simon, T. Conclusion. *Année psychologique, 16,* 361-371.

With Simon, T. Définition des principaux états mentaux de l'aliénation. *Année psychologique, 16,* 61-66.

With Simon, T. La folie avec conscience. *Année psychologique, 16,* 164-214.

With Simon, T. La folie maniaque dépressive. *Année psychologique, 16,* 164-214.

With Simon, T. La folie systématisée. *Année psychologique, 16,* 215-265.

With Simon, T. L'arriération. *Année psychologique, 16,* 349-360.

With Simon, T. L'hystérie. *Année psychologique, 16,* 67-122.

With Simon, T. Les démences. *Année psychologique, 16,* 266-348.

With Vaney. La mesure de degré d'instruction d'après des recherches nouvelles. *Bulletin de la Société Libre pour l'Etude Psychologique de l'Enfant, 66,* 1-14.

1911 Communication au sujet de M. Roussel et Vaney. *Bulletin de la Société Libre pour l'Etude Psychologique de l'Enfant, 72,* 289.

Nouvelles recherches sur la mesure du niveau intellectuel chez les enfants d'école. *Année psychologique, 17,* 145-201.

Qu'est-ce qu'une émotion? Qu'est-ce qu'un acte intellectuel? *Année psychologique, 17,* 1-47.

With Simon, T. Définition de l'aliénation. *Année psychologique, 17,* 301-350.

With Simon, T. La confusion mentale. *Année psychologique, 17,* 278-300.

With Simon, T. La législation des aliénés. *Année psychologique, 17,* 351-362.

* With Simon, T. La mesure de développement de l'intelligence chez les jeunes enfants. *Bulletin de la Société Libre pour l'Etude Psychologique de l'Enfant, 70-71,* 187-248. Translated by C. H. Town, *A method of measuring the development of the intelligence of young children.* Chicago: Medical Book Co., 1913.

With Simon, T. Parallèle entre les classifications des aliénistes. *Année psychologique, 17,* 363-388.

With Simon, T. Réponse à quelques critiques. *Année psychologique, 17,* 270-277.

The following works were published after Binet's death.

1913 With Lorde, A. *La folie au théâtre.* Paris: Fontemoing.

1914 With Simon, T. *Mentally defective children.* Translated by W. B. Drummond. London: E. Arnold.

1915 With Meusy. Notes on the education of backward children. *Training School Bulletin, 12,* 3-14.

1924 With Lorde, A. *Théâtre de la peur.* Paris: Librairie théâtrale.

1926 Données sur la physiologie du sommeil. *Journal medical francais, 15,* 433-439.

Effets de l'ablation des hémisphères cérébraux. *Presse médicale, 26,* 405-406.

1933 *L'amour et l'émotion chez la femme.* Paris: Alcan.

1938 Propos sur la puberté précoce. *Paris médicale, 51,* 470-473.